PROMOTING

SOCIAL

AND

EMOTIONAL

LEARNING

Guidelines for Educators

MAURICE J. ELIAS
JOSEPH E. ZINS
ROGER P. WEISSBERG
KARIN S. FREY
MARK T. GREENBERG
NORRIS M. HAYNES
RACHAEL KESSLER
MARY E. SCHWAB-STONE
TIMOTHY P. SHRIVER

ASSOCIATION FOR SUPERVISION AND CURRICULUM DEVELOPMENT
ALEXANDRIA, VIRGINIA USA

Association for Supervision and Curriculum Development
1250 N. Pitt Street • Alexandria, Virginia 22314-1453 USA
Telephone: 1-800-933-2723 or 703-549-9110 • Fax: 703-299-8631
Web site: http://www.ascd.org. • E-mail: member@ascd.org

Gene R. Carter, *Executive Director*
Michelle Terry, *Assistant Executive Director, Program Development*
Ronald S. Brandt, *Assistant Executive Director*
Nancy Modrak, *Director, Publishing*
John O'Neil, *Acquisitions Editor*
Julie Houtz, *Managing Editor of Books*
Jo Ann Irick Jones, *Senior Associate Editor*
Karen Peck, *Copy Editor*
Gary Bloom, *Director, Editorial, Design, and Production Services*
Karen Monaco, *Senior Designer*
Tracey A. Smith, *Production Manager*
Dina Murray, *Production Assistant*
Valerie Sprague, *Desktop Publisher*

ASCD publications present a variety of viewpoints. The views expressed or implied in this book should not be interpreted as official positions of the Association.

Printed in the United States of America.

ASCD Stock No.: 197157   ASCD member price: $18.95; nonmember price: $22.95

September 1997 member book (pcr). ASCD Premium, Comprehensive, and Regular members periodically receive ASCD books as part of their membership benefits. No. FY98-1.

Library of Congress Cataloging-in-Publication Data
Promoting social and emotional learning : guidelines for educators /
    Maurice J. Elias ... [et al.].
        p.   cm.
    Includes bibliographical references and index.
    ISBN 0-87120-288-3 (pbk.)
    1. Affective education—United States.   2. Social skills—Study
and teaching—United States.   3. Emotions—Study and teaching—
United States.   I. Elias, Maurice J.
LB1072.P76   1997
370.15'3—dc21   97-21198
                                                              CIP

01 00 99 98 97   5 4 3 2 1

Promoting Social and Emotional Learning: Guidelines for Educators

Acknowledgments

A BOOK THAT HAS NUMEROUS AUTHORS, INCORPO-rates on-site visits around the United States, and is based on action research carried out, collectively, over several decades at dozens of sites and involving hundreds of thousands of students and thousands of educators easily could have an acknowledgments section reminiscent of the credits for a Cecil B. DeMille movie. Indeed, each of the authors of this book has mentors, assistants, and collaborators.

What we will do is thank those individuals whose efforts literally made this book possible. Foremost among these are the Founders and Leadership Team of the Collaborative for the Advancement of Social and Emotional Learning (CASEL): Maurice Elias, Eileen Rockefeller Growald, Daniel Goleman, Tom Gullotta, David Sluyter, Linda Lantieri, Mary Schwab-Stone, and Tim Shriver. The core support staff members of CASEL's central office, originally based at Yale (Peggy Nygren, Charlene Voyce) and now housed at the University of Illinois at Chicago (Sharmistha Bose, Bella Giller, Carol Bartels Kuster, May Stern) have provided patient, diligent, and skilled logistical and conceptual assistance.

We thank all those who consented to be part of our on-site visits and who provided information about their programs prior to our deadlines. Contact information for these programs is provided in Appendix C. Most probably, our on-site visit team now has more details about more social and emotional learning programs than anyone else. Linda Bruene-Butler and Lisa Blum conducted most of the visits, and did so expertly. They also did an outstanding job organizing the many tapes and written materials they obtained. Zephryn Conte also conducted two on-site visits, and an ace team of Rutgers undergraduates helped with the transcripts: Debi Ribatsky, Allison Larger, Joanne Mucerino, and Laura Green. Tom Schuyler, a retired school principal with more than two decades of experience working with SEL programs, provided a generous dose of wisdom. Thanks also to Bob Hanson of National Professional Resources, who donated copies of videos that depicted programs we were unable to visit.

Financial support for CASEL from the Fetzer Institute, the Surdna Foundation, and the University of Illinois at Chicago, among others, facilitated our conference calls and meetings. Fetzer also provided the funding for the on-site visits. The Fetzer Institute also hosted the conference at which members of CASEL met with Ron Brandt of ASCD and John Conyers, Betty Davis, and Harriet Arnold, long-time ASCD leaders who served as a kind of focus group discussing this book. Their valuable suggestions helped to shape and ground our thinking.

ASCD has been a true partner in this project. In addition to the individuals listed above, Mikki Terry, Agnes Crawford, and Sally Chapman provided valuable support as they thought about the book's follow-up with professional development institutes and curricular and video projects. Nancy Modrak, John O'Neil, and Julie Houtz have been the shepherds of the manuscript, giving gentle and helpful guidance. The person who has been most directly involved is Jo Ann Irick Jones, and we cannot say enough about her tireless work, her tremendous grasp of the basic concept of the manuscript, and her creative ideas about how to convey those ideas clearly, both in words and in layout. We also salute the many others who provided editorial and production wizardry at ASCD. (What a book cover!) We look forward to a long ASCD-CASEL collaboration in the interests of children and the betterment of schools.

We also want to thank the children, parents, and educators with whom we have worked, and who taught us a great deal. We consider ourselves privileged to be working in the schools, to be able to watch and learn and contribute to this most critical aspect of children's upbringing. The belief that SEL is the missing piece in children's academic and interpersonal success and sound health has fueled our continuing efforts. We are honored to bring this work to a vast education audience through the auspices of ASCD.

Finally, we wish to thank our families. They have supported our action research, our writing, our meetings, and all of the work related to bringing this book to its completion. Three families— those of Maurice Elias, Joe Zins, and Roger Weissberg—bore particular burdens during December 1996 and January 1997, as the struggle to make the publication deadline and pull together vast amounts of materials in a coherent manner grew more intense, and time grew short. Their patience and support show their great reservoirs of social and emotional skills, for which we are grateful.

Preface

DURING THE PAST FEW DECADES, SCHOOLS HAVE BEEN inundated with well-intentioned positive youth development efforts to promote students' competence and to prevent social and health problems. Relevant topics have included initiatives in the following areas:

- AIDS education
- career education
- character education
- civic education
- delinquency prevention
- dropout prevention
- drug education
- family-life education
- health education
- law-related education
- moral education
- multicultural education
- nutrition education
- physical injury prevention
- positive peer bonding
- sex education
- truancy prevention
- violence prevention

It's enough to make an educator's (not to mention a student's) head spin!

Fostering knowledgeable, responsible, and caring students is an important priority for our nation's schools, families, and communities. Yet today's children face unparalleled demands in their everyday lives. They must learn to achieve academically, work cooperatively, make responsible decisions about social and health practices, resist negative peer and media influences, contribute constructively to their family and community, interact effectively in an increasingly diverse society,

and acquire the skills, attitudes, and values necessary to become productive workers and citizens.

Although most people agree that it is important for schools to provide education that produces knowledgeable, responsible, and caring students, there is disagreement about how these outcomes can be best achieved. Unfortunately, in their efforts to respond to the needs of students, many schools have adopted information-oriented, single-issue programs that lack research evidence to support their effectiveness. In this book, we draw upon recent scientific studies, the best theories, and the successful efforts of educators across the nation to provide guidelines to help school administrators, teachers, and pupil-services personnel design, implement, and evaluate comprehensive, coordinated programming to enhance the social and emotional development of children from preschool through high school. A growing body of evidence indicates that systematic, ongoing education to enhance the social and emotional skills of children provides a firm foundation for their successful cognitive and behavioral development.

This book was coauthored by members of the Research and Guidelines Committee of the Collaborative for the Advancement of Social and Emotional Learning (CASEL). As such, it truly represents our collaborative efforts and demonstrates how such a joint approach can greatly enhance what any one of us could have accomplished alone. The coauthors include researchers, practitioners, and trainers, and the final product represents these different perspectives.

CASEL was founded in 1994 to support schools and families in their efforts to educate knowledgeable, responsible, and caring young people who will become productive workers and contributing citizens in the 21st century. As we are painfully aware, rates of drug use, violence and delinquency, damaging health practices, and poor school performance are unacceptably high among youth in spite of several decades of heightened public awareness about these issues. CASEL's purpose is to provide a forum for the exchange of vision, expertise, and ideas regarding effective solutions to promote positive social, emotional, and behavioral development.

CASEL is composed of an international network of educators, scientists, and concerned citizens. Its purpose is to encourage and support the creation of safe, caring learning environments that build social, cognitive, and emotional skills. We have the following primary goals:

1. To increase the awareness of educators, trainers of school-based professionals, the scientific community, policymakers, and the public about the need for, and the effects of, systematic efforts to promote the social and emotional learning (SEL) of children and adolescents.

2. To facilitate the implementation, ongoing evaluation, and refinement of comprehensive social and emotional education programs, beginning in preschool and continuing through high school.

Through research, scholarship, networking, and sharing current information we seek to foster the effective implementation of theoretically based and scientifically sound social and emotional education programs and strategies. Founded in the belief that a collaborative model benefiting from the collective wisdom, experience, and contributions of scientists and educators is the most effective and promising path to developing beneficial programs,

CASEL helps to identify and coordinate the best school, family, and community practices across diverse prevention, health-promotion, and positive youth development efforts.

CASEL strives to foster the development of standards for SEL to assure that well-designed programs are effectively and ethically implemented by competent educators who are well selected and well trained. It seeks to increase opportunities for educators in all phases of their careers to learn about programs and receive training in scientifically tested practices that promote social and emotional development. It educates public policymakers and government administrators about approaches that advance SEL. CASEL believes that the most beneficial SEL efforts are established through school-family partnerships where teachers and parents participate actively in program selection, design, implementation, evaluation, and improvement.

The purpose of this book is to address the crucial need among educators for a straightforward and practical guide to establish quality social and emotional education programming. These guidelines highlight implementation practices that effectively promote SEL among children. As one follow-up to this book, CASEL is systematically and comprehensively conducting an empirical review to evaluate the quality of SEL programs according to criteria that will help educators and parents make informed choices about high-quality curriculums. Results from this review will be available in 1998.

CASEL currently has four active working committees: Research and Guidelines, Education and Training, Communication, and Networking. They are working to create a library and resource center on social and emotional education, to develop technologies that will increase educator access to information about social and emotional education, to conduct diverse research projects to understand and improve processes through which the best SEL practices are implemented and institutionalized, and to forge collaborative relationships with organizations and policymakers committed to encouraging families, schools, and communities that foster knowledgeable, responsible, and caring students. These projects illustrate our mission to promote the exchange of ideas and resources about SEL and to provide educators, parents, practitioners, and researchers with the best of available practices and information.

In keeping with our belief in the importance of collaboration, CASEL invites you, the reader, to share information about your own program efforts, and to request information about current developments and effective practices around the world. CASEL's Central Office can be reached at:

CASEL
Department of Psychology (M/C 285)
The University of Illinois at Chicago
1007 W. Harrison St.
Chicago, IL 60607-7137

We also invite you to visit CASEL's web page to learn what's new at CASEL. The web site contains general information about CASEL projects and events, and information about state-of-the-art social and emotional educational practices. We regularly update our web site, so we recommend that you contact it monthly for current information. Our address is:

http://www.cfapress.org/casel/casel.html

A Study Guide for this book is available on ASCD's Web at

http://www.ascd.org/StudyGuide/

or by calling ASCD's 24-hour Fax-on-Demand service (from your fax or phone) at 800-405-0342 or 703-299-8232.

Finally, we have organized a listserv for individuals interested in the social and emotional development of young people. Members will be able to communicate about important issues in social and emotional education, post questions, and discuss their own work in this area. We believe the listserv will be a useful tool for sharing ideas and information and for generating enthusiasm for high-quality social and emotional learning. You may subscribe for free to this listserv using the following steps:

1. Send an e-mail message to:
majordomo@cfapress.org
2. In the subject area, type: **list**
3. In the message area, type: **subscribe mcasel**
4. Send the message!

We look forward to collaborating with you. We are eager to learn from you and to support your efforts.

Roger P. Weissberg
CASEL, Executive Director
Chicago, Illinois

Timothy P. Shriver
CASEL Leadership Team, Chair
Washington, D.C.

Eileen R. Growald
CASEL Founder & Leadership Team, Vice-Chair
San Francisco, California

1 The Need for Social and Emotional Learning

IT SOMETIMES SEEMS THAT EVERYONE WANTS TO improve schooling in America, but each in a different way. Some want to strengthen basic skills; others, critical thinking. Some want to promote citizenship or character; others want to warn against the dangers of drugs and violence. Some demand more from parents; others accent the role of community. Some emphasize core values; others, the need to respect diversity. All, however, recognize that schools play an essential role in preparing our children to become knowledgeable, responsible, caring adults.

Knowledgeable. Responsible. Caring. Behind each word lies an educational challenge. For children to become *knowledgeable*, they must be ready and motivated to learn, and capable of integrating new information into their lives. For children to become *responsible*, they must be able to understand risks and opportunities, and be motivated to choose actions and behaviors that serve not only their own interests but those of others. For children to become *caring*, they must be able to see beyond themselves and appreciate the concerns of others; they must believe that to care is to be part of a community that is welcoming, nurturing, and concerned about them.

The challenge of raising knowledgeable, responsible, and caring children is recognized by nearly everyone. Few realize, however, that *each element of this challenge can be enhanced by thoughtful,* *sustained, and systematic attention to children's social and emotional learning (SEL).* Indeed, experience and research show that promoting social and emotional development in children is "the missing piece" in efforts to reach the array of goals associated with improving schooling in the United States. There is a rising tide of understanding among educators that children's SEL can and should be promoted in schools (Langdon 1996). Although school personnel see the importance of programs to enhance students' social, emotional, and physical well-being, they also regard prevention campaigns with skepticism and frustration, because most have been introduced as disjointed fads, or a series of "wars" against one problem or another. Although well intentioned, these efforts have achieved limited success due to a lack of coordinated strategy (Shriver and Weissberg 1996).

Based on patterns of child development and on prevention research, a new generation of social and emotional development programs is being used in thousands of schools. Today's educators have a renewed perspective on what common sense always suggested: when schools attend systematically to students' social and emotional skills, the academic achievement of children increases, the incidence of problem behaviors decreases, and the quality of the relationships surrounding each child improves. And, students become the productive, responsible, contributing members of society

1

that we all want. Perhaps the most important rediscovery is that working in classrooms and schools where social and emotional skills are actively promoted is fun and rewarding. As we allow the humanity, decency, and childishness of students (and ourselves, to some degree) to find a legitimate place in the learning environment, we rediscover our reasons for becoming educators.

Thus, social and emotional education is sometimes called the missing piece, that part of the mission of the school that, while always close to the thoughts of many teachers, somehow eluded them. Now, the elusive has become the center, and the opportunities to reshape schooling are upon us.

What Is Social and Emotional Education—And Why Is It Important?

Social and emotional competence is the ability to understand, manage, and express the social and emotional aspects of one's life in ways that enable the successful management of life tasks such as learning, forming relationships, solving everyday problems, and adapting to the complex demands of growth and development. It includes self-awareness, control of impulsivity, working cooperatively, and caring about oneself and others. Social and emotional learning is the process through which children and adults develop the skills, attitudes, and values necessary to acquire social and emotional competence. In *Emotional Intelligence*, Daniel Goleman (1995) provides much evidence for social and emotional intelligence as the complex and multifaceted ability to be effective in all the critical domains of life, including school. But Goleman also does us the favor of stating the key point simply: "It's a different way of being smart."

In recent years, character education has received a great deal of attention, including mention in President Clinton's 1997 State of the Union address. You might wonder about its relationship to social and emotional education. Without going into a lengthy discussion of character education (see Lickona 1991, 1993a), it is apparent that the best character education and social and emotional education programs share many overlapping goals. The Character Education Partnership in Alexandria, Virginia, defines character education as "the long-term process of helping young people develop good character, i.e., knowing, caring about, and acting upon core ethical values such as fairness, honesty, compassion, responsibility, and respect for self and others." Whereas many character education programs promote a set of values and directive approaches that presumably lead to responsible behavior (Brick and Roffman 1993, Lickona 1993b, Lockwood 1993), social and emotional education efforts typically have a broader focus. They place more emphasis on active learning techniques, the generalization of skills across settings, and the development of social decision-making and problem-solving skills that can be applied in many situations. Moreover, social and emotional education is targeted to help students develop the attitudes, behaviors, and cognitions to become "healthy and competent" overall—socially, emotionally, academically, and physically—because of the close relationship among these domains. And, as you will see, social and emotional education has clear outcome criteria, with specific indicators of impact identified. In sum, both character education and social and emotional education aspire to teach our students to be good citizens with positive values and to interact effectively and behave constructively. The challenge for educators and scientists is to clarify the set of educational methods that most successfully contribute to those outcomes.

The social and emotional education of children may be provided through a variety of diverse efforts such as classroom instruction, extracurricular activities, a supportive school climate, and involvement in community service. Many schools have entire curriculums devoted to SEL. In classroom-based programs, educators enhance students' social and emotional competence through instruction and structured learning experiences throughout the day. For example, the New Haven, Connecticut, public schools have outlined the scope of their K–12 Social Development Project, identifying an array of interrelated skills, attitudes, values, and domains of information that lay a foundation for constructive development and behavior (see Figure 1.1).

The goals of New Haven's Social Development Project are to educate students so that they

• Acquire a knowledge base plus a set of basic skills, work habits, and values for a lifetime of meaningful work.

• Feel motivated to contribute responsibly and ethically to their peer group, family, school, and community.

• Develop a sense of self-worth and feel effective as they deal with daily responsibilities and challenges.

• Are socially skilled and have positive relationships with peers and adults.

• Engage in positive, safe, health-protective behavior practices.

To achieve these outcomes, school personnel collaborate with parents and community members to provide educational opportunities that (a) enhance children's self-management, problem-solving, decision-making, and communication skills; (b) inculcate prosocial values and attitudes about self, others, and work; and (c) inform students about health, relationships, and school and community responsibilities. Social development activities promote communication, participation in cooperative groups, emotional self-control and appropriate expression, and thoughtful and nonviolent problem resolution. More broadly, these skills, attitudes, and values encourage a reflective, ready-to-learn approach to all areas of life. In short, they promote knowledge, responsibility, and caring.

Can People Succeed Without Social and Emotional Skills?

Is it possible to attain true academic and personal success without addressing SEL skills? The accumulating evidence suggests the answer is no. Studies of effective middle schools have shown that the common denominator among different types of schools reporting academic success is that they have a systematic process for promoting children's SEL. There are schoolwide mentoring programs, group guidance and advisory periods, creative modifications of traditional discipline procedures, and structured classroom time devoted to social and emotional skill building, group problem solving, and team building (Carnegie Council on Adolescent Development 1989). Of course, they have sound academic programs and competent teachers and administrators, but other schools have those features as well. It is the SEL component that distinguishes the effective schools.

The importance of SEL for successful academic learning is further strengthened by new insights from the field of neuropsychology. Many elements of learning are relational (or, based on relationships), and social and emotional skills are essential for the successful development of thinking and learning activities that are traditionally considered cognitive (Brendtro, Brokenleg, and Van Bockern 1990; Perry 1996). Processes we had considered pure "thinking" are now seen as phenomena in which the cognitive and emotional aspects work synergistically. Brain studies show, for example, that memory is coded to specific events and linked to social and emotional situations, and that the latter are integral parts of larger units of memory that make up what we learn and retain, including what takes place in the classroom. Under conditions of real or imagined threat or high anxiety, there is a loss of focus on the learning process and a reduction in task focus and flexible problem solving. It is as if the thinking brain is taken over (or "hijacked," as Goleman says) by the older limbic brain. Other

3

FIGURE 1.1
NEW HAVEN SOCIAL DEVELOPMENT CURRICULUM SCOPE

Life Skills Curriculum Scope
Preschool through 12th grade

Skills	Attitudes and Values
Self-Management	**About Self**
Self-monitoring	Self-respect
Self-control	Feeling capable
Stress management	Honesty
Persistence	Sense of responsibility
Emotion-focused coping	Willingness to grow
Self-reward	Self-acceptance
Problem Solving and Decision Making	**About Others**
Problem recognition	Awareness of social norms and values—peer,
Feelings awareness	family, community, and society
Perspective taking	Accepting individual differences
Realistic and adaptive goal setting	Respecting human dignity
Awareness of adaptive response strategies	Having concern or compassion for others
Alternative solution thinking	Valuing cooperation with others
Consequential thinking	Motivation to solve interpersonal problems
Decision making	Motivation to contribute
Planning	**About Tasks**
Behavioral enactment	Willingness to work hard
Communication	Motivation to solve practical problems
Understanding nonverbal communication	Motivation to solve academic problems
Sending messages	Recognition of the importance of education
Receiving messages	Respect for property
Matching communication to the situation	

Content

Self/Health	Relationships	School/Community
Alcohol and other drug use	Understanding relationships	Attendance education and truancy
Education and prevention of AIDS	Multicultural awareness	and dropout prevention
and STDs	Making friends	Accepting and managing
Growth and development and	Developing positive relationships	responsibility
teen pregnancy prevention	with peers of different genders	Adaptive group participation
Nutrition	races and ethnic groups	Realistic academic goal setting
Exercise	Bonding to prosocial peers	Developing effective work habits
Personal hygiene	Understanding family life	Making transitions
Personal safety and first aid	Relating to siblings	Environmental responsibility
Understanding personal loss	Relating to parents	Community involvement
Use of leisure time	Coping with loss	Career planning
Spiritual awareness	Preparation for marriage and	
	parenting in later life	
	Conflict education and violence	
	prevention	
	Finding a mentor	

Source: Weissberg, R.P., A.S. Jackson, and T.P. Shriver. (1993). "Promoting Positive Social Development and Health Practices in Young Urban Adolescents." In *Social Decision Making and Life Skills Development: Guidelines for Middle School Educators*, edited by M.J. Elias, pp. 45–77. Gaithersburg, Md.: Aspen Publications.
Copyright © 1991 by Alice Stroop Jackson and Roger P. Weissberg

emotion-related factors can be similarly distracting (Nummela and Rosengren 1986, Perry 1996, Sylwester 1995).

Sylwester (1995) highlights ways in which SEL fosters improved performance in schools (see Figure 1.2). He points out that

> we know emotion is very important to the educative process because it drives attention, which drives learning and memory. We've never really understood emotion, however, and so don't know how to regulate it in school—beyond defining too much or too little of it as misbehavior and relegating most of it to the arts, PE, recess, and the extracurricular program. . . . By separating emotion from logic and reason in the classroom, we've simplified school management and evaluation, but we've also then separated two sides of one coin—and lost something important in the process. It's impossible to separate emotion from the other important activities of life. Don't try (pp. 72, 75).

The basic skills of SEL are necessary for students to be able to take full advantage of their biological equipment and social legacy and heritage. As schools provide the conditions that allow even the students most at risk of failure to become engaged in the learning process, new possibilities open up and new life trajectories become available to students. We know from resilience research that even in the worst conditions, such as decaying inner cities, we still find some children emerging in positive ways. Wherever one looks at children who have remained in school, one will find that SEL was provided to these children by at least one or two caring people, often in the schools.

Social and emotional issues are also at the heart of the problem behaviors that plague many schools, communities, and families, sapping learning time, educators' energy, and children's hope and opportunities. Effectively promoting social and emotional competence is the key to helping young people become more resistant to the lure of drugs, teen pregnancy, violent gangs, truancy, and

---

FIGURE 1.2
BRAIN RESEARCH AND SOCIAL AND EMOTIONAL LEARNING

Robert Sylwester outlines six areas in which emotional and social learning must come together for the benefit of children and schools:

• Accepting and controlling our emotions
• Using metacognitive activities
• Using activities that promote social interaction
• Using activities that provide an emotional context
• Avoiding intense emotional stress in school
• Recognizing the relationship between emotions and health

He also points out that the multiple intelligences are socially based and interrelated: "It's difficult to think of linguistic, musical, and interpersonal intelligence out of the context of social and cooperative activity, and the other four forms of intelligence are likewise principally social in normal practice."

Source: Sylwester 1995, pp. 75–77, 117

---

dropping out of school. Consider, for example, the current interest in the character education movement, which follows years of attention to the violence prevention movement, the values education movement, the citizenship education movement, and the drug abuse education movement. All of these movements have common objectives: to help children acquire the skills, attitudes, values, and experiences that will motivate them to resist destructive behaviors, make responsible and thoughtful decisions, and seek out positive opportunities for growth and learning.

Can any of these movements succeed without teaching social and emotional skills? Clearly not. In fact, the programs that lack such instruction are notoriously ineffective. Among the least successful substance abuse prevention programs are those that provide students information about the dangers of illicit drug use without helping them understand the social and emotional dimensions of peer pressure, stress, coping, honesty, and consequential thinking (Dusenbury and Falco 1997). Indeed, such information-oriented prevention programs have sometimes been blamed for *increases* in substance abuse rates! The truth is, such programs have not been found effective. But this unfortunate outcome cannot be any more surprising than, say, the poor performance of a car with a one-gallon gas tank. Without adequate fuel, neither will get very far. We cannot educate children about the reality of drugs without preparing them for the social and emotional struggles they will confront when exposed to media images about drug use and to opportunities to use drugs.

Some existing prevention efforts do incorporate skills for refusing drugs and other enticements, skills for resisting peer pressure, ways to focus on one's goals, techniques for time management, and steps for making thoughtful, calm decisions—all of which are important skills that prevent problem behaviors. But typically these prevention efforts fail to address the missing piece: feelings that confuse children so that they cannot and do not learn effectively. Children's emotions must be recognized and their importance for learning accepted. By meeting the challenges implicit in accomplishing this goal, we can clear the pathways to competence.

The Significance of Caring

Can children become caring members of a school community without attention to the social and emotional dimensions of their lives? Again, the answer seems obvious. Caring is central to the shaping of relationships that are meaningful, supportive, rewarding, and productive. Caring happens when children sense that the adults in

their lives think they are important and when they understand that they will be accepted and respected, regardless of any particular talents they have. Caring is a product of a community that deems all of its members to be important, believes everyone has something to contribute, and acknowledges that everyone counts.

We work better when we care and when we are cared about, and so do students. Caring is a spoken or an unspoken part of every interaction that takes place in classrooms, lunchrooms, hallways, and playgrounds. Children are emotionally attuned to be on the lookout for caring, or a lack thereof, and they seek out and thrive in places where it is present. The more emotionally troubled the student, the more attuned he or she is to caring in the school environment.

At-risk kids are most vulnerable for growing up without caring. It is caring that plays a critical role in overcoming the narrowness, selfishness, and mean-spiritedness that too many of our children cannot avoid being exposed to, and that replaces these attitudes with a culture of welcome. Caring, the value that most Americans seem to agree is most necessary in adult life, is rooted in the social and emotional development of childhood.

Social and Emotional Skills Matter Beyond the Classroom

If the goal of helping children become knowledgeable, responsible, and caring is a central element of social and emotional development and schooling, then institutions other than schools should be interested in fostering these qualities as well. Ironically, social and emotional skills, attitudes, and values have been embraced most enthusiastically in the boardrooms of corporate America. Moreover, businesses of all sizes have come to realize that *productivity depends on a work force that is socially and emotionally competent.* Workers who are capable of managing their social and emotional interactions with colleagues and customers, as well as their own emotional health, are more effective at improving the bottom line and at making workplaces more efficient. In light of new knowledge about social and emotional development, captains of industry and the moms and pops of neighborhood businesses are rushing to update their techniques for selecting and training workers, organizing the work environment, and developing managers and leaders. They understand that social and emotional competence may be more important than all of the institutions attended, degrees earned, test scores obtained, and even technical knowledge gained. More focus is being placed on problem solving, reflection, perceptive thinking, self-direction, and motivation for lifelong learning—characteristics that are useful no matter what the job (Adams and Hamm 1994). To illustrate this point, Figure 1.3 describes the skills that employers believe teenagers should have.

Goleman (1995) provides insights into this shift of priorities. In contrast to other skills, employers believe their workers show the greatest shortage in the social and emotional areas, and they recognize that businesses are ill-equipped to train employees in these areas. Thus, young people must be prepared for the new workplace with more than the technical and content-specific skills of traditional schooling. Business has made it clear that new qualities are being sought in employees. The accent is on being a flexible thinker, a quick problem solver, and a team player capable of helping the organization adjust to ever-changing markets. Employees are expected to have the basic knowledge necessary to manage the task at hand, but they are also expected to be able to learn quickly and regularly on the job, adapt to new demands and environments, collaborate with others, motivate colleagues, and get along with a variety of people in different situations. In other words, working smarter is now the complement to working harder.

FIGURE 1.3
WHAT EMPLOYERS WANT FOR TEENS: 1980s U.S. DEPARTMENT OF LABOR, EMPLOYMENT, AND TRAINING ADMINISTRATION RESEARCH PROJECT

1. Learning-to-learn skills
2. Listening and oral communication
3. Adaptability: creative thinking and problem solving, especially in response to barriers/obstacles
4. Personal management: self-esteem, goal-setting/self-motivation, personal career development/goals—pride in work accomplished
5. Group effectiveness: interpersonal skills, negotiation, teamwork
6. Organizational effectiveness and leadership: making a contribution
7. Competence in reading, writing, and computation

The report notes that the seventh skill, while essential, is no longer sufficient for workplace competence.

Increasingly, competence in recognizing and managing emotions and social relationships is seen as a key ability for success in the workplace and for effective leadership. Moreover, both health professionals and workplace managers acknowledge that the social and emotional status of an individual may be a substantial factor in determining the person's capacity to resist disease and even to recover from illness (and we suspect school nurses would heartily agree). As educators increasingly recognize the critical role that social and emotional skills play in fostering productive, healthy workers, state departments of education have established core curriculum content standards emphasizing their development (see Figure 1.4).

**FIGURE 1.4
EXCERPTS FROM CORE CURRICULUM
CONTENT STANDARDS FOR NEW JERSEY
(MAY 1996)**

**Cross-Content Workplace Readiness
Standards**
• All students will use critical-thinking, decision-
making, and problem-solving skills.
• All students will demonstrate self-manage-
ment skills.
• All students will develop career planning and
workplace readiness skills.

Health and Physical Education Standards
• All students will learn health-promotion and
disease-prevention concepts and health-enhancing behaviors.
• All students will learn health-enhancing, personal, interpersonal, and life skills.
• All students will learn the physical, mental,
emotional, and social effects of the use and
abuse of alcohol, tobacco, and other drugs.

These standards show the central place of social and emotional skills in the context of workplace skills that go across all areas of traditional
academic content, and as the centerpiece of
comprehensive health education. This is a precursor of future nationwide educational trends.

Issues of SEL have also influenced political writers on democracy and citizenship (Boyer 1990, Parker 1996). Responsible members of a democracy are constantly challenged by changes in technology, communication, and cultural demographics and must filter and integrate large amounts of information from increasingly sophisticated political operatives, electorate pulse-takers, and opinion shapers. Parker asserts that civil competencies cannot fully develop with family influence only, and he calls for civic education in schools and other settings where children learn

and grow. The skills of reflective problem solving and decision making, managing one's emotions, taking a variety of perspectives, and sustaining energy and attention toward focused goals are among many that are called upon at every level, from pulling the lever in the voting booth to enacting laws in state legislatures, making judicial decisions, and issuing directives from the Oval Office. And, it takes a similar array of skills to successfully run a classroom, school, or school district.

How Have Educators Responded to Calls for SEL?

For educators in U.S. schools, the response to the renewed awareness about the importance of social and emotional development has been mixed. In some circles, this task is still seen as solely the responsibility of families. The reasoning sounds traditional: the family should be the place where the child learns to understand, control, and work through emotions; social and emotional issues are essentially private concerns that should be left at the door when a child enters a school to go about the business of acquiring academic knowledge. This thinking has an appealing nostalgia: the school, like the workplace, was always an environment where the agenda was not supposed to be interpersonal relationships, but the task at hand. There is learning to be done—what does this have to do with "feelings"?

On the other hand, educators have always understood on a general level the implications of social and emotional issues for children's learning and development. The best teachers have always been adept at helping children develop socially and emotionally, and many teachers are naturally gifted at promoting the skills, attitudes, and values of competent social and emotional development. It is easy for most people to recall a teacher who made students feel capable of managing the challenges of learning, or who ran the classroom so that everyone understood the importance of respecting one another and resolving problems cooperatively. We would venture to say that the vast majority of readers share with the authors the experience of having such a teacher or being in such a school, and that these experiences—and the feelings associated with them—are part of why we are dedicated to children and to schooling.

Given the growing lack of civility and the related problems educators see around them, it is not surprising that they increasingly acknowledge the importance of addressing social and emotional issues in school. At the same time, some educators believe they are "doing that already." Perhaps this is true. But just as we know instinctively that it makes sense to identify the most effective practices to teach a subject such as mathematics, take those practices and structure them into a sequenced curriculum, and implement that curriculum with trained professionals during dedicated classroom time, we must recognize now that the same effort must be mustered if we are to succeed in the social and emotional domains. It simply makes sense that if we are to expect children to be knowledgeable, responsible, and caring—and to be so despite significant obstacles—we must teach social and emotional skills, attitudes, and values with the same structure and attention that we devote to traditional subjects. And we must do so in a coordinated, integrated manner.

Parallel arguments in academic areas abound. For example, all would agree that quantitative skills, like skills for SEL, develop naturally. But few would argue that just because quantitative reasoning skills develop without formal instruction, there consequently is no need to offer systematic instruction in mathematics. Nonetheless, that is precisely the refrain heard frequently about social and emotional competence: it should be handled intuitively, it should be gleaned from other subjects, it should emerge on its own.

In today's world, and in what we can foresee as we enter the 21st century, nothing could be further from the truth. Reflect for a moment on how the world has changed in just the past five decades. Today, most children grow up in urban and suburban settings in a high-tech, multimedia world that provides constant stimulation, and sends largely unregulated messages about material goods and experiences that few youngsters experience directly or within their families. Many share a classroom with students of diverse cultures and perspectives and various abilities and disabilities.

In this world, millions of good and decent children find that school is but one institution among many influences in their lives. It competes with peer groups, social service institutions, the media, the culture of competition, the pressure to conform, the need to be different, the tug of religious ties, the lure of risk, the fear of loneliness, and the complexities of family relationships in an age on the move. Youth who grow up in this world are all of our children. They come from every ethnic, economic, social, and geographic corner. Their teachers are accustomed to watching them struggle with the pressures and challenges of growing up. Learning at school is but a fragment of these challenges. For this learning to take place effectively, so that classroom lessons become life lessons, students need significant adults and peers in their lives to work with them as part of a community of learners. Only in such supportive contexts can they begin to piece together answers to the sometimes overwhelming social and emotional dilemmas they face.

In a time when our youth need more support than ever to master the tasks of development, we see ironically that the economic and social changes of the last 40 years of the 20th century have reduced those supports (Postman 1996). Many families can make ends meet only when both parents work outside the home—and sometimes at more than one job. Extended families, which once provided a child-care safety net, have all but disappeared. And close-knit communities, once sources of caring adults who guided children and served as role models, are today neighborhoods of strangers.

Schools have become the one best place where the concept of surrounding children with meaningful adults and clear behavioral standards can move from faint hope to a distinct possibility—and perhaps even a necessity.

In our hearts, we know that the outcomes for too many children are negative. Those who drop out, those who go to out-of-district placements, those who get through school thanks to waivers or reduced standards, those who are in alternative schools—all these students are not quite fully visible to us. We often do not know what becomes of those who leave our particular class or school or community. But others know. In every ethnic group, in every geographic region, in every economic bracket, children are letting us know that the vise grip of growing up in a world that diminishes the importance of their social and emotional lives is just too tight.

We will not repeat here the litany of statistics of social breakdown in the lives of children. Read your newspapers and magazines. Look at the stream of books and articles put out by child advocacy agencies. We should no longer need numbers to make us bemoan current conditions. (For statistics about changes in families and communities, see Weissberg and Greenberg 1997, U.S. Department of Health and Human Services 1996.)

The facts spell out a serious message: *We should do more to prepare youngsters for the challenges of life in our complex and fast-paced world*. In particular, these facts must be a wake-up call for educators in every classroom, at every grade level, and in every school district in the United States: *These are our children, and we must teach them in ways that will give them a realistic chance of successfully managing the challenges of learning, growing, and developing.*

How Does This Book Contribute to Efforts to Help Children Learn and Grow?

This book suggests a practical, well-developed, defensible strategy to help educators answer the wake-up call. The strategy is to create programs for comprehensive and coordinated social and emotional learning from preschool through grade 12. Such efforts will be benchmarked by at least three main goals:

1. The presence of effective, developmentally appropriate, formal and informal instruction in social and emotional skills at every level of schooling, provided by well-trained teachers and other pupil-services personnel.

2. The presence of a supportive and safe school climate that nurtures the social and emotional development of children while including all the key adults who have a stake in the development of each child.

3. The presence of actively engaged educators, parents, and community leaders who create activities and opportunities before, during, and after the regular school day that teach and reinforce the attitudes, values, and behaviors of positive family and school life and, ultimately, of responsible, productive citizenship.

These three benchmarks should be assessed along with outcomes in other domains to ensure that schools are playing their part in giving young people the best possible chance to become knowledgeable, responsible, and caring adults. Specific guidelines for reaching these goals and monitoring these benchmarks are identified in the subsequent chapters of this book. They describe social and emotional education efforts that are integrated, comprehensive, and coordinated—qualities lacking in many of today's programs (see Figure 1.5). They lead to students who are ready and motivated to learn, increased academic performance, active learning in the classroom and on the

FIGURE 1.5
AN INTEGRATED AND COORDINATED FRAMEWORK PROVIDES SYNERGY

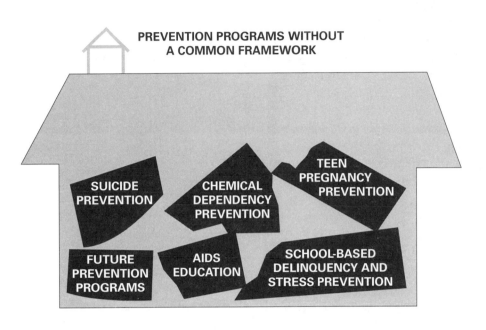

PREVENTION PROGRAMS WITHOUT
A COMMON FRAMEWORK

SUICIDE PREVENTION

CHEMICAL DEPENDENCY PREVENTION

TEEN PREGNANCY PREVENTION

FUTURE PREVENTION PROGRAMS

AIDS EDUCATION

SCHOOL-BASED DELINQUENCY AND STRESS PREVENTION

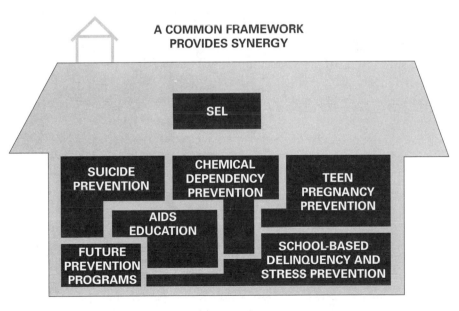

A COMMON FRAMEWORK
PROVIDES SYNERGY

SEL

SUICIDE PREVENTION

CHEMICAL DEPENDENCY PREVENTION

TEEN PREGNANCY PREVENTION

AIDS EDUCATION

FUTURE PREVENTION PROGRAMS

SCHOOL-BASED DELINQUENCY AND STRESS PREVENTION

Source: Maurice J. Elias

playground, greater respect for diversity, better preparation for today's society, and more effective teachers and administrators.

Why are guidelines needed? Why, in the crowded schedule of our school day, must we attend systematically to this task as well? We cannot afford to make social and emotional education a fad; the work of Howard Gardner (1983), Daniel Goleman (1995), James Comer (Comer, Haynes, Joyner, and Ben-Avie 1996), and Carol Gilligan (1987), among others, tells us why. The skills areas these writers have identified are the fundamentals of human learning, work, creativity, and accomplishment. Social and emotional development and the recognition of the relational nature of learning and change constitute an essential missing piece in our educational system. Until it is given its proper place, we cannot expect to see progress in combating violence, substance abuse, disaffection, intolerance, or the high dropout rate.

This book is rooted in the idea that academic and social success are not limited to those of good fortune or privileged upbringing; we can create the conditions for achievement for all children. Success does not occur only through large programs; the necessary conditions are created in families, in individual classrooms, and through relationships with special people in our lives. Here, we provide guidelines to foster these conditions in schools, programmatically and systematically, so that their existence for all children is left less to chance than is now the case.

This, then, is a book about how to promote social and emotional learning in schools—how to promote knowledgeable, responsible, and caring children and adults. In our day, the real challenge of educating is no longer *whether or not* to attend to the social and emotional life of the learner. The real challenge is *how* to attend to social and emotional issues in education. This book suggests a course of action for the "how" questions. It is a clarion call, a shofar blast, a wail from a minaret, a church bell ringing. We ask educators to rethink the ways in

which schools have addressed or failed to address the development of the whole child, and to do so with an eye toward models that have demonstrated success. We ask readers to examine what goes on in their classrooms, schools, and districts, to determine how they can respond best to the opportunities described in this book.

More than anything, this is a book about common sense in education, or perhaps the uncommon sense needed to recognize the missing piece in schooling: enhancing the social and emotional life of each student is part of the educational responsibility of adults. We must remember that

> the democratic way of life engages the creative process of seeking ways to extend and expand the values of democracy. This process, however, is not simply an anticipatory conversation about just anything. Rather, it is directed toward intelligent and reflective consideration of problems, events, and issues that arise in the course of our collective lives (Beane and Apple 1995, p. 16).

An Overview of What Follows

This book reviews the essential elements underlying the effective development, implementation, and evaluation of SEL programs in a straightforward, practical, and systematic manner. In the next chapter we ask you to begin thinking about the social and emotional education efforts already under way in your classroom, school, or district. Doing so will help to make the remaining content more applicable and meaningful for your specific setting.

The following three chapters present fundamental information for social and emotional education. Chapter 3 provides a more in-depth examination of what social and emotional education is, as well as a discussion of its place in our schools. This chapter provides the background information needed for Chapter 4, which explains how teachers can help students develop social and emotional skills in their individual classrooms. In

Chapter 5, important contextual issues related to creating an organizational climate supportive of social and emotional educational programs are examined.

Chapter 6 gets down to practical issues involved in starting and continuing a program. Chapter 7 outlines ways in which social and emotional education efforts can be evaluated to determine whether they are achieving their goals and to provide guidance regarding changes that may be necessary to make them more effective.

Most of the material in Chapters 3 through 7 is presented in a series of concise guidelines that describe the development, implementation, and evaluation of social and emotional education programs. The guidelines have a strong scientific basis and are based on many research investigations and relevant theory. They represent the combined expertise of program developers, researchers, trainers, and practitioners in this field.

In Chapter 8, the self-reflection process is revisited to provide a starting point for you to get your social and emotional education program under way.

This book also includes three appendixes. The first has a social and emotional education curriculum scope, and the second a list of the guidelines presented throughout the book. These are followed by Appendix C, which is a list of programs that emphasize comprehensive approaches to social and emotional education. Under the leadership of Maurice Elias, CASEL conducted on-site visits to schools that have implemented each of the programs included at the beginning of Appendix C. Incidentally, we have included examples throughout the book to give you snapshots of what occurs in SEL programs. Most of the examples were provided in response to questions posed by the site visitors or were developed through observation. Staff at the other programs listed in Appendix C, which were not visited, have indicated to CASEL that they include a strong emphasis on social and emotional education strategies. You can gain additional firsthand knowledge about social and emotional education efforts by contacting or visiting the programs listed.

2 Reflecting on Your Current Practices

TO BEGIN THE PROCESS OF IMPROVING THE OPPOR-
tunities for social and emotional learning that you
already provide, we invite you to begin thinking
about your classroom, school, or district. We challenge you to think about what you *are* doing to promote SEL and what you *could be* doing. This
process will help you begin to think about SEL issues, which will make the rest of the book more
relevant to your particular setting. Further,
whether you are a novice or an experienced hand
at providing SEL instruction, it is important to
regularly reflect on your professional actions and
to develop a thorough understanding of why you
have chosen them.

No matter what your professional position, be
it teacher, principal, or superintendent, we believe
you will find that you and your school or district
are already doing a lot—probably more than you
realize once you begin listing everything. Once
you are finished with this chapter, you will probably be thinking about how you might improve
what you are doing and what more could be done.
At some point, you may want to engage in this self-
reflection process with a team of colleagues representing different positions and perspectives. This
collaborative exploration will likely spark informative discussions and debates about what activities
constitute social and emotional education as well
as creative brainstorming about how to integrate

and coordinate classroom, school, and community
efforts to enhance students' social and emotional
skills.

To get you started, here are some general questions to address. You don't have to answer all of
them now. Some may be more relevant to you than
others, depending on your role in the school or district. The questions are structured around the 39
guidelines presented in Chapters 3 through 7 (Appendix B lists all the guidelines). We encourage
you to initiate this self-reflection process by thinking about and discussing some of the issues raised
in this chapter. Doing so will foster a more focused
and critical approach to reading the next five chapters. As you go through this process, we think you
will find it helpful to put your reflections and ideas
in writing so you can refer to them later.

After you and your colleagues review the first
seven chapters, we urge you to reconvene and engage in the more thorough self-assessment offered
in Chapter 8. That chapter's exercise will help you
identify strengths in current program efforts, identify priorities for new initiatives and directions,
and develop a plan for your next steps. The notes
we are urging you to keep will stimulate your
thinking about specific steps to take and encourage
you to think about all the practical aspects of beginning your renewed SEL programming efforts.

What Is My School Doing to Foster Social and Emotional Learning?

I. Identifying Your SEL Goals and Activities

See Chapter 3 and Appendix A for more information about this area.

1. What are the SEL goals for your classroom, school, or district that will help students become knowledgeable, responsible, and caring?

2. Develop a written list of activities going on in your classroom, school, or district that support SEL. Think broadly when considering what to include on the list. For example, include the following: programs to enhance life skills, problem solving and decision making, positive youth development, self-esteem, respect for diversity, and health; efforts to prevent problems such as substance abuse, AIDS, pregnancy, and violence; conflict resolution and discipline approaches; support services to help students cope with school transitions, family disruption, or death; and positive contributory service, peer leadership and mediation, volunteerism, mentoring, character education, civics and citizenship, or career education.

   - What approaches are you taking to enhance the SEL of students in the classroom (e.g., specific curriculums, variety of focused activities)?

   - On what theory are you basing these activities? In other words, why are you engaging in them?

   - What activities outside the classroom, but within the school context, support SEL (e.g., extracurricular activities, clubs, playground games)?

   - What community activities support the school's SEL efforts?

   - What home activities are taking place that complement the school's SEL program?

3. Are these SEL efforts planned, ongoing, systematic, and developmentally based?

4. Are efforts to prevent problems and promote positive cognitions, emotions, and behaviors coordinated with one another, or are they conducted in a piecemeal fashion?

5. To what extent and in what ways do school-level efforts to enhance students' social and emotional skills reinforce classroom-based SEL instruction and programming?

II. Developing Social and Emotional Skills Through Classroom Instruction

See Chapter 4 for more information on this area.

1. What approaches do you use to build a safe and caring classroom community?

2. Are your SEL training approaches grounded in a comprehensive, theory-based framework that is developmentally appropriate?

3. What instructional methods (e.g., modeling, role playing, didactic instruction) are used to promote SEL?

4. What classroom lessons and follow-up reinforcements do you use throughout the day to improve children's capacities to express emotions appropriately, make responsible decisions, solve problems effectively, and behave adaptively?

5. In what ways do you integrate SEL with traditional academics to enhance learning in both areas?

6. What specific SEL programming is provided for children with special needs? Is there coordination between classroom-based SEL programming and other student support services to achieve an integrated system of special services delivery?

7. How well are staff prepared and supported for building students' social and emotional devel-

opment? Are training opportunities available that provide teachers with theoretical knowledge, modeling, practice, on-site coaching, and follow-up support for providing SEL instruction? How do administrators (or teachers) and colleagues collaborate with you to support your SEL efforts and develop long-range SEL plans?

III. Creating the Context for SEL Programs

See Chapter 5 for a discussion of this area.

1. How are students and teachers involved in designing, planning, and implementing SEL programming? Describe the process used to select specific SEL activities.

2. In what ways are your SEL efforts coordinated within the curriculum, across grades, and throughout schools?

3. Are your school's SEL programming efforts aligned with district-level goals and supported by the administration? How do your school and district policies support and encourage SEL efforts?

4. In what way are parents and community members involved in SEL in your classroom, school, or district? How do they support social and emotional education?

IV. Introducing and Sustaining Social and Emotional Education

See Chapter 6 for more information on this topic.

1. What is your school's planning process for selecting SEL programs and activities?

2. What mechanisms and resources exist for training and supervising staff who implement SEL programs? Is there a coordinator or planning committee to ensure that the social and emotional education efforts are effectively conducted?

3. How are new SEL initiatives coordinated with related programs and services that are currently under way?

4. How are staff, parents, the central office, and the community informed of new SEL initiatives?

5. To what extent are resources provided to conduct SEL activities?

6. What specific actions are you, your school, or your district taking to foster the long-term success and positive impact of SEL programs?

V. Evaluating SEL Program Efforts

See Chapter 7 for a discussion of this topic.

1. In what ways are you evaluating SEL efforts to ensure that you are on the right track?

2. How do you evaluate the program's effects on children, staff, parents, and the community?

3. What evidence do you have that you are making progress toward reaching your SEL objectives and that the program is succeeding?

4. What uses are made of information about the extent to which SEL activities are achieving their goals? In what ways is the information applied to improve future practice?

There are no preconceived right or wrong answers to these questions. Rather, our intent is to encourage you to think about what you are doing with respect to SEL, and to help you see how broad the scope of these activities is.

What Comes Next?

Now that you have begun to think about what you are doing, we bet that you are surprised at how many relevant efforts are taking place in your classroom, school, or district. Even though some educators may not be aware of all the ways in which they are promoting social and emotional development, we think that teachers must provide at least some instruction in this area in order to be effective.

At the same time, you are probably also aware of various efforts you could be making to foster social and emotional competence that you are not pursuing right now. As you proceed through the book, we will introduce many ideas to help you think in SEL terms and to understand how to weave these new ideas effectively into what you are already doing.

3 How Does Social and Emotional Education Fit in Schools?

IT IS THE SECOND WEEK OF THE SEMESTER. TWENTY-two high school juniors sit in a circle on the floor of their classroom, desks and chairs pushed to the sides of the room. They just completed a "Day Starter" activity in which each student chose a piece of colored paper and was asked to use it to express one of the emotions he or she felt coming into class today. Some students were content to express their feelings only through their choice of a particular color or the way they folded or drew upon the paper. Others verbally shared the meaning of what they did.

Now the teacher puts in the center of the room a variety of objects brought in by students that represent something very important in their lives. One at a time, students choose an item that intrigues them—a ring, a cupcake, a small box, a stone, a set of keys, a locket, a picture. They speak briefly about what attracted them to the object, and then ask for the story behind it. The student who brought the item then explains its meaning.

This storytelling creates an interconnected narrative of what youngsters care about in their lives today. Many stories are about the preciousness of relationships—with family, with friends, with a brother, or with a father recently lost to death. Some are about the passion to create through art, dance, or theater. Some are about the joy of being part of a team, or being alone with nature, or the frustrations and dangers of living in their communities.

When it is time for this activity to end, the teacher asks the students to say a word or phrase that captures what they are feeling as they prepare to leave for their next class. Words like "happy," "excited," "peaceful," "calm," and "pensive" fill the air. The teacher thanks the class and, if all students didn't have time to share, says that when they meet again, the rest of the students will have their stories heard. Together, the students then restore the desks to their original positions.

Creating the Personal-Academic Connection

To anyone who has been around adolescents, it is clear that they are generally more focused on themselves, their peers, and their outside lives than they are on the school curriculum. Their strong feelings compete with the teacher for their attention and, more often than not, the feelings win. But when teachers allow those feelings to take a constructive place in the classroom and then use the concerns of the students as a bridge to academic assignments, they are providing the "missing piece" to students' learning. They are integrating social and emotional needs with academics. This process allows students to personalize and internalize their learning in ways that high school teachers are most accustomed to seeing from students taking electives, from "gifted and talented" students, or from those who are in an academic or vocational track to which they feel genuine commitment.

Activities like the sharing session described earlier create new opportunities for teaching and learning. Depending on the class—English, literature, history, civics, art, music, family life, biology, earth science—the teacher who has used such an activity can link an assignment to the sharing the students have done or to the words they have used to describe their feelings. One assignment might involve writing a story, play, video script, or docudrama about their concerns. Another might involve finding a work of literature that has similar themes and comparing and contrasting life and fiction. Relationships might be explored, such as those with peers and parents. Or students might enjoy looking at the way in which climate and topography influence how people come together and live, thereby helping adolescents choose where to spend their college or early adult years. An increasing number of articles in the popular media help make the biology of everyday life—influencing emotions, learning, sports performance, and schooling—interesting and relevant to teenagers.

What Do We Want Our Students to Achieve?

Most people would agree that social and academic success and a sense of personal well-being and efficacy that enable students to participate in school, home, family, workplace, and community life with skill, thoughtfulness, and integrity are high on the list of what we want students to achieve. In other words, we want them to be knowledgeable, responsible, and caring.[1] How can we increase the odds of

this happening? There are certain *tasks* that students need to master along the way, certain *competencies* needed to accomplish those tasks, and certain *values* and *attitudes* they need to develop. Knowledge, skills, values, or attitudes by themselves are insufficient; they must all work together, be nurtured and encouraged, and occur within a supportive climate.

In the example above, the teacher is creating a receptive climate for learning that reflects the developmental stages of the high school students. Such a climate is urgently needed in the schools. Media influences, a powerful consumer culture, and household pressures compete with our hope that family life will inculcate in children a love of learning and respect for academic routines, traditions, and requirements. The teacher in our example was tired of swimming upstream, of fighting the forces of development within the students. By going with the flow of social and emotional development, educators have found that academic as well as interpersonal success is enhanced. SEL is indeed the "missing piece" in schooling today, and we have learned a great deal about it in recent years.

Applications of Social and Emotional Skills to Diverse Areas of Development

"Who ya gonna hang out with on the school yard?"

"C'mon, let's spray paint the school."

"I can't believe you're worried about school work. Forget it, and forget class. Come with us."

"You gotta smoke—everyone else does."

"Are you gonna listen to what they tell you about health in those stupid assemblies?"

"How can you listen to that teacher? I'm gettin' myself thrown out, and if you do too, we can hang out in the office. Here's what we gotta do . . ."

"I'm gonna punch him out!"

These situations—familiar to anyone who has been

---

[1] Primary source material for this chapter and the developmental scope and sequence in Appendix A are Asher and Coie (1990); Bartz (1991); Berk (1989); Brooks (1981); Copple, Sigel, and Saunders (1979); Damon and Hart (1988); Dorman and Lipsitz (1984); Eisenberg and Mussen (1989); Elias (1993); Erikson (1954); Nummela and Rosengren (1986); Sylwester (1995); and Wood (1994).

in a school—place children at personal and interpersonal crossroads. Are they aware of their conflicting feelings as these situations unfold? Are they able to manage their emotions, whether they feel threat, anger, temptation, joy, or relief? Can they understand the perspectives of the others involved? Can they tell which of their peers are their genuine friends? Do they have an ethical or spiritual framework to guide their decision making? Do they have the interpersonal skills needed to handle the situation as they would most like to? Can they refuse appropriately and assertively? Can they stall others while they think things through more carefully? If they try something once, can they stop if they realize they are uncomfortable or that the consequences are worse than they expected?

If students are to gather accurate information from themselves and their environments, make decisions, and follow through with competent action, then they must possess social and emotional strategies and skills. These "life skills" guide children as they face situations like those presented above. Such skills are even more critical as we look ahead to the time when children become adolescents and then move on to take adult roles as citizens in a democracy, with all of the many opportunities and responsibilities that follow. They will be called upon often to work in groups and in partnership with classmates and adults. They inevitably will face all manner of academic, workplace, and interpersonal challenges. Their success in navigating the currents of daily life—both in and out of school—will require a capacity to think clearly and make decisions under emotionally arousing circumstances.

As children mature, they must learn to assume greater responsibility for their behavior as adult supervision becomes less direct and intensive. Their capacity for sound social and emotional judgment and appropriate personal decision making truly becomes as important as their basic academic abilities. Kolbe (1985) points out that one's "independent" health decisions are connected to one's social relationships and therefore can in no real

sense be viewed as "autonomous." If a teenager smokes, her act affects others. If a middle school student goes off by himself and drinks beer in the park, or does so with a few friends, there are clear ramifications for parent-child and other family relationships. Children's sleep habits may lead to distractible or lethargic, inattentive behaviors that may affect peer and teacher relationships in school. Violence and prejudice in a classroom or school act as poisons, tainting academic learning, coloring personal goals, and creating a climate in which schooling becomes highly difficult to carry out effectively. The entire atmosphere becomes unhealthy, leaving no one untouched. Goleman (1995) echoes others when he says that success in the adult world depends on both academic ability and interpersonal, intrapersonal, or practical intelligence—that is, social and emotional skills (Blythe and Gardner 1990, Sternberg and Wagner 1986).

For these reasons, it is important to outline clearly the social and emotional education that children need to acquire in the course of their school years—skills and capacities that schools must impart in partnership with parents and the surrounding community. Starting now, and continuing through the next five chapters, we will present key guidelines for social and emotional education (see Appendix B for a list of the guidelines). Each guideline is followed by a brief rationale as well as discussion of its implications and applications for educational practice. You will find examples throughout the book of various SEL applications; the examples are numbered to correspond with the appropriate guideline (e.g., Example 1A is an example of Guideline 1; Example 2A is an example of Guideline 2).

GUIDELINE 1 ▼

Educators at all levels need explicit plans to help students become knowledgeable, responsible, and caring. Efforts are needed to build and reinforce skills in four major domains of SEL:
   1. Life skills and social competencies

2. Health-promotion and problem-prevention skills

3. Coping skills and social support for transitions and crises

4. Positive, contributory service

Rationale

Learning skills requires ongoing exposure and practice. Social and emotional skills are similar to other academic skills in that the initial building blocks are elaborated upon over time and can be combined to address increasingly complex situations that children face. New skills, such as coping with the greater independence of high school and learning workplace skills, are built on earlier foundations. Hence, it is necessary to address these skills at each key grade level and for each domain (Weissberg and Greenberg 1997).

1. Life skills and social competencies. These include *generic* life, health, citizenship, and workplace skills. Examples include self-control, stress management, decision making, problem solving, conflict resolution, appropriate assertiveness, social skills, listening, self-expression and other communication skills, and skills related to identity and spiritual development. This last competency includes such things as knowing how to access one's creativity; how to set academic, career, and relationship goals; and how to discover constructive personal meaning and purpose. These skills are the foundation of successful social interaction in all contexts, and shortcomings in these areas diminish potential accomplishments in academic and other areas (Elias et al. 1994, Gardner 1993, Goleman 1995).

2. Health-promotion and problem-prevention skills. These are strategies and behaviors to reduce the likelihood of experiencing specific problems such as drug use (including alcohol and tobacco), violence, AIDS, sexually transmitted diseases, premature sexual activity, delinquency, and suicide at-

tempts. These skills complement the life skills above, but with the addition of context-specific information related to a particular problem or risk area (see Figure 1.1 on p. 4 for the New Haven Social Development Curriculum Scope, which offers an example of a program that combines life skills and competencies with problem prevention and risk reduction across several social and health areas). The National Commission on the Role of the School and the Community in Improving Adolescent Health[2] (1990, p. 36) describes a "new kind of health education" that highlights the importance of social and emotional skills in efforts to promote health and prevent problems. This sophisticated, multifaceted program goes light years beyond present lectures about "personal hygiene" or the food pyramid:

• It provides honest, relevant information about disease and injury prevention, family life and sex education, drug and alcohol abuse, violence, mental health, and nutrition.

• It teaches students the skills and strategies needed to make wise decisions, develop positive values, generate alternatives, deal with group pressure, work cooperatively, and avoid fights—skills that are better learned through role playing and other small-group participatory activities than through lectures.

• It includes participation in physical activity programs that foster lifelong exercise habits.

• It begins before students are pressured to experiment with risky behaviors and continues throughout adolescence. It should begin in kindergarten and continue in a planned, sequential manner through grade 12.

3. Coping skills and social support for transitions and crises. These skills involve children's capacity to deal with stressful life events. The creation of support systems of caring adults and peers to help students handle challenging situ-

---

[2]A collaborative effort between the National Association of State Boards of Education and the American Medical Association.

EXAMPLE 1A
HELPING CHILDREN COPE WITH DIVORCE

Joanne Pedro-Carroll oversees the implementation of the Children of Divorce Project, which operates out of the Primary Mental Health Project in Rochester, New York, in numerous schools. She points out that while administrators are sometimes hesitant to delve into this personal area, parents typically are avid supporters of this well-researched and acclaimed program. They appreciate the option of having a short-term skill-building and peer support group for their children. There are structured curriculums for older and younger groups of elementary-aged students. The structure of this program can be extended to a range of other event-triggered problems.

We work with the feelings of the children: fear that parents will stop loving them, sadness, misconceptions about why parents divorce, and so on. For younger children, "Tenderheart" is a doll who takes on the characteristics of a child whose parents are divorced. The children in the group talk to Tenderheart about their feelings and the difference between problems that are solvable and unsolvable by children. For K–3, we aim at correcting misconceptions. We have a board game that has emotion cards and divorce situations, for example, "Do you think that you can get your parents together?" The group talks about how to solve the problem.

For grades 4 to 6 we emphasize feelings. We use creative writing. We also help students to learn problem-solving skills by role playing and considering the consequences of their solutions. A group of 10-year-olds who felt very isolated started a newsletter. Amanda, who was put in the middle of a vicious custody battle, wrote a poem for the newsletter and "accidentally" left it on her mother's desk. The poem read, "Anger, fear, and worry sometimes turn to fury. And when this happens, parents must try not to turn to dust with anger, fear, and worry." The group was very interested in her feelings. The mom wrote back, and this opened up lines of communication through leaving notes for each other. The newsletter is used to express feelings of members of the group. It is also used for thinking through ways to deal with day-to-day problems. The group helped Adam role play possible ways to discuss with his mom changes in the visitation schedule and what her response might be. Eventually he got up the encourage to confront her and it worked out well. The weekend after it happened he told the group. They were so proud of him that they cheered and gave him high fives. That day, Adam's shoulders were back, not sunken, and his head was held high instead of [his face] being covered by his hair.

Overall goals are the same for each grade: Reduce stress and anxiety, let students know they have support, develop skills to cope. The kids choose names for their groups. Two are "KICS= Kids Incorporated in Caring and Sharing" and "The Cosby Group" because they long for a family like that.

ations and circumstances is an important element of any SEL program. So-called "event-triggered services"—that is, those initiated upon the occurrence of critical life events—need to be available. These services are designed to *prevent* children from experiencing severe behavioral or learning disruptions as a result of events such as parental separation and divorce or making the transition to middle school (see the end of Appendix A [p. 133] for additional examples).

In this domain, students need specialized skills to help them address the personal and interpersonal turmoil and conflict that accompany significant life change and loss. Students need to know how to cope, how to reduce tension, and where to look for support. This information is best conveyed through structured programs of conflict resolution, support groups, and so on, as illustrated in Examples 1A, 1B and 1C (Johnson and Johnson 1989/ 1990; Johnson, Johnson, Dudley, and Burnett 1992; Pedro-Carroll, Alpert-Gillis, and Cowen 1992; Wolchik et al. in press; Zins and Elias 1993). While these interventions may be coordinated with classroom-based programming, they are often delivered individually or in small groups by various other school personnel.

4. Positive, contributory service. In this domain, we recognize that our society is becoming more complex, interdependent, and diverse. The demands of citizenship are growing. Our communities need dedicated leaders and volunteers. From where will they come? How will they be prepared? A critical part of the answer includes such school-based activities as in-class and cross-age tutoring and mentoring; classroom, school, or community service; and serving as peer mediators and orienters for new students, "buddies" for studying, and assistants for students with special needs. Example 1D speaks to the benefits of service for students of different ages.

We live in a time of changing social institutions, and the schools have a critical role to play in preserving children's sense of belonging and pur-

---

EXAMPLE 1B
COPING EFFECTIVELY WITH AN ILL TEACHER AND HER SUBSTITUTE

SEL provides students with both individual skills and skills for solving problems as a group. We were having a big problem with a class of students who were upset about having substitute teachers while their teacher, who they had learned to care for and trust, was absent for an extended period of time because she was receiving chemotherapy. I was able to go into the class and work with the children, using the skills we had learned in "Second Step" [*Authors' note*: See also p. 28 for more on Second Step], to help them share their feelings and then move into problem solving what THEY could do to make the situation better. With the help of Jackie (SEL program coordinator), the students were able to make themselves and the new visiting teacher feel comfortable in the classroom.

The students role-played to see what it felt like to be the new person in the classroom. The students then made sure they welcomed the teacher and gave small tokens of their appreciation, thanking the substitute for coming into their classroom and helping them. They also decided to reinstitute something they had done with their teacher: making every Wednesday a time to give written friendship-grams letters to their teacher on their class computer.

—Jacqualine Brown,
Seattle Public Schools, Committee for Children,
describing the Second Step program

---

pose. Students are seeking to feel a sense of positive relatedness and community, whether as a complement or an alternative to having strong religious or family guidance. A key to attaining this outcome is positive, contributory service (Brandt 1991, González 1991, Lewis 1991).

EXAMPLE 1C
RESOLVING CONFLICT AND CREATING PEACEABLE RELATIONSHIPS

The Resolving Conflict Creatively Program (RCCP) teaches students (and teachers, administrators, and parents) a process that enables them to find creative solutions to conflicts. This is done by teaching de-escalation and negotiation skills, but also by structured lessons to increase appreciation of their own and other cultures and ways to live in a school as a peaceful learning community. In a typical model, older students in a school are the mediators for younger ones. Here is a story about the program in action.

With tears streaming down her face, 7-year-old Veronica picks herself up from the asphalt of the playground and charges toward her friend, Jasmine. "Why'd you trip me?" she screams. "I didn't trip you." "Yes you did, and I'm gonna trip you right back on your face!"

Suddenly, two 5th graders wearing bright blue T-shirts appear. Across the front and back of their shirts, the word *mediator* is emblazoned. "Excuse me!" says one. "My name is Jessica." "And I'm Angel," says the other. "We're mediators. Would you like us to help solve this problem?" "I guess so," the younger girls say grudgingly. Jessica and Angel first obtain the disputants' agreement to some ground rules (including no name-calling and no interrupting), and then the mediators suggest that they all move to a quieter area of the playground to talk things out.

"You'll speak first, Veronica," says Jessica. "But don't worry Jasmine, you'll get your chance. OK, Veronica, tell us what happened."

Within two minutes, the girls have solved their problem. Jasmine acknowledges that she tripped Veronica by accident as she was trying to tag her. She says she is sorry. Veronica agrees to accept the apology and to be Jasmine's friend again. After being congratulated by Angel and Jessica for solving their problem, the girls resume their game.

—Lantieri and Patti (1996), RCCP, New York City

Implications and Applications

Success in each of the four domains involves the coordination of skills in emotion, thinking, and behavior. Many of these skills are basic to human functioning, so they begin to appear in rudimentary form in infancy. As children get older, they apply these skills to increasingly complex situations and learn to differentiate, label, and integrate them. Even in adolescence, skill development continues, primarily through the feedback, reflection, learning, and growth that result from new experiences.

Helping students develop and coordinate skills in emotion, cognition, and behavior is a necessary activity at the classroom, school, and, ideally, district levels (Shriver and Weissberg 1996, Weissberg and Greenberg 1997). In the rest of this chapter, we highlight the main areas of skill development that research so far has identified as important and worth addressing in the schools, both formally and informally. For the sake of clarity, we next present some starting points for your consideration.[3]

[3]See also both the later section on Development in this chapter (pp. 37–41) and Appendix A, both of which present more detailed, though not comprehensive, scope and sequence outlines.

EXAMPLE 1D
POSITIVE CONTRIBUTORY SERVICE FOR DIFFERENT AGE GROUPS

Positive, contributory service provides benefits at all age levels. Here are some examples:

La Salle Academy's Big Brothers/Big Sisters Program

Principal Ray Pasi: On the first day of classes, freshmen are paired up with seniors. The seniors are asked to become a role model and assist the freshmen in making the transition to La Salle. The parents love it because it helps them to have people take an interest in their children, to help them adjust and give them encouragement. The seniors feel needed in the school; 210 out of 300 seniors participated in the program.

Student: The program is great because it gives the freshmen somebody to listen to and give them guidance. I have to go see my little brother soon because he's having a little trouble with English, and I'm pretty good at it and I am going to help him with it.

Student: My little sister was having trouble with someone who wanted to beat her up. She wanted me to beat the person up.

Bob Lisi, Freshman Transition Coordinator: We got both parties together because I knew about it and did a little conflict resolution.

Student: Freshmen know where to find the seniors, and the seniors know where to find the freshmen so they can visit before homeroom. It feels good to make a difference to somebody.

Student: Some of the kids who couldn't be bothered or only did it for their resumes now are doing it because they see its importance.

La Salle's Senior Service Program

Student: I went to the day care and worked with 4- and 5-year-olds who didn't really get a lot of attention at home. They were neglected. I walked into the classroom, and this little girl grabbed me by the knee and said, "Do you want to be my brother?" And it was a really great feeling. The last class the teacher let me conduct a whole lesson, and the kids really looked up to me and it felt good. Then, as I was leaving, the kids gave me a book that each of the kids had drawn a page for. I'm going to visit them on my next half day because I miss them.

Fourth grade students from Hazelwood School in Lexington, Kentucky, had these comments about their Buddy Program:

"I like the buddy program with the 1st grade because I get to read to them. I like to do things for them."

"I like to stop fights when they start by helping them talk it out."

"We feel happy because we get to teach them stuff that we know how to do."

"They help you learn, too. For example, I got to read an "Arthur" book. My buddy reads to me, and I feel proud that my buddy can read."

Emotion. The skills related to becoming emotionally competent begin in infancy. At their simplest, the skills involve recognizing cues from the faces, postures, and vocal tones of others, followed by labeling and verbalizing emotions. Gradually, children expand their vocabulary for feelings and their ability to link feelings appropriately to an increasing range of situations. It takes only a moment's reflection, however, to recognize that children come to school with a range of emotional skills and a range of consistency in the use of these skills. Much of what educators observe about children's emotional awareness and regulation depends also on the skills of memory and language, and how emotion, events, and their labels become integrated, coordinated, and recalled. The ability of children to learn, access, and apply their learning is interwoven with their emotional skills.

Cognition. To live and learn in a social world, we need to be able to listen accurately, pay attention, remember what we hear and learn, and guide ourselves in thoughtful decision making and problem solving when facing choices or problematic situations. More specifically, we need a social decision-making and problem-solving strategy that includes the following skills:

• Understanding signs of one's own and others' feelings.
• Accurately labeling and expressing feelings.
• Identifying one's goals.
• Thinking of alternative ways to solve a problem, especially when planning a solution and making a final check for possible obstacles.
• Thinking about long- and short-term consequences for oneself and others.
• Reflecting on what happens when carrying out one's strategies, and learning for the future.

These cognitive skills foster integration and are interdependent with skills in the emotional and behavioral areas; consequently, they are subject to any limitations in those areas. We see the effects of

not accomplishing this task in the classroom when children with great intellectual problem-solving abilities are not socially successful because of difficulties in dealing with feelings or in carrying out desired behaviors. Further, carrying out thoughtful decision making and problem solving under stress requires an even higher level of ability in these areas. Example 1E shows problem-solving strategies from several different programs.

Behavior. *Self-control skills* are necessary to accurately process the information contained in social encounters, to engage in thoughtful social decision making, and to be able to approach others in difficult situations without provoking anger or annoyance. These skills include the ability follow directions, calm oneself down when under stress, manage anger effectively, and communicate clearly in a respectful and civil manner.

Group participation skills underlie the exercise of social responsibility, constructive task-oriented contributions in groups, and the building of meaningful communities. They include the following:

• Recognizing and eliciting trust, help, and praise from others.
• Recognizing others' perspectives.
• Choosing friends wisely.
• Sharing, waiting, and participating in groups (including cooperative learning groups).
• Giving and receiving help and criticism.
• Resisting pressure from peers and the media to engage in antisocial, illegal, or dangerous behaviors.
• Exercising leadership, accepting diversity, and demonstrating desirable attributes such as honesty, responsibility, compassion, and caring.

Integration. Although the three skills areas are presented separately here, they are of course integrated in actuality. Emotional intelligence serves as the integrative concept, in that competence in social and emotional functioning is a product of an interrelationship of skills in the emotional, cognitive,

EXAMPLE 1E
PROBLEM-SOLVING STEPS USED BY DIFFERENT PROGRAMS

Social Decision-Making Skills: A Guide for the Elementary Grades
When children and adults are using their social problem-solving skills, they emphasize eight skill areas:

1. Noticing signs of feelings.
2. Identifying issues or problems.
3. Determining and selecting goals.
4. Generating alternative solutions.
5. Envisioning possible consequences.
6. Selecting their best solution.
7. Planning and making a final check for obstacles.
8. Noticing what happened, and using the information for future decision making and problem solving.

An instructional and easily prompted version of the social decision-making and problem-solving skills, given the acronym "FIG TESPN":

1. Feelings cue me to problem solve.
2. I have a problem.
3. Goals give me a guide.
4. Think of many possible things to do.
5. Envision end results (outcomes) for each option.
6. Select my best solution.
7. Plan the procedure and anticipate pitfalls (roadblocks), practice, and pursue.
8. Notice what happened, and now what?

—Elias and Tobias (1996)

The Second Step Violence Prevention Program
The Second Step Program for 4th and 5th graders offers a five-step process:

1. What is the problem?
2. What are some solutions?
3. For each solution, ask:
   - Is it *safe*?
   - How might people *feel*?
   - Is it *fair*?
   - Will it *work*?
4. Chose a solution and use it.
5. Is it working? If not, what can I do now?

—Committee for Children (1992)

EXAMPLE 1E—*continued*
PROBLEM-SOLVING STEPS USED BY DIFFERENT PROGRAMS

The Social Competence Promotion Program for Young Adolescents
The Social Competence Promotion Program for Young Adolescents presents the following six-step social-information processing framework for solving a wide range of real-life problems. A traffic light poster is used to display the following sequential, six-step process:

1. Stop, calm down, and think before you act.
2. Say the problem and how you feel.
3. Set a positive goal.
4. Think of lots of solutions.
5. Think ahead to the consequences.
6. Go ahead and try the best plan.

The traffic light links a familiar image to three central, sequential phases of problem solving. The red light—or "stop" phase—symbolizes stopping to calm down in preparation for problem-solving thinking and action (step 1); the yellow light—or "thinking" phase—offers a process for identifying problems and evaluating options for implementation (steps 2 to 5); and the green light—or "go" phase—represents taking action to resolve the problem (step 6). Through explicit instruction in the six steps, teachers and students learn a common language and framework for communicating about problems. Furthermore, the traffic-light poster may be used as a visual reminder to prompt students to apply problem solving throughout the school (e.g., in the cafeteria, on the playground) and at home.

—Weissberg, Caplan, Bennetto, and Jackson (1990)

---

and behavioral areas (Goleman 1995, Mayer and Salovey 1995). Example 1F shows the key skills that make up emotional intelligence and cut across different domains of human functioning. Although there is value in presenting the skill areas separately, particularly as part of the learning process, we actually apply these skills simultaneously. For example, when students have just been handed a surprise quiz, knowing how they feel, managing these feelings effectively, focusing on the task at hand, and communicating appropriately afterward to friends all are part of effective problem solving.

Acquiring an integrated set of skills such as these often occurs best in an experiential context, where the skills are learned through practice and role modeling. These considerations are reflected in the guidelines that follow.

GUIDELINE 2 ▼

Successful efforts to build social and emotional skills are linked to developmental milestones as well as the need to help students cope with ongoing life events and local circumstances.

Rationale

Students who are at risk for problems such as violence, school failure, and substance abuse typically lack the skills to meet normative developmental challenges or the special challenges posed by highly stressful life events. In some cases, the students are skilled, but their values or expectations conflict with those of the school. Although blind conformity to all rules is clearly not an intended outcome of education, thoughtful reflection about rules and the interests of oneself and others is desirable. Specifically, social and emotional skills are necessary to reduce the incidence of what Goleman (1995) calls "emotional hijacking," which takes place when one's feelings overwhelm the balance of behavioral and cognitive checks and balances that are a necessary part of everyday living.

EXAMPLE 1F
EMOTIONAL INTELLIGENCE: KEY SKILLS IN SOCIAL AND EMOTIONAL LEARNING

Self-Awareness
- Recognizing and naming one's emotions.
- Understanding of the reasons and circumstances for feeling as one does.

Self-Regulation of Emotion
- Verbalizing and coping with anxiety, anger, and depression.
- Controlling impulses, aggression, and self-destructive, antisocial behavior.
- Recognizing strengths in and mobilizing positive feelings about self, school, family, and support networks.

Self-Monitoring and Performance
- Focusing on tasks at hand.
- Setting short- and long-term goals.
- Modifying performance in light of feedback.
- Mobilizing positive motivation.
- Activating hope and optimism.
- Working toward optimal performance states, flow, manage inverted U relationship between anxiety and performance.

Empathy and Perspective Taking
- Learning how to increase these, and develop feedback mechanisms to use in everyday life.
- Becoming a good listener.
- Increasing empathy and sensitivity to others' feelings.
- Understanding others' perspectives, points of view, feelings.

Social Skills in Handling Relationships
- Managing emotions in relationships, harmonizing diverse feelings, viewpoints.
- Expressing emotions effectively.
- Exercising assertiveness, leadership, persuasion.
- Working as part of a team/cooperative learning groups.
- Showing sensitivity to social cues.
- Exercising social decision-making and problem-solving skills.
- Responding constructively and in a problem-solving manner to interpersonal obstacles.

Implications and Applications

Guideline 2 has a number of practical implications. First, learning that is developmentally appropriate, as well as brain-friendly and appealing to diverse learners, uses skill-based, experiential approaches. These approaches greatly increase students' use of social and emotional skills outside the classroom. Unfortunately, in many instances, particularly in high school, fact-oriented and lecture-based approaches predominate. When students are in emotionally charged and high-pressure situations, however, they have trouble accessing information and skills learned from such approaches. We see evidence of this in evaluations of information-oriented health education programs (Weissberg and Elias 1993, Weissberg and Greenberg 1997). Guideline 2 suggests that we carefully note what constitutes sound educational procedure in this area.

Second, this guideline acknowledges that state and federal guidelines and mandates for alcohol, tobacco, steroid, and other drug abuse, AIDS, health education, violence prevention, and so on, must be met. However, it also challenges us to examine their focus on persuading children to avoid risky behaviors that may lead to dangerous outcomes. Problem prevention alone is not sufficient to provide the "missing piece" children need in their lives. Building the social and emotional skills required for all endeavors and relationships in their lives—including the discipline and motivation to successfully navigate what are literally nearly two decades of academic hurdles—must be emphasized.

To be able to teach students, educators must clearly understand when students will be called on to use social and emotional skills. Here is a range of examples:

• When waiting in a long line, waiting to get on a computer, or waiting to use a paint set.
• When being pressured to smoke, to vandalize property, or to speak in a disrespectful way to students who are members of minority groups.

• When dealing with the anxiety of taking a major test like the SAT, preparing to speak in front of an assembly, playing competitive sports, or participating in a musical, artistic, or dramatic performance.

Indeed, it is real-life events that are the best practice field for learning to use skills that are called upon under stressful, difficult, rare, and unpredictable conditions, as Example 2A illustrates.

The Importance of Character, Values, and Self-Esteem

G U I D E L I N E 3 ▼

SEL programs emphasize the promotion of prosocial attitudes and values about self, others, and work.

Rationale, Implications, and Applications

The Four C's. Healthy self-esteem develops when children are given the four C's: Confidence, Competencies, Chances, and Caring. Throughout their school careers, our children need the adults around them to inspire them with *confidence* that they can learn, accomplish, and interact successfully in a range of situations. They need adults around them to design experiences that will impart the *competencies* needed for academic and social successes, to back up their confidence. They need adults around them to create *chances* to use their skills, to learn in the protected and supervised arena of the school so that they will be less at risk in the relatively unsupervised and unscripted world in which they interact.

Would we send students in front of an assembly to do a skit without giving them a sense of confidence, the skills they need, and lots of rehearsal? No way. How is it, then, that we seem content to do less to prepare students for the major chal-

---

EXAMPLE 2A
DRAWING ON COMMUNITY TO PROVIDE SUPPORT WHEN SCHOOL TRAGEDY STRIKES

"Over the Christmas vacation, one of our students, a young man named Frank, was killed as a result of injuries from a car accident. And I thought Social Problem Solving (SPS) was a lifeline for me and also for the students. It gave us all something to fall back on to face a very difficult situation.

"For me, as the teacher, I was very glad that I had done the background work of establishing group unity and trust in our sharing circles. We had an opportunity to do that before anything so serious and difficult happened. When we came back to school, I remember the first morning that we entered the building. It was a Thursday. And immediately the students and I entered the room and put the chairs in a circle. No one said anything about it. So, we had a chance to share our feelings, and at that point weren't processing anything. We were just feeling. We used the circle to work that out.

"I was really surprised those first few days of dealing with Frank's death that the students relied so much on having that sharing circle and wanted to share. And these are students that came to us with minimal self-awareness skills and minimal self-control skills. And actually, as I tried to get the routine back to normal, they stopped me at one point and said, 'Wait, Miss Krah. Can we take a vote and see if everybody wants to have a sharing circle?' And they did. It seemed like a really good forum for them to deal with what we had to deal with.
"As time has gone on, we've had some ideas come up from students about alcohol-related car accidents and what kind of decisions people could or couldn't make. We used the process a little more to think that through."

—Marge Krah, Middle School Special Education Teacher
Cape May, New Jersey, Special Services School District

---

lenges they face all the time on the stage of life? This is where the fourth C, *caring*, becomes so important. Each student needs to feel valued as a meaningful member of the class and school. What is particularly important is how we *show* caring to students so that they are more likely to respond with caring toward themselves and others.

Character. Thomas Lickona (1991) is one of the leaders in the character education field. His view of character, values, and self-esteem shows the inherent linkage of these areas. Character is defined as values in action; values refer to "knowing the good." Clearly, in different families, communities, and cultural groups, there may be varying definitions of what is "good." Self-esteem is a feeling or attitude that accompanies believing that one is fol-

lowing the "good" in a given community or valued group. This is why, as Lickona notes, people of "good character" can be quite different from one another.

These differences also explain why disaffected youth seek out peers and other groups that will validate their actions and serve as a source of self-esteem. Gangs take on this role for many students who do not or cannot derive esteem from school or family. Bullard (1992) notes that schools may encourage an allegiance to gangs if they have a narrowly academic or culturally bound definition of "the good," particularly when families are not serving as alternative sources of positive support.

Religious schools have definitions of "the good" linked to worship and observances that may not be interchangeable across denominations. Nevertheless, Lickona (1991) and others point out that there are common denominators amidst these differences, and these are proper topics of concern for the public schools (Ryan 1995). Lickona cites respect and responsibility as two of the most consensual and important, and caring clearly could be included, too. From the perspective of SEL, it is virtually impossible to imagine a classroom, school, community, family, or workplace that can function in the absence of respect, responsibility, and caring (among other attributes). Thus, ensuring that children have the skills to convey respect and responsibility—and make no mistake about it, there are many skills involved, it is not simply an "attitude" or "orientation"—is a valid and necessary part of basic education (Wynne and Walberg 1986). Families may have their own ways of wanting children to show respect, responsibility, and caring, and their teaching of these behaviors is essential. However, schools, workplaces, community organizations, and social groups also have their own definitions, and children must be prepared for these as well. Example 3A outlines one method of teaching about values and character.

Self-esteem. It should be clear that self-esteem is generated when students perform valued behaviors and are recognized for doing so. For this to happen, students' emotional intelligence must be put to work so that they can accurately perceive values around them and act in ways that are consistent with those values. Naturally, decisions must be made locally about what aspects of character and values will be emphasized, and how. Some maintain that desirable values are best learned in the crucible of interaction with positive adults and peers (Taffel 1996). However, Lickona (1991) and others believe that it is in students' interest for schools to address core values (such as honesty, fairness, and responsibility) that are likely to be endorsed, and thus encouraged, by most settings.

Providing Developmentally Appropriate Social and Emotional Education

It follows from what has been presented thus far that social and emotional skills cannot be reserved for periodic instruction; nor can they be expected to develop in the absence of continuous practice and opportunities for feedback and improvement. Therefore, it is necessary that developmentally appropriate instruction be provided in a planned way throughout children's time in school.

G U I D E L I N E 4 ▼

It is most beneficial to provide a developmentally appropriate combination of formal, curriculum-based instruction with ongoing, informal, and infused opportunities to develop social and emotional skills from preschool through high school.

Rationale

The interpersonal situations students face in school require that they make constant choices about how to behave. Being in a school community exposes kids to many influences on their choices, and life events occur that do not follow any prescribed curriculum guides. Social and emotional instruction, therefore, must be *anchored* by being *systematic* and *curriculum-based* at each level of schooling. Such learning provides a forum for skill building to help address ongoing, developmentally expected issues. But there is also a need for *flexibility* to help address unexpected life events in ways that are minimally disruptive of academic progress and that sustain healthy, positive relationships with others. This process occurs through encouraging the informal use of skills and by infusing skill building into academic activities (Elias and Clabby 1992; Hawkins, Catalano, et al. 1992; Weissberg and Greenberg 1997).

EXAMPLE 3A
HOW TO ADDRESS VALUES, VIRTUE, AND CHARACTER USING AN SEL FRAMEWORK

1. Select a focal value (character aspect, etc.).

2. Define it via group discussion and by looking at the dictionary definition, especially the derivation of the word.

3. Provide an age-appropriate literature example that explores, addresses, and involves that value. Integrate this material with your current reading program and areas of emphasis, making relevant assignments. Include aspects of the value in class and small-group discussions.

4. Help students identify life examples of the value. Several useful approaches include an individual or class chart in which examples of the value "in action" can be recorded for a given week (or other period of time) or having a circle or sharing time in which students identify and share times when their behavior involved that value, might have involved that value, or when they saw that value enacted by others. Interesting discussions will take place, for example, as to whether "caring" was appropriate or perhaps overdone or not genuine, or whether "assertiveness" turned into aggressiveness, or whether what seems to be a behavior seen as aggressive in minority students or girls is seen as assertive in majority students or boys.

5. Assign academic projects related to that value that fit with broader learning goals.

Personal: Individual students can set personal goals around the expression of a particular value with their classmates, toward other teachers, and so on.

Paired, small-group, class, or schoolwide projects can be assigned, related to a particular reading or series of readings; can be integrated with a civics unit; or can be applied to life on the playground, on the school bus, in the lunchroom, the hallways, the classroom, the surrounding school environment, or the community. Paired students can be empowered to hand out "Gotcha!" stickers to people seen enacting a focal value in the classroom or in other areas of the school. Other books can be assigned, and small groups can report on how the value was expressed differently by different characters. Associated art and music projects can be carried out. Adolescents often find it quite informative, engaging, and thought-provoking to look for the varied expressions of values in song lyrics and teen magazines.

Some of the values that schools from varied socioeconomic, geographic, and cultural backgrounds appear to emphasize include:

caring	honor	respect
confidence	justice	responsibility
courtesy	kindness	reverence
creativity	love	self-discipline
enthusiasm	loyalty	service
excellence	peacefulness	thankfulness
friendliness	purposefulness	tolerance
helpfulness	reflectiveness	trustworthiness
honesty	reliability	truthfulness

EXAMPLE 4A
LA SALLE ACADEMY'S SUCCESS FOR LIFE PROGRAM: EMBODYING THE PRINCIPLES OF SEL

La Salle Academy, in Providence, Rhode Island, incorporates all four social and emotional learning domains in a developmentally sensitive manner. The school also includes milestone and event-triggered and crisis programs, and a combination of curricular and informal, infused opportunities for SEL skill development and recognition.

"Success for Life," a schoolwide, curriculum-based program, assists students with issues connected to social and emotional intelligence. Not an "extra," it is incorporated into classes and activities and linked with La Salle's existing goals. These include the nurturing of all aspects of the child: spiritual, intellectual, social, and emotional. Administrators, teachers, and coaches explicitly incorporate a decision-making approach in their dealings with students.

Underscoring all our educational endeavors, we try to challenge students to consider what choices confront them, to remember to think before responding, and to choose the best alternative. Given the developmental levels and needs of adolescence, every attempt is made to infuse the program with the variety and engagement that typify successful secondary school educational strategies. Given the constraints of time and curriculum in the classroom component, only a limited number of "target" lessons may be included during a particular semester. A decision-making or problem-solving structure, however, can often be used as an instructional strategy.

Success for Life seeks to strengthen adolescents' awareness of themselves, their relationships, and situations in which they make important decisions in their lives. An ultimate goal is to help strengthen self-esteem and self-respect, as well as attitudes of caring and responsibility toward others. The program includes an interaction of cognitive, affective, and behavioral components:

• A *classroom program*, providing instruction across disciplines on issues of social competence and the intelligent management of one's emotions.

• A *schoolwide program*, starting with a daily morning reflection (by students or staff), designed to reinforce classroom efforts that promote healthy development.

• An *Adult Contact Program* for sophomores; a *Freshman Transition Program* (and Coordinator); a *Big Brother/Big Sister Service Program* for freshmen (and for the upperclass students working the program).

• *Small-group meetings* for students with more serious or chronic behavior problems to help build self-control and social awareness skills.

• A *computer-based education program* for specific types of disciplinary problems (a decision-making model).

• *Career Awareness and Wellness programs* that span four years, while concentrating on the decision-making, problem-solving focus of the junior year.

• *Theme-based assemblies* for each year, geared to particular competencies and the developmental level of each group.

• A *Senior Service program*, in part to foster post-high school transition.

• *Inclusion of the part-time coaching staff* in the orientation session on the school's mission, the Success for Life program, and their practical implications for dealing with student athletes (including the Student Athlete Contract).

• Ongoing *parent communication* to keep parents informed of our specific efforts and various *schoolwide activities* (designed with the help of the parent organization) to enhance parents' knowledge of program norms and values.

—Raymond Pasi, Principal, La Salle Academy

EXAMPLE 4A—*continued*
LA SALLE ACADEMY'S SUCCESS FOR LIFE PROGRAM: EMBODYING THE PRINCIPLES OF SEL

Three Examples of SEL in Action at La Salle
1. Celebrations of Success/Reinforcing School Climate. Students are issued wallet cards containing the La Salle Seal and the mission statement and goals:

Goals of Community Behavior
La Salle Academy
Mission:
To create a learning community which fosters acceptance, generosity, and mutual respect

OUR COMMON GOALS:
Our interest in the growth of each person urges us toward
Respect for Self
A high regard for the worth of each person
Respect for Others
An interest and concern for one another
Respect for Property
A vested interest in and respect for the property of
La Salle Academy

Art adorns the school entrance. Everyone created a separate panel depicting something that was important and involved principles he or she had been learning. One was a picture of Respect for the Environment. Another was a picture of the school and a picture of the world. All dealt with the main theme of respect. A banner embodying all three areas of respect hangs in our entrance.

2. Assemblies Linked to SEL Themes by Grade Level. Excerpt from Memo to all faculty from Leo Butler about the Sophomore Assembly:

As part of our Success for Life program in social and emotional education, the first of two assemblies for sophomores will be held . . .

Mr. Jim Hopkins will address students on the topic of interpersonal understanding and conflict resolution. He will share with us his experience over the years with peer mediation at Johnston High School. He will stress the importance of students' using peer mediation when a dispute occurs, as well as the importance of their eventually becoming involved as peer counselors.

Mr. Hopkins will also speak about appreciating the individuality of each person, by looking for and respecting the special talents unique to each person.

EXAMPLE 4A—*continued*
LA SALLE ACADEMY'S SUCCESS FOR LIFE PROGRAM: EMBODYING THE PRINCIPLES OF SEL

3. SEL must be taught formally, as well as infused, and linked to all aspects of education; for this to happen effectively requires ongoing staff development and curricular leadership.

Letter from Principal Ray Pasi to staff, October 31, 1996

When teaching students some aspect of social and emotional intelligence—whether it's empathy, some aspect of self-awareness, the importance of delaying gratification, etc.—it is essential that we are explicit about what we are doing. If we are not, students tend to think we are simply taking a break from the math or science or foreign language lesson. We should specifically tell them something to the effect that we are now covering something very important, and explain what social and emotional skill is being presented. When an assignment or lesson is given with this focus in mind, tell the students specifically what you want them looking for and considering, in relation to their own lives. If this is not done directly and explicitly, students will not appreciate the fact that they are deliberately getting something "extra" as part of a lesson or assignment. They should leave your class, at the end of the year, appreciating that you dealt on occasion with certain social and emotional skills that you consider quite important—as well as the academic content of the course.

Again, it is this combination of explicit instruction across the disciplines, plus our schoolwide programs, that combine to make our educational program in this area different from others.

Implications and Applications

It is common to see discussions of "ages and stages" of development in children; it is less common to see such a discussion focused on the details of what we know about social and emotional skills development (Consortium on the School-Based Promotion of Social Competence 1991; Elias et al. 1994; Hawkins, Catalano, et al. 1992). An overview of each of the major developmental periods follows.

Pre-school and early elementary grades (pre-K to grade 2, ages 3–7). Erikson's *stages of trust and autonomy* cover the years from birth to the age of 2 (approximately—the sequence is more reliable than the specific age boundaries). A successful outcome of these stages is linked to children receiving physical and emotional security (Carnegie Task Force on Meeting the Needs of Young People 1994). Even infants begin to make "if I do this, then that happens" connections as they learn what they must do to have their needs met. They learn how to get people to hold them, feed them, and change their diapers long before they can ask for such things directly. From these early experiences, children begin to develop a nonverbal sense of how to get their needs met. They also develop a sense of how likely they are to be successful in getting what they want. Later, a sense of self-efficacy emerges from this early, generalized sense of trust. Their early verbal behavior also is part of their current and future ability to make positive connections to others and get their needs met as they begin to recognize their capacity to explore and interact with their environments.

Preschoolers tend to become less and less impulsive and more likely to follow directions and rules even when no adult is present—but the range of variability is huge. Their use of language for self-regulation is helpful here. Getting along with peers is fostered by social approach skills, perspective taking, and empathy. Fears characteristic of the previous period should diminish; however, it is hard for young children to hold onto two strong emotions at the same time. As a result, moods can shift quickly.

Next, the *stage of initiative* brings new requirements for social interaction as children encounter day care, preschool, and school environments. Children must improve their motor and verbal control and begin to respond to social rules (in addition to parental rules). In early childhood, growing language and cognitive abilities fuel advances in social decision making and problem solving. Children can be expected to identify basic feelings, pick up on a central theme in social situations, be more aware of how to communicate successfully with others, consider alternative ways to reach a goal, and recognize alternative consequences to their actions.

Language and conceptual skills, needed for mature social decision making, evolve at this time. Children acquire terms to help them with key cognitive concepts: *is/is not, and/or, same/different, all/some*. These words are all about similarities and differences. *Other* and *else* reflect divergent production. *If/then* and *why/because* promote causal inferences. *Where, with whom, when, now/later,* and *before/after* are critical for social understanding and for specifying events. Preschoolers also get better at understanding patterns of related occurrences, and they begin to develop an early sense of what Rotter (1982) calls an "expectancy" for the usefulness of being a good problem solver—something adults should actively encourage.

Elementary and intermediate grades (grades 3–5; ages 8–10). Elementary school brings increases in understanding others' emotional reactions, reading social cues, and understanding others' verbal and nonverbal communications. Children are better able to help others, share, and feel empathy; there are more attempts to seek harmony with others, such as parents and peers, when there are tensions. Impulsivity declines and angry outbursts and aggressive behaviors decrease. Sustained, focused attention and effort emerge along with the pride at accomplishing goals. Assertiveness can replace aggressiveness, with verbal forms occurring far more often than the physical. Fearfulness decreases. Unhappiness, however, can be more sustained and can become more of a source of concern. Shyness is not typical, and cooperation with peers should be encouraged.

Cooperation, sustained attention, and harmonizing skills are essential because children enter the *stage of industry* during what is usually called middle childhood. School and extracurricular activities require children to display more focus and persistence than in prior stages. The skill of keeping track of their goals and how they are progressing toward them is important if students are to be able to carry out projects and participate in teams and performances. The attributes of persistence and sustained attention also are behind their penchant for collecting things and reading book series during the latter part of this age period.

Key social and emotional abilities include a broadening vocabulary to label a range of feelings in self and others, an improved understanding of how events relate to one another over time, and a more accurate sense of perspective. Further, an expanded ability to consider alternative solutions and consequences, increased planning to achieve goals, and the beginning of an ability to anticipate obstacles to one's plans contribute to interpersonal and school success.

Middle/junior high school (grades 6–9; ages 11–14). Early adolescence—the middle-school years—is most obviously a time of intense physical changes. Perhaps most significant are the varying rates at which these changes occur, both for a given child and across children. This variation means that the middle-school child can look like an elementary-school child or as old as an adult. As children see their schoolmates reach various milestones at different times, they inevitably make comparisons, and all too often see themselves as deficient.

Nevertheless, it is a myth that adolescence must be defined as a period of stress, turmoil, and rebellion. The developmental tasks that early adolescents must work through on their path toward adulthood can be sources of both exhilaration and consternation (Carnegie Council on Adolescent Development 1989, Dorman and Lipsitz 1984).

Adolescents are making a transition from the *stage of industry* to the *stage of identity*. They awaken to the world of possibility and potential, and they become more adept at abstract thinking and going from the specific to the general. They retain a certain egocentrism, which leads them to believe they are unique, special, and even invulnerable to harm (this mind-set, naturally, increases risk-taking behavior). At the same time, these youngsters care a great deal about what the anonymous "they" think.

To help deal with the vast cognitive awakening they are experiencing, early adolescents often see things in black and white, good versus bad terms, leading to the possibilities of exaggeration, denial, and overgeneralization. At the same time, middle-school students can be wonderfully idealistic, thoughtful, and incredibly immature and silly—all in the space of a typical school morning! Some of their idealism comes out as increased social concern, fueled by outrage with what is "wrong" in the world and their emerging realization that what they do in the present will affect what they do in the future.

Erikson (1954) noted that a sense of "industriousness" characteristic of early adolescence can be seen both in a strong orientation to certain tasks and in a faddish commitment to certain things for relatively short periods of time. Thus, middle-school-aged children can become avid collectors or focus intensely on a particular game or hobby. These kinds of activities prepare them for the stage of identity, which extends from preadolescence into the teen years. Students build on prior experiences to attempt to answer the questions "Who am I?" and "What can I become?"—questions that take on an emotional charge and a sense of reality as children move into formal operational cognitive capacities. Spiritual development also stirs, as children begin to glimpse the possibility of larger purpose and greater meaning to life. Many religions contain rituals in early adolescence that guide students in exploring these questions and mark the rite of passage into greater responsibility.

Unfortunately, the tendency toward industriousness does not necessarily translate into motivation related to school achievement. Having the best baseball card or audiotape collections may be more than sufficient for some children. Therefore, it is beneficial to bring students' own industriousness into the school and connect it with some area of academics. By linking school with students' own efforts to construct an identity, we can guard against disaffection, underachievement, failure, and dropping out.

Even though peer relationships are increasingly influential during the early adolescent years, adults must not be lulled into thinking that their influence as adult role models and guides is in any way diminished. What is most likely to occur is that children are more reluctant to admit or acknowledge this influence during the middle-school years than they might have just a few years earlier. Accordingly, providing support will often be quite thankless, and at times frustrating. Nonetheless, it can be a lifeline for youth who otherwise would derive most of their views from their peers. What adults can do to stimulate these children's social and emotional skills is to create environments where peers can relate to one another in positive, reflective, constructive ways, addressing important topics and questions about life in the community, social issues, the environment, rights and justice, or diversity.

Indeed, one of the markers of the transition to adolescence is a growing capacity for reflectiveness. This capacity includes increased awareness of sexuality and the ability to articulate "who am I?" in terms of strengths and weaknesses or preferences. It also can be seen in a heightened awareness of one's own and others' thoughts and feelings. (It is not unexpected to encounter some fears about the future, especially about success in jobs, and parents' health and well-being.) There is an interest in learning about one's own patterns of handling impulses, stress, difficulties, and so on. Awareness of these patterns can be taught, and goal-setting strategies to improve behaviors can be carried out, though more for short-term than long-term benefits.

Having arenas where there is a sense of mastery and control is important. Art, hobbies, sports, games, phone calls, collecting, magazines, music, clubs, cliques, groups, diaries—all are part of being unique and special and having something that is "theirs." Often the value of these is enhanced when they are shared with peers. Yet for the student lacking social and emotional skills, success in any of these arenas—and sharing them with peers—is quite difficult.

High school (grades 10–12; ages 15–17). Adolescents are involved in an ongoing process of consolidating and articulating who they are, where they are going, and what they intend to do. Key areas for emotional functioning are listening and understanding; self-expression; honesty; facing difficulties; trust; being more future-oriented than past-oriented; compromise; and expressions of loving, caring, and support.

For many, adolescence is a time of awakening to the energies, wonderings, and questions that accompany spiritual development. Some adolescents have an intense experience of their "inner life" and feel that school is irrelevant to their concerns.

Some students have a religious or cultural framework in which to express and explore their broad questions about life and themselves. Many students who lack spiritual guidance may engage in misguided attempts to seek experiences of "deeper meaning" and "transcendence of the ordinary."

Sometimes this search results in what we might call experimentation—with drugs, cults, gangs, sexual behavior, leaving school, or living elsewhere. Adolescents benefit from outlets that allow their questions to be heard and answered in relatively safe ways. SEL programs at the high school level can meet some of these needs through opportunities for reflecting on and discussing students' questions and goals, through community service, and through activities that challenge students to discover their courage and stamina and foster a sense of connection to other individuals and groups.

Against this backdrop, it is clear that adolescence requires a coordinated set of expectations about oneself and others and well-integrated social and emotional skills for handling complex life situations, especially when under emotional pressure. What are healthy perspectives for adolescents to maintain?

- An appropriate internal locus of control.
- A realistic sense of which situations will have positive outcomes.
- A general tendency to consider multiple alternatives, consequences, and plans before acting.

With regard to skills, the following are characteristics of SEL that are desirable for both college and workplace success:

- The ability to take the perspective of others and oneself into account at the same time and weigh each.
- The ability to identify a broad range of emotions in oneself and others.
- The ability to think about different reasons for why interpersonal events happen.
- The ability to consider multiple alternatives, consequences, and plans.

• The ability to form contingency plans.

• The ability to develop flexible responses to obstacles.

• The ability to exhibit a range of self-control and social awareness and group participation skills.

There must be no mistaking the strong link between poor self-monitoring and the inability to deal constructively with tension and crises.

Summary

In general, the psychosocial stages are the engines of development, fueled by the emergence of new emotional, cognitive, behavioral, and integrative capabilities at each level. However, a strong role is played by the living environment of the child; by the joint effects of families, school and extracurricular programs, community and religious-related activities; and by the opportunities, challenges, and resources that support students' mastery of the developmental pathways just outlined. Successful efforts to promote social and emotional learning are characterized by coordinated efforts to build students' skills and to create sound classroom, school, and district programs that encourage students to develop these skills and reinforce them.

Appendix A includes concrete examples of the developmental guidance that can be provided for the key life tasks children need to accomplish at different developmental stages. It focuses on experiences that integrate the various SEL components that are important for students to achieve, and that will help build their understanding and commitment to values. It is divided into Personal, Peer, Family, School-Related, and Community domains to reflect the influence of socialization on social and emotional skills development. The chart includes examples of experiences, opportunities, key concepts, values, attitudes, and skills drawn from a wide range of groups that have worked on these issues. The topics are organized according to task areas but overall should be seen as integrated and complementary rather than as separate and unrelated.

4 Developing Social and Emotional Skills in Classrooms

STUDENTS OF THE 1990S DIFFER FROM WHAT MOST veteran teachers have experienced in the past. For example, a 3rd grade class can have readers that are reading from the K to 6th grade level. Kids are all over—there is not as tight of a bell curve as there once was. We have to teach the kids who are in the classroom, not the kids we want to be there. Their background should not be judged, but to realize you have to teach all the kids the skills they need to be successful in the classroom—teach the kids where they are. Many educators today are mourning the loss of students they used to have, or would like to have.

—Kevin Haggerty,
Social Development Research Group

Fostering SEL to enhance knowledge, responsibility, and caring is both a challenging and a highly rewarding aspect of teaching. Despite the fact that many preservice teacher education programs pay scant attention to the importance of social and emotional influences on all learning in the classroom, increasing numbers of educators have come to recognize it as a keystone to effective education. A coordinated approach in which teachers receive necessary training, support, and recognition is among the essential aspects of a successful education program. In this chapter, specific factors that influence how thoroughly teachers are able to promote SEL in the classroom are discussed, including classroom practices that foster SEL, adaptations for different populations, and conditions that prepare and sustain a teacher who provides SEL instruction.

How Do Teachers Foster Social and Emotional Skills, Healthy Attitudes, and Competent Behavior?

Although our focus is on SEL, it is increasingly clear that teaching practices that promote SEL are intrinsic to good teaching practices in general. We can see this in the observations of a 4th grade teacher who took great pains in the first week of class to help her students become comfortable with one another and work on common elements of the classroom routine. She started by exploring the standards for classroom behavior (e.g., "With your partner, make a list of things we can do in our classroom that show respect for others, respect for ourselves, or respect for our environment."). The teacher then pointed out that these standards are the basis for all class routines; even simple things like lining up and listening to others speak can be done in ways that show respect. The entire class was asked to suggest ways to accomplish different routines, starting with, "How do you want me to call for your attention?" As students discussed different methods, they addressed which ones respected people's feelings, which were fair, and which enabled everyone to get their work done. Once students decided on a method, volunteers demonstrated and the class provided feedback. Finally, the whole class practiced the routine until it went smoothly.

During this activity, students got to know one another better, practiced communication skills, and developed a sense of responsibility for their behavior. In particular, they became aware of different perspectives in the classroom.

In the short run, this teacher's efforts left less time for academic pursuits than those of another 4th grade teacher who introduced class routines with brief admonitions or "reminders" of appropriate behavior. One month later, however, the teacher who had expended time the first week on these elements spent very little time attending to basic management issues. Routine events occurred smoothly with little obvious input from the teacher. In contrast, the other teacher was still searching for an efficient mode of operation. This difference continued through the last observations in winter. Others have found that over the course of the school year, teachers who spend valuable class time on these so-called "nonacademic" pursuits end up with considerably more time for teaching academic subjects.

Why is the first teacher's approach so much more powerful than simple reminders of class protocol? None of these class routines is new to 4th grade students. Both teachers communicated the expected behavior. But the first teacher introduced the concept of showing respect. By showing concern for students' feelings, encouraging a group spirit, having students play an active role in determining the protocol, and communicating important reasons for having efficient and respectful routines, this teacher stimulated a sense of belonging and the motivation to cooperate. In the next section, we explore how teachers at all grade levels create a sense of respect, caring, and belonging by attending to students' social and emotional needs.

Building a Responsive and Empowering Classroom Atmosphere

G U I D E L I N E 5 ▼

SEL programs engage students as active partners in creating a classroom atmosphere where caring, responsibility, trust, and commitment to learning can thrive.

Rationale

Adler (1930) proposed that a sense of belonging motivates children to develop their skills and contribute to the welfare of all. Much of the foundation of SEL is the conscious effort of school personnel to increase a sense of belonging or attachment with the school (e.g., Charney 1992; Lewis, Schaps, and Watson 1996). Research indicates that educators who establish firm boundaries, foster warm personal relationships in the classroom, and enable students to have an impact on their environment strengthen students' attachment to school, their interest in learning, their ability to refrain from self-destructive behaviors, and their positive behaviors (Hawkins, Catalano, et al. 1992; Solomon, Watson, Battistich, Schaps, and Delucchi 1992).

Implications and Applications

Students' participation in classroom decisions and responsibilities provides an excellent opportunity for them to experience the satisfaction and responsibility of influencing their classroom environment (Glasser 1969). An added benefit is that students—like educators—are most likely to act in accordance with group decisions or rules if they have had some part in forming them (Lewin, Lippitt, and White 1939).

Some teachers make an explicit link to the U.S. system of government by creating a "Class Constitution" or "Bill of Rights and Responsibilities" (e.g., Elias and Tobias 1996). In one such session, the teacher starts out by having students discuss the classroom goals, teacher and student duties, and possible problems. He asks students to brainstorm possible "laws" or guidelines. The students quickly suggest prohibitions for various problem behaviors (e.g., "no put-downs," "no talking behind someone's back," "no laughing when somebody is talking"). The teacher helps students restate their ideas in general, positive terms, such as, "Listen respectfully until it is your turn to speak."

As the activity continues, students are involved and paying attention until one student makes a rambling, confused suggestion. Ignoring the student's grammatical errors, the teacher clarifies the speaker's intent with a brief paraphrase. The student looks pleased to have made a contribution, and the attention of the class returns now that the suggestion is understood. Students who have been holding back in order to see how the teacher responds to student suggestions and gaffes start to contribute. When a lull occurs, the teacher waits, giving students time to think. More thoughtful and creative responses seem to follow.

The teacher makes a concerted effort to avoid having the brainstorming session become a mindless parroting of "the rules." This class has yet to suggest any inappropriate rules, so the teacher says, "How about this: students can leave the classroom whenever they like"? Students laugh and yell, "Yeah!" The teacher adds, in a matter of fact way, his suggestion to the list of ideas. In this way, he models the nonjudgmental approach necessary for brainstorming, takes the steam out of silly responses, and enables students to practice evaluating and correcting poor ideas.

When the class starts to discuss the importance of the various suggestions, we see the teacher elicit a lot of reasoning about the effects of our behavior on other people's feelings, well-being, and ability to learn. He uses a rich vocabulary related to emotions, fairness, and shared goals. He emphasizes the long-term consequences of various actions, and asks students to consider how their parents feel about various behaviors. Eventually, the class arrives at a set of classroom rules or agreements. Often, the exercise concludes with everyone signing the list of rules.

Developing a Safe and Caring Classroom Community

In a safe and caring community of learners, students feel they can freely express themselves and risk making mistakes because they know they will be accepted no matter what. Teachers create such a learning community by providing safe, firm boundaries and modeling respectful, supportive interactions with others. They insist that their students also be respectful and supportive of others, and they provide specific learning experiences that nurture and serve the community. An emotional attachment to teachers, peers, and school is a vital link to academic success (Hawkins, Catalano, et al. 1992; Solomon et al. 1992). Educators accomplish this goal by communicating caring in their teaching and inspiring students to identify with them and feel hopeful about their ability to learn. Equally important is fostering students' abilities to form and maintain mutually supportive relationships, which serves as a buffer against developing social, emotional, physical, and academic problems (Parker and Asher 1993, Rutter 1990). In this way, the classroom becomes a microcosm of the larger community, giving students an opportunity to try out and develop the social skills that elicit caring and support.

The personal bonds between teachers and students influence much of the learning in schools. When teachers share parts of their personal lives to illustrate elements of an SEL curriculum, they nourish those bonds and excite student interest in the lesson. Elementary students in particular love hearing about the teacher's own childhood experiences. By talking about and demonstrating healthy

---

EXAMPLE 5A
GOOD MORNING IN THE RESPONSIVE CLASSROOM

The children drift into school in the morning and make their way into the classroom. The teacher stands by the entrance and welcomes them.

"Good morning, Leah . . . Hi, Andy . . . Morning, William. Morning, Renee. I like your new scarf."

At morning meeting time, she informs the group, gathered in a wide circle, that she looks forward to seeing them and she likes to show this with a "Good Morning." What is she to think, she asks in a somewhat joking way, when she says hello and someone says back, "Mmmf," or "Grrr," or pulls back—she imitates a turtle receding into a shell. Giggles. The children enjoy the pantomime. How nice it feels, she tells them in a more serious vein, to hear a hearty round of "Hello" or "Good Morning!" or "Nice Day." Perhaps we just need some warm-ups, she suggests?

"Good morning, Eddie." Eddie smiles and looks around. "What might Eddie say now?" the teacher asks.

"Good morning, Ms. Charney?"

"Yes. I'd like that. Eddie?"

"Good morning," Eddie manages in a quiet voice.

"Good morning, Justin."

Justin replies with spirit, "Good morning, Mrs. C."

"I like that nice strong voice, Justin. I also like hearing my name."

Then, Justin is asked to greet someone else in the circle, until there is a full round of "Good Mornings" and every single person in the class has been named. Every student has been greeted, and has named and greeted another. In this "game," each child is spoken to, named in a friendly manner, and is responsible for continuing that manner. The mood of the circle is now awake. "Yes, we are glad to be here. Yes, we are glad to see each other." The "Good Morning Game" initiates each morning meeting until there is a spontaneous flow.

—Charney (1992), pp. 3–4

---

relationships with friends and family, a teacher in Kent, Washington, communicated a lot about the ability of those bonds to weather adversity. She also made her students feel as though they were somehow part of a healthy family.

Class Meetings, Sharing Circles, Councils. Many teachers use class meetings or sharing circles as tools for building a sense of community (e.g., Elias and Tobias 1996, Lewis et al. 1996). These activities offer a structured opportunity for each student to speak without interruption. Students may be asked to "check in" by describing how their week has been, what they think about topics being explored in lessons, or how they are feeling about a class, school, or civic event. Often they are asked to share something about themselves to help other students get to know them better. Those who do not wish to respond are "passed" and may contribute later. Such an activity offers a welcome buffer at the beginning of the day to help students get ready to learn, and has been used in both general and special education settings to start off every morning and afternoon.

Some teachers pass "talking sticks," toss Koosh™ balls, or have another "Speaker Power" object to designate the speaker and remind students to speak in turn. Turn taking provides a built-in delay that discourages impulsive responses to provocative statements. Students are thus more likely to relate their contribution to the theme of the meeting rather than build reactively on the previous comment. More reserved students may become more vocal in this situation because they do not have to fight for a turn. The safety and opportunity for expression provided by this format contributes to the growth of respect, empathy, and recognition of shared experience, thereby strengthening the sense of community in the classroom.

Using a Comprehensive Framework for All Content Areas

G U I D E L I N E 6 ▼

Academic and SEL goals are unified by a comprehensive, theory-based framework that is developmentally appropriate.

Rationale

Having a consistently used framework is a key component of effective instruction in any domain, but in the case of SEL, it is especially important. As the number of written curriculums, workbooks, videos, and other materials in the area of SEL multiplies, teachers, principals, and curriculum coordinators are inundated with diverse approaches and methods. Often, curriculums cover only specific problems or issues (e.g., bullying, substance abuse, sexually transmitted diseases). As a result, teachers in a single year may work from various curriculums, perhaps picking bits and pieces from each in an effort to reduce the time commitment. This smorgasbord approach can lead to confusion for students and teachers because of the differing orientations of each curriculum. In contrast, the most effective SEL instruction has a conceptual thread woven through all topics and classrooms.

There are a variety of frameworks on which to base SEL teaching. While sharing many features, models use different unifying themes and strategies such as problem solving, classroom community building, social bonding, or emotional intelligence. Essential to being a reflective educator

is adopting a consistent framework to foster the development of social and emotional skills, rather than a fragmented focus on isolated issues. Effective SEL teachers provide students with generic tools (as identified in Chapter 3) that can help them maintain healthy relationships and make wise choices. Using consistent language and strategies, the framework is then applied to the specific developmental issues of concern in a particular classroom, school, or community.

Implications and Applications

A veteran 6th grade teacher reported the following observations after two years of using the PATHS curriculum (see Appendix C) in his school:

> In 6th grade we're under a lot of pressure to stress basic academic subjects, and yet at the same time we're being held responsible to cover new curriculums in family life and sexuality, and drug, alcohol, and violence prevention. In the past there was no integration, and the students weren't well prepared to handle these topics.
>
> Since our school adopted a consistent problem-solving model, we have posters of the model in the classroom and around the school environment. The teachers at different grade levels are teaching these skills, and we now have a common language to talk about them. It doesn't matter if we're talking about health, smoking, or sexuality, we and the kids share a problem-solving approach to talking about these issues and dilemmas.

Instructional Methods That Enhance Social and Emotional Learning

G U I D E L I N E 7 ▼

SEL instruction uses a variety of teaching methods to actively promote multiple domains of intelligence.

EXAMPLE 5B
WALLS SPEAK VOLUMES ABOUT SEL

It is difficult to imagine an effective SEL classroom that does not display on its walls the steps, rules, values, and principles by which it operates. The best are generated by the children. Typically, one finds procedures and problem-solving steps used by specific programs; here are some "created" wall vignettes:

Respect	Rights	Responsibility
yourself	to be respected	to be kind
parents	to be safe	to be careful
teachers	to learn	to do my best
friends	to hear and be heard	to listen quietly and wait my turn

"No Violence"
by Emily, Grade 2
May 1996, Washington

There should not be any Violence at this school. Not even at any other school. We need to Stop, Choose, and Move on. We need to persevere and not fight. We have to respect other people's boundaries. No Violence! Persevere! Be kind to others! Take care of yourself! Keep persevering!

—From Lynnwood Intermediate School, Edmonds School District, Lynnwood, Washington:

"Life Skills: Learners Under Construction for a Better Tomorrow"

—a sign posted by Brenda Stingley, Teacher

Pledge to Myself
This day has been given to me fresh and clear
I can either use it or throw it away
I promise myself I shall use this day to its fullest
Realizing it can never come back again
I realize this is my life to use or throw away
I make myself what I am.

Pledge to the Universe
I pledge allegiance to the world
To cherish every living thing
To care for Earth, Sea, and Air
With Peace and Freedom everywhere!

—Steve VandeGrind, Teacher

The most potent variable is being clear what the vision is and what we are going to accomplish, and having very clear models of change. Just as public health researchers have identified smoking and a diet high in fat as risk factors for heart disease, we have identified a set of risk factors for adolescent health and behavior problems. In the Social Development Model, we focus on protective factors to reduce the risk: It's giving opportunities for kids to be involved in prosocial roles, teaching them the skills they need to be successful, and providing consistent systems of recognition and reinforcement for prosocial involvement. This is the foundation of where we start.

—David Hawkins and Richard Catalano
Social Development Research Group/
Raising Healthy Children
University of Washington, Seattle, Washington

Rationale

Research makes it clear that various domains of intelligence are interrelated (Gardner 1983, Sylwester 1995). An athlete's thoughts and feelings while competing will dramatically affect the level of physical achievement, a child's ability to learn academic material is profoundly affected by emotional state, and social problem solving is a product of the integration of emotional intelligence and analytical cognitive processes (Damasio 1994). Nevertheless, any SEL activity will emphasize some of these domains over others. Within Gardner's multiple intelligences framework, for example, SEL is most closely linked to the intrapersonal and interpersonal intelligences. SEL can also enrich—and be enriched—by the other intelligences: verbal, artistic, musical, logical/mathematical, spatial, and bodily/kinesthetic. By using activities that call on a variety of intelligences, teachers allow for the strengths and weaknesses of a broad range of children.

Implications and Applications

Varying the methods for introducing SEL lessons can be important to engaging the students. A 3rd grade teacher in Tyrone, Pennsylvania, reported that "the class begins to zone out if I always introduce a lesson on feelings by starting with a story." On the other hand, children often look for

EXAMPLE 6B
CONSISTENCY MATTERS

Alfie Kohn (1996) provides an example of what happens when there is incongruity between an SEL approach and an example of how an approach was applied during the formal lesson but not to nonlesson interaction:

> In a 3rd grade classroom in New Jersey, I once watched a teacher whose approach to academic instruction could be described as a model of student-centered discovery and constructivist learning. . . . Then the class meeting began. "Where do you sit?" she asked the boy—and then cut him off as he started to answer, chasing him back to his assigned seat. The meeting's purpose was to discuss a scheduled field trip, but it consisted mostly of telling students what she thought they needed to know. . . . Students offered several suggestions, which were brushed aside until she got the answer she wanted. . . . At no point during the meeting had students been asked to make a decision or think through an issue or even address each other (pp. 91–92).

and seek regularity. A 3rd grade teacher in Nashville reported, "The children always want to end each lesson by making a compliment list; if I forget they always remind me. It gives a sense of closure to the topic and ends things on a positive note." These two examples indicate that sensitivity to the interests and needs of one's class as well as flexibility of methods are hallmarks of effective SEL instruction. By recognizing that the needs of the class are constantly shifting, teachers are able to fully respond to the teachable moment.

Which instructional techniques a particular teacher will use to introduce or explore a particular concept on a given day will depend on a variety of factors, including the developmental level of the classroom, the teaching style and strengths of the instructor, the needs and interests of the students, and the goals of the lessons. Different methods commonly used in SEL instruction include:

- Storytelling and biography
- Group discussion
- Rehearsal and practice (role play)
- Self-awareness and self-regulation
- Self-reflection and goal setting
- Artistic expression
- Play
- Cooperative and small-group learning

Storytelling and biography. Teachers often use storytelling or biography to introduce topics to a class. This indirect approach can be especially effective when introducing feelings, dilemmas, or situations that may be sensitive or difficult for students. For younger students, teachers might begin by reading a children's book that raises the topic. If truthful speech is an issue, for example, a teacher may use a story, myth, or fable about other children (e.g., "The Boy Who Cried Wolf") or a story about his or her own childhood to provide insight and material to which students can react. For older students, teachers may refer to an aspect of a story, historical context or figure, or current event. If the class is struggling with issues regarding ethnic or racial conflict, teachers may use literature and videotaped accounts of movements for equality and human rights as a way to begin discussions of issues that are now affecting students. These stories or videos can be dovetailed with reading, language arts, or social studies goals for improved curriculum integration.

In one elementary classroom, the teacher was concerned and frustrated with the arguments, pushing, and shoving that occurred when the class lined up after recess. She brought in an article from the newspaper about the tragic death of soccer fans at a match in which there was a rush to the exit and people were trampled. She had the children discuss the feelings of the different people involved and then examined how their own problem of lining up involved similar issues. Given the wide availability of high-quality videos on many social and interpersonal issues, teachers have many opportunities to enliven lessons and provide examples of real issues that students are facing (Elias and Tobias 1996).

Group discussion. Group discussions are a primary instructional method for SEL programs. There are a variety of types of discussion that have different goals and functions. A didactic whole-class or small-group activity with the teacher imparting new information may be followed by discussion. These are likely to be curriculum-driven and follow a developmental sequence of topics. At other times, real social situations will stimulate group discussions (e.g., a new student arriving, problems with tattling, having wronged someone, discrimination). Some discussions, focused on solving a problem, will be structured so that students (1) adopt the perspectives of all participants in the problem, (2) generate solutions, (3) discuss possible consequences and obstacles, and (4) perform role plays of viable solutions (see Chapter 3 for examples of problem-solving models). Other discussions may focus more on the feelings generated than on solving the problem—for example, understanding the perspectives of partici-

EXAMPLE 7A
A CURRICULUM-BASED SEL LESSON

What does a curriculum-based lesson on SEL look like? A single lesson is like looking at a frame from a movie. Further, there are many versions, tailored to a program's age level and theoretical framework. However, some examples from the PATHS program provide an indication of the most common structure, which involves integration of emotion, cognition, and behavior:

One lesson that was really successful was Lesson 31. This is about a boy who separates himself from his parent at the mall. We discussed how the boy was feeling and how his parents felt. We made a long list of consequences that the boy could experience as a result of leaving his parent's side and what steps the parent would have to take to find his or her son. Many children felt the need to share stories of becoming separated from their parents and the feelings they felt. I enjoyed the many children's comments concerning the fear that the parents might feel and expressed the danger of being alone in our world today (e.g., being kidnapped and possibly never seeing their parents or friends again).

* * *

The lessons on Best Friends were really interest grabbers for my students. We had been talking about play writing, and several children were writing plays in small groups. These lessons brought it all home for them. They quickly caught on to the potential conflicts in the beginning of the lessons with two friends auditioning for the same part, and their predictions were confirmed as the lessons went on. They put themselves in the place of the characters. The situations portrayed in the curriculum are generic enough that the children don't view the lessons as addressing specific personal issues that would make them uncomfortable, yet allow for discussion.

* * *

I read "What Do You Say, Dear?" as an introduction to the manners lessons. The children enjoyed the book a lot, and it helped to focus them on the common polite phrases which were the subject of the lessons. Many of my students were quick to strike out or call names when they thought they had been deliberately insulted or bumped, pushed, kicked, or in some cases even touched or stared at. Many times these actions were unintentional, but the "offending" student didn't bother to say "Excuse me" or "I'm sorry." I found that I was able to get a good idea of who knew these manners words and who didn't, so I was better able to plan the succeeding lessons. The truth, I found, was that most of my students did not know a lot of the appropriate manners responses when we began, but as we continued with the manners lessons, I began hearing them start to use these phrases proudly (and with an eye toward me for acknowledgment). Manners often avert conflicts. Just saying "Excuse me" or "I'm sorry" can stop a fight from starting.

—Teachers of the PATHS program in Washington

pants, providing students with opportunities to share their emotional reactions, and developing empathy for the different feelings and perspectives of the participants.

Rehearsal and practice (role play). A man in New York City is walking around with a musical instrument. He approaches a stranger and asks, "Excuse me, can you tell me the best way to get to Carnegie Hall?" "Certainly. Practice, practice, practice." Humor teaches many lessons. Here, it reminds us that when we want children to learn something and be able to use it, especially in a stressful situation, we need to provide many rehearsal and practice opportunities. In almost every school, who gets the most practice? Those performing with the band or chorus, on sports teams, or on the stage. They come into school early, stay late, and work on their own on weekends. Why? Because this is how skills are learned. When students do not have extensive opportunities to rehearse and practice valued skills—such as those involved in being civil to one another, or helping, caring, and working well in academic groups—we should not be surprised to see that their behavior does not meet our expectations.

Rehearsal and practice foster assertiveness, empathy, and socially responsible behavior through the development of three skills:

• The ability to understand what another person is likely to be thinking and feeling.
• Knowledge of what to say or do.
• The ability to use the appropriate voice tone, gestures, and expressions that promote constructive communications.

Youngsters unwilling to attempt a new social behavior are often uncertain of their ability to successfully navigate the situation, such as initiating a conversation, handling conflict with a peer, or describing their qualifications for a potential job. Rehearsal develops both knowledge and confidence that encourages children to put their skills to real use. A nonthreatening way to begin is to have stu-

dents practice reading aloud and acting out dialogue from assigned books, or to practice telling jokes, like the Carnegie Hall story or knock-knock jokes. Only after working for a while with hypothetical situations can most students shift to rehearsal and practice with actual situations they are facing (Elias and Clabby 1992).

Self-awareness and self-regulation. Developing awareness of one's own feelings and behavior is a critical step in development (Greenberg and Snell 1997). Many SEL programs provide concepts like "Feelings Fingerprints" and tools like the "Anger Thermometer" to assist in the self-monitoring of feelings (see Example 7B). The next step, of course, is to balance awareness, expression, and inhibition—the domain of self-regulation. Many things that go on in the classroom influence children's ability in this vital area.

The complexity and sophistication of these tasks naturally varies with age and experience, and so do the methods of instruction that support them. Teachers of primary-grade children encourage students to pause and consider how they are feeling. When getting students seated on the floor, the teacher asks, "Are you comfortable? See if you have enough room around you." "Ask yourself if you are ready to pay careful attention to the person who is speaking. Is everyone ready?" A 4th grade teacher cues self-monitoring and suggests how students can regulate their behavior: "Ask yourself if there is any part you do not understand. If so, you might need to ask for more information." A 7th grade teacher also encourages students to applaud their successes: "How many people felt they really used their time wisely? If you didn't, think about what you could do to improve next time. If you did, tell yourself you did a good job." A high school football coach instructs players to monitor their emotional states: "If you are thinking about punching that guy who has been giving you a rough time, you are not thinking about the game and you are not playing your best. You need to recognize that and get yourself back on track."

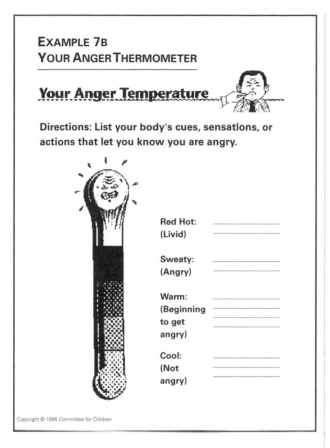

EXAMPLE 7B
YOUR ANGER THERMOMETER

Your Anger Temperature

Directions: List your body's cues, sensations, or actions that let you know you are angry.

Red Hot:
(Livid)

Sweaty:
(Angry)

Warm:
(Beginning
to get
angry)

Cool:
(Not
angry)

Copyright © 1995 Committee for Children

Teachers may also demonstrate self-monitoring by thinking aloud: "I am feeling frustrated because we have lots to get to and we are running out of time. I need to calm down and think. I will take a deep breath. Now what? I can list on the board everything we need to do and then decide which ones are really important to do today. That sounds like a good idea. Where is my marker?" By verbalizing what otherwise is only an internal dialogue, and linking it with the steps of problem solving, this teacher allows "hidden" cognitive elements of the problem-solving process to become visible and understandable to students.

Finally, teachers may give students opportunities to practice self-regulation by reducing overt supervision of the class for short periods. The teacher may become involved in a conversation or step outside the classroom very briefly, gradually increasing the length of time he or she is out of sight. A 5th/6th grade teacher in Kirkland, Washington, taught her class to start their work without her. She worked in her adjoining office for several minutes after the bell rang. Students were usually working quietly when she came in. This was simply part of the routine.

Self-reflection and goal setting. A crucial dimension of developing decision-making and problem-solving skills is the ability to set goals that are meaningful and appropriate to the individual student. Small day-to-day decisions, as well as larger ones involving career and family, require the ability to set both short- and long-term goals. With increasing cognitive and social development, identifying personal goals becomes more important and assists students in planning and setting priorities that lead to personal success and to satisfying lives.

Quiet periods for self-reflection are important to this process. By providing freedom from outside stimulation or pressure, teachers enable students to access their own values, priorities, and sense of purpose. High school students in particular may find quiet, reflective periods to be sources of refreshment and focused attention. Others, especially younger students, may become fidgety and distracted during quiet times. Relaxation exercises and art materials can help these students focus their attention, and enable them to gradually extend their periods of concentration.

The types of goals chosen by students will vary widely depending on the grade and developmental level of the classroom as well as the immediate context. In high school, some goals reflect student efforts to find a sense of purpose in life. Others simply reflect the desire to raise one's grade in biology class. Using Personal Problem Solving worksheets and Student Conflict Manager software (Elias and Tobias 1996), and by rehearsing and practicing plans, students learn to think through all aspects of their goals. They consider the role of other people—parents, teachers, clergy, peers, and popular culture—in shaping their personal goals, and they learn to identify the steps necessary to achieve their goals. Some programs clearly define a timetable for those steps in "contracts" between teachers and students. This approach enables students to evaluate progress, know when additional effort or adjustment of goals is necessary, and celebrate when goals are attained.

Artistic expression. Because art often has emotional content, it can enhance student understanding of emotions and how to express them in safe and appropriate ways. Artistic activities are often an excellent "starter" to gain children's engagement in a new topic. Elementary students may work with a palette of colors to symbolize various emotions. As a transition between analytical and self-expressive activities, a high school teacher in Boulder, Colorado, asks students to sculpt clay into a symbol of how they are feeling. The students decide whether to display their sculpture to classmates and describe the feelings that stimulated the sculpture, or to pass. According to this teacher, "The freedom to choose one's level of participation conveys respect for the students' right to control their inner world and provides a sense of security that fosters self-expression. Particularly for adolescents, this indirect communication of their emotions provides the freedom to explore and express feelings which they may find uncomfortable to discuss."

The dramatic arts form a natural link between literature, writing, and social and emotional skills. Working with other students to produce skits, plays, and musicals fosters expressive communication skills. At Assumption School in Seattle, the drama teacher worked closely with classroom teachers to incorporate rehearsal and SEL-program practice vignettes into his class. "Since the lessons focus on accurate communication of emotional states through voice tone, facial expression, gesture, and posture, it is a great way to develop acting skills and support our school's social goals at

the same time." A class at Decatur Elementary in Washington wrote and staged a "peace opera" using principles they had learned in their SEL program. The teacher assigned students with problem-solving difficulties the role of characters who displayed expertise in that area. As rehearsals progressed, she noticed a particular improvement in students whose parts required repeated rehearsal of problem-solving strategies. Rehearsals also provided a natural, real-world context in which to work on skills development with students.

Play. Play also has a role in SEL programs, particularly in secondary school classrooms, where there is a tendency to view social behavior as a series of problems or conflicts. Observations of exemplary teachers suggest that using play provides a strong readiness to learn. A high school teacher in Santa Monica, California, uses games as warm-up activities. Group juggling requires that each student receive a ball from one specific person and toss it to another specific person. As the game progresses, more balls are added. Concentration increases and laughter erupts frequently. When discussing the game afterward, students mention that having a group goal led to a sense of responsibility to group members—everyone had to be fully alert to achieve the group goal. The laughter further added to the sense of closeness among students.

Cooperative and small-group learning. The ability to cooperate with others is an important skill that is likely to become increasingly crucial for future success. Having students work in well-structured cooperative learning formats helps develop SEL skills that are particularly important in today's team-oriented work environment. However, the use of cooperative learning methods in any subject area requires that some component SEL skills be in place, such as basic self-control, role taking, and communication skills. Although many teachers report that using cooperative learning in SEL lessons is exciting and effective, this is true only when the children are well prepared and developmentally ready for such lessons.

When teachers prepare students to work through the disagreements that naturally occur in team situations, cooperative learning promotes sharing of ideas and resources, creativity, and a sense of shared purpose (Johnson and Johnson 1994). Cooperative learning enables students to practice listening to others, taking others' points of view, being sensitive to the needs and concerns of group members, negotiating and persuading, and using the generic steps of problem solving.

The instructional approaches presented may be applied to a wide variety of contexts. Stories, discussion, and role playing, for example, can be shared by the entire class. Alternatively, the teacher may ask students to work in pairs or small groups for particular activities. The use of paired or small-group exercises is often useful for building self-confidence and trust. Within large groups, these small-group configurations give more students an opportunity to be heard and to actively engage in conversation and problem solving.

G U I D E L I N E 8 ▼

Repetition and practice are vital to the integration of cognition, emotion, and behavior.

Rationale

Whether applied to recognition, scientific notation, irregular verb conjugation, or SEL, repeated rehearsal using many different instructional modalities provides benefits (Ladd and Mize 1983, Mize and Ladd 1990). There is one main difference between SEL and many academic subjects, however. While SEL entails the learning of many new skills, it may also require the unlearning of habitual patterns of thought and behavior. For instance, students rarely come to class having repeatedly practiced an incorrect version of the multiplication table, but they may have become well schooled in

not waiting their turn or not listening carefully to others.

Implications and Applications

Research on neurological development provides some insight into the challenges of changing problem behaviors and their cognitive, emotional, and interpersonal components. Throughout childhood and adolescence, maturation and experience lead to both the strengthening of some neural connections and the "pruning" of others. Connections that are unused are lost, while those that are stimulated by frequent behaviors or thought patterns become dominant pathways for nerve impulses (Edelman 1987). Well-entrenched behavior patterns are likely to have a rich network of neural connections throughout the brain. Alternatives to those patterns will not be able to "compete" on either behavioral or physiological levels unless they have been practiced repeatedly, thereby strengthening the neural pathways that are necessary for integrating emotion, cognition, and action.

Promoting the Use of Social and Emotional Intelligence Throughout the Day

G U I D E L I N E 9 ▼

Educators can enhance the transfer of SEL from lesson-based or other formal instruction to everyday life by using prompting and cuing techniques throughout all aspects of school life.

Rationale

Young people face many situations that are extremely challenging emotionally. How many adults could comfortably deal with having peers cruelly tease them about their appearance, physical talents, or mental competence? When individuals feel anxious, angry, or sad, their ability to solve problems or concentrate on learning diminishes (Forgas 1994). Students who have shown improvements in their behavior may revert to earlier, more dominant habits when emotions are strong. When this happens, it is as if the "thinking brain" in the frontal cortex is overrun by the more automatic responses of the subcortical limbic system (Damasio 1994, Goleman 1995, Sylwester 1995). To avert this occurrence, social and emotional skills must be strengthened through practice in a wide range of contexts. Direct facilitation of classroom instruction may be provided by teachers, school counselors, psychologists, social workers, or paraprofessionals trained in SEL. In schools using the family group model, each adult in the school—including administrators and staff—works with a small group of students to provide SEL. But whether or not each adult has responsibility for a group, all personnel play an important role in actively encouraging and reinforcing the use of skills and attitudes they see displayed. Throughout the day—on the playground, in the halls, in the lunchroom, on field trips, on the bus, in aftercare programs—every adult has the opportunity to help students in real-life situations use what they have learned in the classroom. Typically, this practice is aided by reminders, usually in the form of tangible prompts.

Implications and Applications

Real-life situations during the school day provide many opportunities to exhibit self-control, express feelings, or engage in problem solving. By exploiting teachable moments, teachers provide support when it is actually needed, enabling students to make considered choices about their behavior and making it less likely they will be overrun by strong feelings (Greenberg and Snell 1997). In high school, for example, educators may target sports programs for teaching social and emotional skills. These are ideal real-life laboratories, because athletic competition engenders many

emotional highs and lows. The ability to regulate those emotions is often credited as providing the "winning edge" (Iso-Ahola and Hatfield 1986), a significant incentive for students and coaches. Educators appreciate that the prestige and respect accorded to athletes by their peers often make them role models for other students. By focusing efforts on this highly visible group, educators hope to foster socially responsible behavior for students to emulate. For example, a program run by the football coach and team doctor at Franklin High in Seattle makes use of the teachable moments inherent in sports competition to advance SEL and academic achievement. In New Brunswick, New Jersey, teaching "Keep Calm" is part of every after-school and midnight basketball program. SEL prompting techniques such as modeling, cueing, coaching, and scaffolding dialogue can be used by all school personnel (see Example 9A).

Modeling. Teaching by example, or modeling, is the most powerful technique that educators employ, intentionally or otherwise. All aspects of teacher behavior reflect their social and emotional relationships, making a powerful statement of values and expectations. Not surprisingly, students who observe discrepancies between what is "practiced" and what is "preached" are most likely to imitate what they see modeled (Mize and Ladd 1990). Thus, students are unlikely to respond to others empathically or use problem-solving steps to resolve conflicts until they see teachers also employing those skills.

One aspect of modeling that can affect students' willingness to try new skills is the teacher's use of humor. "I like to be goofy and remind students that it is OK, even fun, to make mistakes or look a little foolish sometimes," reports a teacher in Tacoma, Washington. Seeing a teacher enjoying himself and at ease when he makes mistakes reinforces the idea that mistakes are an essential part of the learning process and reduces student concerns about looking foolish themselves.

EXAMPLE 9A
SEL AND SPORTS: PERFECT TOGETHER

Michael J. Murphy, Athletic Director at La Salle (H.S.) Academy in Providence, Rhode Island, has fully integrated SEL into all aspects of the athletic program:

> Each student athlete receives a booklet that includes Player Guidelines, the Player's Contract, and Player's Goals. The Contract affirms that students will abide by the Guidelines.

The following excerpt is from the introductory letter to the contract, from Michael Murphy:

> Every individual in this athletic program must become unified. We must function together, "One Common Goal." No contribution is too small; all contributions to these teams are significant. Everyone is vital to the success of this program.

He introduces the idea of off-season personal and team goals:

> The goals are done in a confidential manner. Only the athlete and the Athletic Director ever view these goals.... During the course of the season, many juniors and seniors are called in to discuss their goals. The reason we focus on them is due to the proximity in their lives to the change from high school to college or the workforce. This allows them to see the importance of goal setting in all aspects of life.

> We hope, through this program, to teach our students how to prioritize events or circumstances in their lives. We aspire to also teach them the value of goal setting and hard work.

Michael notes, "There has been a surprisingly positive amount of support by the student body, and especially the seniors, about suspensions of athletes who did not follow the guidelines. We are trying to teach more than just athletics. They are not going to leave this school as a senior and get a job playing volleyball. They are going to go out in society and function. It's telling kids that nobody is more important than anyone else no matter how good an athlete you are. Each athlete is a representative of the school and the community.

"There was an incident during a half-day of school during a walkathon. The kids were allowed to show up out of dress code, and they walk and get people to sponsor them. Two athletes went out and had a "power breakfast" and came back intoxicated. They underwent the (discipline) process and were suspended from school and athletics. They violated not only school codes but the athletic guidelines as well. This shows that the rules are enforced no matter who the party is. If you disobey, there are consequences to the actions. It's not enough just to sign the contract."

EXAMPLE 9A—*continued*
SEL AND SPORTS: PERFECT TOGETHER

La Salle Academy Athletics

PLAYER'S GOALS

I, _____ am signing this GOAL SHEET to sig-
nify that I have and will continue to make a committed effort toward reaching "ONE COMMON GOAL" for La
Salle Academy Athletics. I further agree to fulfill my obligation to the team and its members by achieving the
goals listed below.

Signature: _____ Date: _____

Sport: _____

OFF-SEASON GOALS:
1.

2.

3.

PERSONAL GOALS:
1.

2.

3.

TEAM GOALS:
1.

2.

3.

Cueing and coaching. It is a common error in social and emotional instruction to assume that, because the subject matter—everyday actions and feelings—is so "obvious," children learn the skills once they are presented. This misconception is a key reason why we see less carryover from classroom to schoolyard, bus, and home life than we would like. When some of us provide training to teachers, we offer them a money-back guarantee—if they ever see children spontaneously carrying out something from a program after its first presentation in a class or group, they will get their money back. Teachers ask if we have it backwards—and we say, "No." It is the fundamental responsibility of adults to prompt and cue and coach students to use the skills to which they have been introduced. This is the third "C"—Chances—of the four "C's" concerning self-esteem presented in Chapter 3.

Teachers and playground supervisors may have to coach students to think of other perspectives, construct positive solutions to problems, make a request in an engaging voice tone, or keep calm when upset. Teachers in Highland Park, New Jersey, use the prompt, "Listening Position" (face the speaker, keep your rear end in the seat, and put your feet on the floor) to help their elementary school students focus on the teacher, a classmate, or an assembly speaker. A Florence, South Carolina, principal has her waiting room supplied with notepads, pencils, and an anger management poster. The school secretary instructs students to answer questions on the poster (e.g., Why was I angry? What did I do? What would I do differently?). According to the principal, students have calmed down and have often written a constructive solution to the problem by the time she sees them (Guzzo 1995). Tangible reminders in the forms of posters, signs, and bulletin boards are a hallmark of classrooms where social and emotional skills are an essential part of the culture.

Scaffolding dialogue. In rushed or chaotic moments (e.g., dismissal, on the playground) reminders often need to be brief. In more controlled situations, teachers are sometimes able to engage in a more prolonged dialogue. In a scaffolding dialogue, teachers and administrators rely on questions that serve as a catalyst for creative thinking and new insight on the part of the child. The goal is to enhance the child's ability to think independently and share ideas and feelings with others. Here is an example of how one teacher worked with an 8-year-old girl. The student was in a peevish mood all morning. During an art lesson, she encountered yet another frustration:

Student: [Whining, near tears] Look! It's all messy! [Showing paper to her teacher.]

Teacher: [Neutral tone] Oh. How do you feel about that?

Student: Frustrated!

Teacher: You feel frustrated. What can you do about it?

Student: [The student uses a gesture indicating "calm down."]

Teacher: That's one thing you can do. Maybe there's something else you could do too.

Student: I don't like black.

Teacher: You don't like black. OK, what could you do about that?

Student: I don't know.

Teacher: Hmm, let's see. You have a problem and you feel frustrated because you don't like black, but you don't know what to do about it.

Student: I want blue.

Teacher: OK, what could you do if you want blue?

Student: Ask for the blue pen.

Teacher: That's a good idea. You could ask Purcell for the blue pen.

Student: [To Purcell] May I borrow the blue pen? [Purcell hands the pen to Samantha.] Thank you. [Student begins to draw again.]

Teacher: What a very good idea. You asked Purcell for the pen, and you also thanked

---

EXAMPLE 9B
PROMPTING SELF-REGULATION, SELF-CONTROL, AND SKILL TRANSFER

A 6th grade boy with a lot of behavior and emotional problems stemming from the 3rd grade (and probably earlier) had spent a lot of time coming to the SPS [Social Problem Solving] Lab once a week. We found that his biggest problems happened when he seemed to be in a free atmosphere (e.g., physical education). After speaking to the phys. ed. teacher I found out that she would, at key times, tell him, "This is the time to use 'Keep Calm.'" The best was when he was able to catch himself before he'd lose his cool. He'd step into the hallway and use Keep Calm in order to be able to think about what he really wanted and things he could actually control and do to reach his goal. He would then come back to the gym and continue playing. Self monitoring . . . AAAHHH— an educator's dream!!

Another 6th grader was having a problem with her teacher. She was referred to our Social Problem Solving Lab to work on solving problems in a better way than verbally lashing out at the teacher and just not trying in class. After about four months of attending SPS Lab once a week, this girl was not only doing better in class but also was now actually coaching her friends when they were having problems among one another. In other words, if her friends started verbally attacking other girls, she would ask them what the real problem was, how they were feeling about the problem, and what they'd like to see happen. She would then begin to pump them for solutions, making them think through what would happen with each solution they would give her. She probably single-handedly kept about five different situations from escalating into something much worse. This girl also received the health award for trying out the many skills learned in health in different situations, not just in the health room for a grade.

—Vicki Poedubicky
Health Teacher, Grades 3-6,
Bartle School, Highland Park, New Jersey

---

him! How do you feel now?

Student: I feel happy. [She resumes drawing.]

Even without hearing this child's emotional intonation, it is likely that this exchange required real patience from the teacher. It might have been tempting for the teacher to tell the child her drawing was all right or to sit down and draw another one. Neither alternative would have improved the child's mood or demonstrated to the child that she could create solutions for herself. Instead, the teacher provided a supportive scaffold for the child's newly acquired problem-solving skills, and the child succeeded in reaching an original resolution that was internally satisfying. Research indicates that this style of questioning is also important for developing literacy skills (Heath 1982).

Scaffolding dialogues can be conducted with the whole class, and can benefit from making use of relevant SEL lessons. They not only provide an excellent opportunity for transfer of learning, but also save the teacher extra time and effort in dealing with difficult situations individually. Children can accept responsibility for solving problems and agree to abide by solutions they create for themselves. Extended samples of dialogues are part of the Interpersonal Cognitive Problem-Solving, Social Competence Promotion Program for Young Adolescents, Social Decision Making and Problem Solving, Second Step, and PATHS program materials (see Appendix C).

G UIDELINE 10 ▼

The integration of SEL with traditional academics greatly enhances learning in both areas.

Rationale

Research on brain function shows that learning takes place in an emotional and behavioral context (Nummela and Rosengren 1986). To the extent that students attach academic skills to feelings and actions that are part of their everyday world, they are more likely to use those skills in real life. In this way, the skills and process of SEL enrich the teaching of academic subjects and infuse the curriculum with interest and challenge. Further, because SEL programs teach a range of thinking skills, they are easily connected to other curriculums that promote skills such as analytical thinking, prediction, synthesis, analogy, and metaphor.

EXAMPLE 9C
SEL ON THE OP-ED PAGE

One of my 6th grade students defended social problem solving in a letter to the editor. A parent had written a letter to the editor expressing many misconceptions about our schoolwide concept. This student explained not only the benefits to himself (he happened to be quite small in size and would use the many skills when dealing with bullies or on safety patrol) but to his peers. Needless to say, when an educator sees his or her students applying skills appropriately to situations or they are able to see the value on an adult level, you just want to cheer! YESSSS!!!

—Vicki Poedubicky
Health Teacher, Grades 3-6,
Bartle School, Highland Park, New Jersey

Implications and Applications

Language, literature, and writing. The world's great literature deals with themes that are universal, such as friendship, courage, duty, jealousy, grief, and loss. And the not-as-great literature students also read is similarly imbued with issues of loyalty; freedom; growing up and growing older; relating to strangers, family, friends, bosses, and teachers; and even just plain having fun and fostering imagination and creativity. By asking students to relate these themes to their own lives, teachers vividly create a new context of meaning for what otherwise are likely to be perceived as irrelevant or "dead" works. Students' understanding of character is also enhanced when they are asked to identify with the viewpoints of each actor.

EXAMPLE 10A
SEL AND ACADEMICS

A lot of things that kids used to come to school knowing, the kids today don't know anymore, so we have to integrate them into the curriculum every day. Unless the kids know how to express their feelings and talk about their problems, they might not be able to increase their reading scores, for example. First they are overwhelmed with emotion, and then they won't pick up on what you are teaching. The teachers have to take as many opportunities as they can to combine the SEL lessons with reading lessons or other subjects throughout the day and throughout the school. If you are with children who don't have social and emotional skills, it becomes a disruptive situation. It's as if we have this huge piece of furniture in the middle of the room, and we keep bumping into it. We need to find a way and time to say, "How can we rearrange the room?" That's what SEL programs do.

—Vivian McCloud, Principal
School #29, Rochester, New York
Primary Mental Health Project

EXAMPLE 10B
READING, WRITING, AND CONFLICT RESOLUTION

Kids want to open up and discuss books that we are reading, and they follow through in their writing. The children are anxious to help get the character out of conflict. Their writings are different now than before when they were asked how a character would get out of conflict.

—Elementary School Teacher, RCCP
South Orange-Maplewood, New Jersey

At the elementary level, teachers can choose books for paired reading, silent reading, or read-alouds that contain SEL content and the appropriate developmental reading criteria. Teachers ask questions for discussion or writing assignments that encourage empathic identification or use of a problem-solving strategy (e.g., How would you feel if this happened to you? What is the little boy's problem? How do the other characters feel? What do you think he will do? What do you think will happen if he does that? What would you do in this situation?)

Older students may create plays or videotaped dramatizations of the book's events. Another more advanced skill is to analyze the author's intentions in the book: Why was it written? What theme(s) did the author want to communicate? Thus, teachers at all levels can meet the goals of language arts, literature, and SEL learning simultaneously.

History, social studies, and current events. Emotional identification and the analytic reasoning of problem solving can similarly be used with history lessons, social studies, and current events, which can help make the facts more relevant for students. Almost any historical or current event can be approached effectively with a problem-solving model (see the sample worksheet in Example 19A). In almost all these situations,

difficult decisions had to be made, and there were often competing needs, attitudes, and values on different sides of the issue. For example, "Why did the colonists throw the English tea into Boston Harbor? What were their goals? Why did they think that England's rulers were acting unfairly? How do you think the colonists felt when they had dumped the tea? How do you think England's rulers felt? Do you think the colonists knew what would happen as a result? Do you think they picked a good solution?" When these questioning frameworks follow the same pattern as dialogue around social and emotional issues, great synergy is possible.

EXAMPLE 10C
SEL AND LITERATURE

The essence of SEL is in the substance of literature. In "Encounter," a Native American boy speaks of how he lost his land, his customs, his dreams. Having kids write a passage about how they would have felt if they were him—integrating SEL with academics—the social web!!—also fits in with U.S. history.

—Lorna Dunson
Grade 4 teacher, Cedar Way Elementary School
Mountlake Terrace, Washington
School Development Research Group

Using SEL in an integrated curriculum. In a similar manner, the general problem-solving model can be used to create an integrated series of lessons that link many subjects together. For example, teachers have created integrated units on ecology, using reading, writing, mathematics, biology, and social studies. The students use problem-solving models to explore the interrelations among plants, animals, and water supply in a particular ecology (e.g., the rain forest), discuss the compet-

EXAMPLE 10D
BOOK TALKS

Decision-making and problem-solving steps or strategies used in interpersonal situations are fully applicable to the analysis of all kinds of stories. Here is a format used in Language Arts as part of the Social Decision Making and Problem Solving Program (Elias and Tobias 1996).

Questions Assigned to Students in Problem Solving Applied to Literature Analysis/Book Talks

1. Think of an event in the section of the book assigned. When and where did it happen? Put the event into works as a problem.
2. Who were the people involved in the problem? What were their different feelings and points of view about the problem? Why did they feel as they did? Try to put their goals into words.
3. For each person or group of people, what are some different decisions or solutions to the problem that he, she, or they thought of that might help in reaching their goals?
4. For each of these ideas or options, what are all of the things that might happen next? Envision and write down short- and long-term consequences.
5. What were the final decisions? How were they made? By whom? Why? Do you agree or disagree? Why?
6. How was the solution carried out? What was the plan? What obstacles were met? How well was the problem solved? What did you read that supports your point of view?
7. Notice what happened and rethink it. What would you have chosen to do? Why?
8. What questions do you have, based on what you read? What questions would you like to be able to ask one or more of the characters? The author? Why are these questions important to you?

Simplified Book Talk Format for Young Readers

I will write about this character: _____

My character's problem is

_____

_____

How did your character get into this problem?

_____

_____

How does the character feel?

_____

_____

What does the character want to happen?

_____

Which questions would you like to ask the character you picked, one of the other characters, or the author?

_____

_____

ing demands that come from human populations living in or near these ecologies, explore students' hopes or fears about the environment, and consider how to plan ahead to maintain delicate economic and ecological balances (e.g., Johnsen and Bruene-Butler 1993). This can be done in formats that naturally use students' multiple intelligences. By integrating SEL concepts and skills with academic subjects, teachers enrich the learning of basic skills by placing them in the vivid context of social relationships and creative activities. That context provides memory "prompts" that help students use the information at a later time (Sylwester 1995).

Teachers report that the longer they teach social and emotional skills, the more likely it is for SEL to be a seamless part of the school day. As one teacher in Shoreline, Washington, reported,

> At first, Second Step seemed like just another add-on, and that's how I taught it the first year. I had the usual trouble finding time to do everything. Now it's just a basic part of my school day. The problem-solving strategies are so applicable to what we think of as our academic program. They enable me to do a lot more interesting things and really challenge the kids' thinking.

How Is SEL Adapted for Different Populations?

The skills, attitudes, and opportunities that were presented in Chapter 3 are needed by everyone in our society (see Guidelines 1, 2, and 3). These social and emotional strategies are critical life skills that promote effective decision making in everyday interpersonal challenges as well as in academic performance. At each grade level children face new developmental challenges that can be mastered by learning life skills, finding new ways to manage risk situations, using peer and adult support for coping, and becoming involved as a positive contributor to others. This section ad-

dresses issues that may arise when an SEL program is implemented in an inclusive classroom.

G U I D E L I N E   1 1   ▼

The SEL curriculum may have to be adapted for children with special needs.

Rationale

All classrooms contain learners of widely different levels of accomplishment and need. Given the movement toward inclusion, the average teacher faces increasing variability in students' ability to control their own behavior and to interact and communicate with others. Many teachers find they are highly stressed by the inclusion of children who have problems with attention, aggression, and learning in general. In the inclusive classroom, the use of SEL programs can be critical to supporting the development of all children (Elias and Tobias 1996). Teachers find that building a cohesive classroom community, focusing on the development of all students' social competence, and providing opportunities for using these skills in mixed-ability groups can greatly improve the inclusive experience (Gager, Kress, and Elias 1996). Ultimately, it requires less disruption of the academic program than isolating the misbehaving, impulsive, or immature student (Johnson and Johnson 1994).

Implications and Applications

A 3rd grade teacher at Hazel Valley Elementary in Washington State remarked:

> One concern we had this year in our class was a child who was far behind academically and not working very hard. At first other students were angry and showed little compassion; they were basically resentful and mean to this child. I did a lot of work on the "Golden Rule" lesson and tried to focus the children on how to keep thinking about

the other guy and how you would feel if this was you. I began to pair her up with both older and younger students, and as they began to have more one-to-one interaction with her, they showed more compassion and interest. By focusing on friendship, cooperation, and caring for others, everyone appeared to benefit.

EXAMPLE 11A
SEL AND INCLUSION

A psychologist in Seattle was planning an SEL group to focus on the special social needs of youngsters with cerebral palsy. Other staff members were enthusiastic, but cautioned against including one youngster with a reputation for disruption. The psychologist did include this child, and noticed that some of the more compliant youngsters looked dismayed to see him in the group. Feelings of the other children began to change, however, when it was apparent that the boy had lots of ideas that were valued by the leader. His enthusiasm and skill with role playing made the sessions fun, and encouraged the more inhibited children to join in. The new respect this boy received from the other children bolstered his self-confidence and made him eager to try new social and emotional skills. With so much attention for his constructive contributions, disruptive outbursts disappeared. In retrospect, the psychologist attributed much of the group's success to inclusion of this initially impulsive youngster.

In classrooms composed of children with a large range of abilities, it may be more challenging to conduct whole-class SEL lessons. Teachers often report success in using small-group activities that give students greater responsibilities, provide fewer distractions, and allow teachers to connect with students' prior knowledge and personal experiences. Work is presented using multisensory in-

structional techniques and includes substantial opportunities for practice and repetition. The small-group strategy works well when it is coupled with regular sessions that include the whole group (e.g., putting on plays, reading stories, holding group problem-solving meetings).

Even special pull-out groups may include a mix of abilities. Some programs for children who are rejected by peers allow other class members to be guests on a rotating basis. This approach provides skilled role models and also helps raise the social status of children who are rejected (Bierman, Greenberg, and the Conduct Problems Prevention Research Group 1996). Also, youngsters who are disruptive may have a lot to offer to their more restrained peers.

It is well documented that children with learning disabilities (Kavale and Forness 1996), language disorders (Craig 1993), mild mental delays (Bramlett, Smith, and Edmonds 1994), neurological disorders (Moffitt 1993), and hearing loss (Greenberg and Kusche 1993) often have related difficulties in the areas of social and communicative competence. They are more likely to show difficulties in effectively reading social cues from others and managing frustration and other high-intensity emotions. They are also more likely to be rejected by peers. For these reasons social and emotional development is often specifically outlined as an objective in their Individualized Educational Plans (IEPs). Self-contained settings focus on building for success in the mainstream as well as specialized settings. SEL programs meet these needs and are often quite successful in specialized classroom settings (Amish, Gesten, Smith, Clark, et al. 1988, Greenberg, Kusche, Cook, and Quamma 1995). At-risk learners, however, require support as they move between the self-contained classroom and the mainstreamed classroom, lunchroom, and playground. Consistent use of SEL procedures across these environments is extremely beneficial.

Children in self-contained classrooms for severe learning and behavior disorders generally present significant challenges. Poor impulse control and the inability to appropriately regulate emotions contribute to out-of-control, aggressive behavior and poor attention and performance. Standardized behavior management programs often are used in such classrooms. What is also necessary are strategies to help children develop the inner competencies to manage themselves and handle the stresses of a normal classroom environment. SEL adds skill building in needed cognitive and emotional competencies. Thus, it is important to develop a plan that integrates behavioral management with SEL (Elias and Tobias 1996, Kusche and Greenberg 1994).

GUIDELINE 12 ▼

Coordination between the SEL curriculum and other services creates an effective and integrated system of service delivery.

Rationale

For many children with severe behavior disorders, either individual or some type of family therapy or counseling is advisable. SEL programs are valuable adjuncts to such treatment. When counselors or therapists are familiar with the skills and concepts being learned in class, they are able to draw on those skills during the treatment process. In those cases where school-based psychologists or counselors are regularly involved with particular children, there are advantages to their involvement in SEL lessons. SEL programs can play a critical role in the success of full-inclusion programs, even for students who are severely troubled (Epstein and Elias 1996).

Implications and Applications

A program by the Conduct Problems Prevention Research Group (1992) illustrates this guideline quite well. They have created a series of

services for children and families at different levels of need and concern. All children in the school receive SEL programming throughout the elementary years. Then, children identified as at risk for behavioral and academic difficulties receive small-group social skills training, while their parents par-

---

EXAMPLE 11B
ADAPTING SEL FOR STUDENTS WITH SPECIAL EDUCATION NEEDS

The Children's Institute—a private special education school for children with severe emotional, conduct, and learning difficulties in Livingston, New Jersey—has been a flagship of the Social Decision Making and Problem Solving Program for nearly a decade. Staff members there have become expert at creating adaptations of lessons to their populations. Among their innovations are (1) combinations of classroom-based lessons with academic infusion and special skill-building groups; (2) activities that use the computer; (3) uplinks to public school districts for collaboration in science; and (4) activities that promote self-reflection and self-regulation through self-monitoring sheets, sharing circle questions that ask about their preferences and experiences, and activities like, "Who are you?" as ways to promote self-understanding as a precursor to building friendship skills. Foremost, however, is an extensive focus on feelings, building feelings vocabularies, reading social cues in others accurately, and self-control skills to avert "emotional hijacking."

We have got to give these kids skills for living, and we can't wait for parents or anyone else to do it. The next stop for many of these kids is residential treatment or prison.

—Dr. Bruce Ettinger, Director
The Children's Institute

EXAMPLE 11C
HOW STUDENTS AT A RESIDENTIAL SCHOOL VIEW SEL

Among the students at North Country School, a residential school in Lake Placid, New York, are some who have experienced significant losses and other difficulties in their lives. At one of their weekly Town Meetings, students commented on what it is about the school that helps them:

I think it is really a great learning experience because it's not a normal school. We get to get in touch with nature. We go out and hike on the weekends; we learn how to build fires even when the wood is wet. On the farm, you get to be with new people because you change chores every week.

* * *

We get a lot closer to each other. You know if something is wrong with someone else if they're quiet and they're normally not.

* * *

This school isn't only about just taking out your books and pencils; when I was in public school, I didn't do anything on my days off except watch TV and go to movies. We never knew what to do with ourselves. If some grown-up had said, "Do you want to climb a 4,000-foot mountain?" I would have said, "You've got to be kidding!" But now, it's different.

* * *

I like that you learn about a lot of different cultures and there's no real problems racially.

* * *

I keep all of the pictures I draw here.

A teacher summed it up well: "There is a real search for positively identifying the child and what he or she is good at. We really try to find success for the kids. There is so much communication among the staff about the kids' individual needs."

ticipate in parent education and support groups. The concepts established in the SEL program for the entire school are transferred and reinforced in both the child and parent programs. Thus, common principles and language are used across the different levels of service.

What Prepares and Sustains a Teacher in Effective SEL Instruction?

G U I D E L I N E   1 3   ▼

Staff development opportunities provide teachers with theoretical knowledge essential to teaching social and emotional skills.

Rationale

Taking on an SEL program can seem daunting at first. With the possible exception of special education, teacher training programs often provide inadequate training in understanding motivation, emotions, and social competence. At first, some teachers are concerned that by taking on a social and emotional curriculum, they are being asked to take on the role of a school counselor or psychologist. It is important to clarify that while classroom SEL programs can complement specialists' efforts to help certain high-risk students, the focus of the classroom teacher is, in fact, education and healthy development. The goal of a classroom program is to help develop personal qualities essential to well-being and success in school, on the job, and within families and communities.

Implications and Applications

In the early stages of SEL program implementation, teachers are given opportunities to learn about the full scope of the program and the developmental sequence of instruction from grade to grade. Such familiarity enables teachers to see the links between simple self-monitoring, for example, and mature self-regulation. They are then better able to set goals and design lessons appropriate to the developmental qualities of their particular age group (see Chapter 3). As teachers are able to integrate the overall principles, scope, and sequence of the program, they can bring more of their own creativity and spontaneity to this work.

EXAMPLE 12A
DEFUSING PROBLEM BEHAVIORS

Two boys were on their way to the office all upset. They were going to report each other to the principal. I asked each of them what their problem was. Apparently, one boy made fun of the other by saying he was annoying. The (annoying) boy's feelings became hurt because he thought they were friends. I asked each of them what they wanted, and they both said to remain friends. They each came up with ways to remain friends, one of which was to tell each other when they would get on each other's nerves. We never did make it to the office that day. What is so very rewarding here is not just that they parted as friends but that a process/framework was reinforced by our common language. Also, if this concept were to follow them, they would no longer need adults to "coach" them as I did. They would be able to deal with this situation themselves.

—Vicki Poedubicky
Health Teacher, Grades 3-6,
Bartle School, Highland Park, New Jersey

Group facilitation skills likewise are not always emphasized in preservice education. As a result, many teachers don't appreciate the usefulness of training in the process of group development—

the stages through which most groups pass as they grow and reach completion. Teachers learn to help the class move from strangers who test one another and maintain maximum distance, to a cohesive group of individuals who find emotional support and empowerment in their connection. Although some groups may reach stages that involve trust and self-disclosure, others may not progress beyond becoming respectful acquaintances. Teachers learn to adapt their lesson plans and pace lessons appropriately for their groups.

Another example is that training in group dynamics emphasizes the importance of closure at the end of the term. This process assists students in saying goodbye to their classmates and provides students with skills that are applicable to many situations that involve the ending of relationships. Teachers who are aware of, and responsive to, the changing classroom relationships are able to provide the most effective and positive learning experiences for their students.

G U I D E L I N E   1 4   ▼

Staff development provides modeling and practice in experiential learning.

Rationale

Effective staff development provides educators with opportunities to explore and experience their own social and emotional skills, so they become increasingly effective models for their students. In teaching students to understand and effectively manage and negotiate the challenges and opportunities of feelings and social relations, teachers use not only technique and theory but also ways of relating with students. Coaching and inservice exercises have supported teachers in creating a positive view of discipline as an act of protection and guidance. Teachers develop skills and attitudes that help them give students clear feedback about what is and is not safe and appropriate behavior in dif-

ferent situations. By setting firm boundaries, teachers help students create a classroom increasingly free of disrespect; as described earlier, clear rules and standards are used to promote responsibility in each student. Such a structure promotes a healthy bonding between student and adult that motivates young people to learn from their teacher.

EXAMPLE 14A
HASSLE LOGS FOR TEACHERS

You know a concept like social problem solving works when even other teachers use the skills to help solve their own personal/professional problems. One of our teacher associates was having a professional disagreement with a colleague. Imagine my reaction when the teacher associate asked me for a hassle log to fill out and give to the teacher. I have filled out my share of hassle logs and have given them to various people. The motto that hangs in my room is: "Hassle Logs . . . They're not just for kids!"

—Vicki Poedubicky
Health Teacher, Grades 3-6,
Bartle School, Highland Park, New Jersey

Implications and Applications

Those designing training programs in SEL will find it useful to draw upon the following elements of caring, openness, and responsiveness:

Caring. Earlier chapters described how caring is a key part of constructing the relationships that make learning possible (Noddings 1992). Teachers demonstrate caring—the respect for and appreciation of the essential worth of each student—in two fundamental ways: empathizing with the feelings and dilemmas of students and protecting students by providing clear boundaries.

Caring from teachers includes listening for and validating the value and wisdom of what each student is offering instead of listening for only the "right answer." With this atmosphere of acceptance, the SEL classroom is an ideal setting for teachers (and students) to discover the value of mistakes and apparent detours to the learning process. When the goal is understanding rather than critical judgment, teachers model an acceptance of a range of feelings and ideas, and students respond with greater sharing.

Firm guidance is the other side of caring included in teacher preparation for SEL. Because of the interactive style of teaching in SEL lessons, students have more opportunities to be disruptive than in a strictly didactic classroom. And because the goal is to encourage open expression and independent thinking, SEL teachers may be particularly challenged to find a style of providing limits and structure that prevents chaos without suppressing any student's expression (Elias and Tobias 1996).

Openness. Because much of the inspiration and reinforcement for social and emotional skills comes through the modeling of the teacher, staff development opportunities should help teachers become more open with their students in ways that feel appropriate for the particular teacher. Like the teacher earlier in this chapter whose students loved to hear the ongoing "learning stories" that emerged from challenges and fiascos with her own children, many teachers discover a new freedom in sharing their personal stories and wisdom with students. Students delight and learn from the stories teachers share about their own reactions as children or teenagers to the dilemmas students are discussing now. SEL training provides guidelines for appropriate self-disclosure, and ongoing collaboration between colleagues allows teachers to check out a particular story when they are in doubt about its value for their students. Through the experiences of teaching an SEL curriculum, educators report that they become more comfortable with their own interpersonal and intrapersonal intelligence; they learn how to express their feelings and when to contain them.

Teachers demonstrate their openness not only through what they say but also through how they listen to their students. Refining their ability to interpret body language and hear the feelings between and beneath the words, teachers become increasingly skilled at understanding the whole child. With experience, teachers find they can listen with increasing compassion to their students, knowing that they may bring up feelings that are initially uncomfortable for themselves and their students as well. A teacher's openness can contribute to a climate of tolerance in which students more easily learn to distinguish feelings from behavior. When negative feelings can be acknowledged in this climate, students more easily learn to manage them so that they do not lead to destructive behavior.

At times, students bring up issues and feelings that are difficult for both students and teachers to manage. Those may require individualized support beyond what classroom teachers can be expected to provide. Staff development can provide teachers with guidelines and mechanisms for coordinating with other teachers and pupil-services staff to help their students find the right place and time to get the professional help they need.

Responsiveness. Another skill teachers develop through training and increased experience in teaching SEL is being aware of and responsive to the needs of students at a given moment. Teachers often adapt or deviate from a lesson plan for a moment to effectively meet the needs of the class. Staff development experiences can offer teachers support in gaining skills that allow them to fully respond to the "teachable moment": being responsive to the changing needs of the group and its individuals, becoming increasingly comfortable sharing and learning from one's own mistakes, and being flexible enough to shift gears.

Teachers report that as they grow more experienced in working with curriculum materials and themes, as well as this responsive style of teaching, they are rewarded by an expanded repertoire, creativity, and imagination, which allow them to invent new approaches in the moment.

The spirit of spontaneity, flexibility, and responsiveness is strengthened by learning experiences that enable teachers to express their own humor, playfulness, and creativity. Just like classroom students, teachers learn best when they feel comfortable, are most creative when they are playing, and are most engaged when "serious" learning is punctuated with laughter. A successful staff development program gives teachers a range of SEL experiences. This outcome is more than can be accomplished in a single session or even a series of sessions. Ongoing support and coaching provide opportunities for teachers to gain experience, reflect on their teaching practice, and feel a sense of renewal.

G UIDELINE 15 ▼

Staff development activities are visibly and regularly supported by feedback from colleagues, administrators, and others.

Rationale

Because teachers are often exploring new territory when they embark on teaching SEL, most find it essential to have ongoing support. A supportive environment is one in which the following are true:

- Administrators empower teachers by encouraging them to have an active voice in decisions that affect them.
- Administrators model and encourage clear communication and a constructive strategy for resolving conflicts among the staff.
- Administrators foster a sense of shared purpose and enjoyment among the staff.
- Administrators provide active support for teachers who want to try new approaches.

Implications and Applications

Some administrations have actively promoted opportunities for teachers to observe other teachers and to co-teach new programs with teachers, psychologists, or the principal. Ongoing faculty meetings that foster collaboration among colleagues reinforce and refine the capacities and

---

EXAMPLE 15A
ONGOING COMMITMENT AND EXPERT SUPPORT PRODUCE GENUINE CHANGES IN PRACTICE

The first year there was a 10-day conference, and Developmental Studies Center (DSC, the program center in California) staff gave training to the core group. They came to the school for one week four times the first year. We communicated on the phone all of the time. The following summer there was a five-day conference to help the core group train others. The second year the DSC staff visited again four times for one-week periods. The following summer there was another five-day conference. The people are always helpful and are always available.

The staff development uses frequent meetings to try to reflect the way the project operates in the classroom. The teachers use partner chats, talk about goals and strategies, and learn about one another. The teams of primary and secondary teachers share planning time while the kids go to different specials during the same time slot. This is done because it is too hard to get people together outside of school hours.

Originally, we didn't count on it to change us as people. We interact differently now with our own children at home. We have developed a sense of awareness. We reevaluate why things do and don't work. It has developed me [become] a much more reflective person.

—Sheila Koshewa
Child Development Project
Lexington, Kentucky

---

knowledge gained by teachers in introductory training. Such meetings can include group supervision from mentor teachers, administrators, or social services personnel who can help teachers identify red flags that require further specialized support or referral, or SEL consultants who provide ongoing curriculum development and troubleshooting for the faculty. Teachers are also supported by one-to-one coaching from mentor teachers or supervisors, and from having the opportunity to visit SEL lessons in other classrooms (see related discussion in Chapter 7).

Teachers value help they get from other teachers more than any other source. Peer coaching is most successful when teachers have a framework to use during the coaching process (Nelson, Lott, and Glenn 1993) or when working in a group (Elias and Tobias 1996, Summers 1996). Ongoing collaboration and staff development ensures that teachers have support at their school and that they know the limits of what they can and cannot provide for their students' social and emotional needs, as noted in Guidelines 12 and 13. In the safe setting of the SEL classroom, students may reveal emotional disturbances or traumatic experiences that need to be addressed outside the classroom. Teachers usually welcome guidance in identifying these situations, finding ways to protect students in class, and obtaining the necessary services for students who are troubled. Administrative leaders can create opportunities for teachers to get to know and trust support personnel. This effort will help teachers to make the most effective use of the psychologists, social workers, or deans in their school. Schools should also have a clear system for dealing with disclosure of abuse or neglect so that classroom teachers alone do not carry the burden.

G U I D E L I N E   1 6   ▼

SEL programs are most effective when teachers and administrators adopt a long-range perspective.

Rationale

Ongoing teacher support is one aspect of the long-range perspective needed for effective SEL programs. For teachers and students alike, the effects of SEL appear to get stronger the longer a program is implemented at a particular setting (Slavin, Madden, Dolan, Wasik, Ross, Smith, and Diana 1995). Teacher commitment to a new program develops during implementation as teachers start to see practical benefits. Furthermore, teacher presentation of a program tends to be relatively superficial until the second or third year, when teachers really make a program their own (Hord, Rutherford, Huling-Austin, and Hall 1987). Teachers of many SEL programs, for example, commonly report that they do not spontaneously use the techniques with their students, their own families, and colleagues until the second year of the program.

Implications and Applications

Changes in student behavior seem to follow a similar progression. An elementary principal commented about the changes she observed: "By the end of the first year, I was hearing a new vocabulary. After two years, both teachers and students were using the problem-solving strategies more consistently." She continued to see improvements, stating that "the longer students worked with the strategies and the more they saw their teachers use them, the more students were able to problem-solve in 'hot' situations."

Like any basic skill, social and emotional skills develop gradually throughout childhood and adulthood. And because emotional patterns are relatively slow to shift, teachers benefit from gentleness and respect when encouraged to develop these new social and emotional skills. Having realistic expectations about timing can buffer discouragement in the early phases of implementation. When teachers feel supported in taking this long-range view of developing skills and perspectives that go beyond their original training, they often discover that teaching SEL allows them to experience ease and effectiveness in fostering the quality of relationships that allow learning to flourish even more in the classroom.

Students' benefits are accompanied by teachers' benefits. Teachers report that problem-solving strategies help them deal more effectively with stresses in both their personal and professional lives (Caplan, Weissberg, and Shriver 1990). A teacher in Shoreline, Washington, told interviewers that explicitly teaching social and emotional skills made it much easier to deal with late afternoons. "I used to dread all the little conflicts that pop up when everyone is tired and needs to rush to the bus. I sometimes avoided the problems, or quickly imposed my own solution on them. Neither approach worked very well. Now that I've been teaching Second Step, it takes much less time and is less stressful."

Teachers also report that their growth as caring, open, and responsive teachers spills over into their relationships with colleagues, families, and friends. They discover more enjoyment, a greater sense of effectiveness and reciprocity in their relationships, and more satisfaction with themselves. Ultimately, these intrinsic benefits will sustain teachers.

Summary

Many teachers already use important elements of SEL. What is less common is a comprehensive framework that provides coherence and consistency to specific objectives and instructional methods. Effective teaching requires consideration of how the class structure, teaching methods, and class climate will affect both academic and social and emotional development. Having a specific SEL program brings unity to these aspects of school life and frees educators to focus their creative energies on special projects and adaptations that enrich any program.

Despite the importance of SEL for all aspects of student functioning, teacher educators and administrators have been slow to provide teachers with training, support, and recognition in this area. Adopting a new program inevitably requires the use of some unfamiliar teaching methods; thus, teaching SEL can be challenging for several reasons. First, educators who wish to create a caring learning community must "walk the talk" in a way that may require them to change their way of relating to others and structuring the classroom. Second, the empowering nature of SEL may initially encourage students' attempts at disruption, as the "rules of the classroom" undergo change. Third, potential growth in students' SEL skills and teachers' efforts is impeded to the extent that grade-level, school, and district colleagues are not joined in a common effort. Meeting these challenges requires an ongoing commitment from teachers and administrators, and this is often provided through networking opportunities (see the list of programs in Appendix C).

Fortunately, the motivation to make this commitment is strengthened by the intrinsic benefits of providing SEL instruction. Educators discover professional and personal satisfactions as both learning and social relationships are enhanced in the classroom. Teachers often find that the theoretical framework and methods of SEL are intellectually stimulating for themselves as well as students. Perhaps most important, teachers derive satisfaction from addressing the skills that educators believe are most essential for the citizens of tomorrow. As just noted, though, teachers are best able to persist in their commitment when their personal efforts are embedded within those of their school and a supportive community.

5 Creating the Context for Social and Emotional Learning

EVERY YOUNG PERSON HAS A DEEP NEED TO belong. Children with the greatest unmet needs for relationships are often those most alienated from adults and peers. Schools and youth work programs must make a planned and concerted effort to nourish inviting relationships in a culture of belonging.

—Brendtro, Brokenleg,
and Van Bockern 1990, p. 69

Social and emotional learning is best taught and learned in school and classroom environments in which young people are respected and valued, and in which they experience a sense of personal fulfillment and responsibility. Schools and classrooms in which adults are nurturing, supportive, and caring furnish the best contextual opportunities for SEL programs to be introduced, sustained, and effectively provided. It is also true that an approach to SEL that connects with other aspects of students' learning and development within and outside the school setting is likely to be the most sustainable and effective (Dryfoos 1994).

In this chapter, we discuss six major contextual factors related to the effective planning, implementation, and coordination of SEL programs. They include the classroom and school climate, student participation and empowerment, program coordination and integration, school district support, home and school collaboration, and community involvement and support.

The Importance of Creating a Supportive Classroom and School Climate

GUIDELINE 17 ▼

A caring, supportive, and challenging classroom and school climate is most conducive to effective SEL teaching and learning.

Rationale

How students experience and perceive their school and classroom climate has been shown to be significantly related to their psychosocial and academic development, and to their school adjustment and performance outcomes (Garmezy 1989, Haynes et al. 1996). A context that is caring, supportive, and challenging also leads to better SEL outcomes.

Implications and Applications

The staff of a middle school in a major northeastern city reviewed school climate data from a survey of students and staff. Most students reported feeling a lack of respect and trust between themselves and their teachers. The teachers were surprised, as they had reported a high level of student-teacher respect and trust. Focus groups involving mixed groups of students and teachers were organized, and discussions revealed that students expected direct and palpable demonstrations of respect and trust (e.g., students expected teachers to greet them more in the hallways and classrooms, and to be more willing to listen to their concerns and more accepting of their ideas and points of view).

Subsequently, a "respect and trust" campaign was developed. It involved posting notices around the school that identified the school as a place where teachers and students respect and trust one another, and where active expressions such as daily greetings, attentive listening, and responding to one another's concerns are the norm. When school climate surveys were re-administered one year later, the results showed significant increases in student, staff, and parent assessments of the levels of respect and trust. There were also many

more palpable demonstrations of the change in the attitudes and behaviors among and between students, staff, and parents.

Numerous examples and consistent research suggest that in supportive organizational environments, school staff and classroom teachers help to create a climate that reflects the following:

• *Free and open interaction and dialogue among and between staff and students.* Students are able to express their ideas and feelings in an atmosphere that is nonjudgmental and respectful of their individuality.

• *High standards of behavior and achievement, including the ability to think critically and make informed judgments about behavior and related consequences.* Students are challenged to be the best they can be. Staff create opportunities for students to be creative and innovative, and to engage in active learn-

---

EXAMPLE 17A
STUDENT, PARENT, AND STAFF VIEWS OF POSITIVE SCHOOL CLIMATE

At a New Haven school, a major focus was on improving school and classroom climate and supporting SEL activities. After introduction of the program, many students, staff, and parents made positive comments about the climate of the school (Haynes and Perkins 1996). The following are examples:

Student: You can't feel safe around any school this year because this world is not a very good place to live in because a lot of things happen, but I feel safe at this school. Like when we talk to our teachers, and when I play with my friends, and they stay with me, and like we never get hurt or nothing, and if we get hurt, my friends and I help each other.

Parent: I feel that the school's climate is wonderful; it's a nice secure place for children here. You feel comfortable coming to the school. You feel that the school is not a separate place anymore where it's them and us. Now *we* are *we.*

Staff: When the parents enter the building, they know that we're always thinking of the welfare of the youngsters as well as our own. It is important that we have rules and guidelines. The children have a good sense of how things work. We try to communicate love to them. We don't stand off from the children; we try to move to their eye level. We try to talk in a manner in which they can respond back to us, in a quiet way as opposed to intimidating children to respond back to your questions.

ing experiences that allow them to realize their fullest potential for success as students and as individuals.

• *Collaboration, cooperation, and constructive group problem-solving activities.* Students gain significant social skills and develop positive attitudes of altruism, kindness, and respect for others when given structured opportunities to participate as members of organized problem-solving teams. Teachers and staff create opportunities for students to become engaged in meaningful, creative, and stimulating activities that enhance their social interactive skills and reinforce prosocial values.

• *Equity, fairness, and respect for diversity of race, culture, ethnicity, social class, religion, gender, ability, and other factors.* Students come from diverse backgrounds and expect to be treated fairly and equitably. They expect their teachers, other staff, and peers to be sensitive to their individuality and to understand and respect them. Teachers and staff encourage and support cross-cultural sharing and competence, and create environments that promote mutual respect and understanding among and between adults and students.

• *Supportive, positive learning experiences.* There is a strong relationship between self-esteem, self-efficacy, and students' general behavior and academic performance in school. Teachers and staff should provide opportunities for students to experience success, positive reinforcement, and validation of their worth as individuals in a challenging and nurturing environment.

• *Strong connections between adults and students, and commitment to the mission and goals of the school.* Students adjust and learn best in school and classroom environments in which they intellectually and emotionally identify with the adults and the program. Teachers and staff are cognizant of and responsive to the special and diverse needs that students have and are available to listen, advise, counsel, and provide guidance to them when necessary. There are routines and structures that send students a clear message: "Welcome. You are important."

Information obtained through interviews and focus groups with students and staff demonstrate the importance of these dimensions of school and classroom climate in preparing students and enabling them to confidently and successfully face the many academic and social challenges in and outside of school.

Is Empowering Students the Latest Bandwagon, or Is It Really Important?

GUIDELINE 18 ▼

Students derive more benefit from SEL programs that they help to design, plan, and implement.

Rationale

Especially as students enter high school, programs in which they have meaningful influence show higher levels of student participation and deeper commitment. When their suggestions are sought before a program is fully developed, students can often identify barriers that may impede the program, giving teachers and others a chance to remove those obstacles. Naturally, one must recognize that the appropriate degree of involvement depends on the nature of the endeavor. For example, students may have more input and direct involvement in activities designed to improve the social climate of the school than in matters affecting the design of the academic curriculum. Nevertheless, as described in Chapter 3 and in the quote that begins this chapter, involvement is a part of being valued, and children in today's society need reaffirmation and a sense of belonging and mastery.

Implications and Applications

To encourage students' interest and to give them a sense of shared ownership of the curricu-

---

EXAMPLE 17B
MORNING REFLECTIONS

At La Salle (H.S.) Academy, each day begins with a Morning Reflection that can come from students or any staff. The main selection criterion is that the statement reflect the mission of the school. Here is an example:

Ed Sirois, Faculty Member, October 1996

Good Morning, Everyone — Me-You-Us.

Me: Self-respect, self-confidence, self-worth, self-esteem. I have inalienable value, dignity, and worth simply because I am a human being. Inalienable dignity—no one gives it to me, and no one can take it away—it just is. And because I value and respect myself, I take my own needs seriously. Not necessarily my wants and whims, but my needs—physical needs (food, shelter, clothing, clean air and water, medical services), social and emotional needs (self-control, friendship, acceptance, love), intellectual and spiritual needs (learning, beauty, art, music, character, prayer, God).

You: You're just the same as me. You have the same inalienable dignity and value and worth. Because I truly respect myself, I respect you. It's not "hate yourself and love your neighbor"—it's "love others as you love yourself."

Us: All the you's and all the I's together, we form an "us," a community of individuals, each with dignity and value and worth.

Together, we, us: A community that has needs and rights that deserve to be acknowledged and protected. Our building, our grounds, our furniture, our library books, our lockers, our computers—they belong to us. Me—Respect for Self; You—Respect for others; Us—Respect for the Community and its property.

---

lum, a Bronx, New York, school uses the "Mysteries Questions" to engage students in refining the curriculum for their particular needs and interests (Kessler et al. 1990). Briefly, four or five weeks into the semester—once the teacher and class have created an environment of caring and respectful listening in which honest self-expression is possible—the teacher asks students to write about three topics: mysteries about myself, mysteries about others, and mysteries about life or the universe. Mysteries are explained as our worries, wonderings, fears, curiosity, confusions, or excitement.

After a period of quiet reflection to clear their minds, the students are invited to write their questions anonymously. The next week the teacher reads aloud to the students with a tone of respect and honors their "class mysteries." After the students have heard the questions, they're given a copy of the collection, some quiet time to look it over, and encouragement to notice common themes that particularly interest them. Students usually comment that they feel much closer to and safer with this group now that they know what's on their classmates' minds. In discussions, students often comment that they are surprised they are not alone with their concerns. Sometimes the teacher invites them to identify one question they're really committed to having discussed in class.

Through this process, students experience the power of expressing what's most pressing in their lives and also the ability to influence the curriculum. They also discover a wealth of wisdom and depth in their peers that they didn't anticipate. And, the teacher discovers a way to learn more about the students, to adapt the sequence of topics to respond to the group's priorities, and to develop a new lesson plan when students bring up an important issue that has been left out. Teachers and staff can engage students in the design and planning of SEL programs in a number of ways:

1. Use focus group discussions to identify student issues and concerns and to get reactions to specific proposed activities, and then incorporate students' input in the design of the program (e.g., time and place for SEL activities, format for presentations).

2. Conduct surveys to identify students' perceptions of issues, their needs, and their likely responses to program activities.

3. Obtain students' input to help guide the design, development, and implementation of the program.

4. Talk individually to students about their interests, challenges, and desires, and use that information to help select SEL activities.

5. Involve students on SEL planning teams with staff, parents, and community members.

In schools with site-based decision making, involving students on teams can turn adversarial relationships into collaborations. By making room for student ideas and thoughts—not student control—in SEL planning and implementation, teachers and staff provide a sense of empowerment to students and increase the probability of the program's success.

Why All This Talk About Coordinating and Integrating SEL Activities?

G U I D E L I N E   1 9 ▼

SEL programs and activities that are coordinated with and integrated into the regular curriculum and life of the classroom and school are most likely to have the desired effect on students, and are also most likely to endure.

Rationale

A major obstacle to SEL program success occurs when the skills taught are not part of the regular curriculum, but instead are add-ons. In such cases, SEL activities are perceived as less important than other content areas, and consequently are not given as much emphasis. In addition, program skills, attitudes, and beliefs are not reinforced throughout the curriculum or throughout the entire educational program, including during after-school or extracurricular activities. As a result, there may be far less generalization and maintenance of these skills than is possible with a well-coordinated, integrated program in which SEL is on par with academic subjects such as math, English, and reading.

During the planning stages of any SEL program, it is important for goals to be clearly defined and operationalized. These goals can include ways in which the classroom and school building, as social units, will be tangibly affected by the program. In Piscataway, New Jersey, one such goal was a measurable increase in the ethnic diversity of student-selected work groups as a result of a social problem-solving program. Including goals that call for the results of an intervention to affect classrooms or schools compels the program to include elements that will create such outcomes (see Chapters 6 and 7).

EXAMPLE 18A
SETTING UP A SUPPORTIVE ENVIRONMENT FOR ALL CHILDREN

The Child Development Project operates on a schoolwide basis in the elementary grades. It cannot be implemented without strong staff consensus because SEL works more effectively when the entire climate that children are exposed to reflects the program's philosophy and methods. In the words of teachers:

> The program builds a sense of community in the classroom so that all the kids fit in and feel a part of the community. They band together as a class so that you don't have these children any more who don't feel like they belong. Those are usually the kids who don't make it.

> The principles support the way we all want children to learn about living in this world. You're not the only person in the world. What you do affects other people. We talk about that a lot en there are rough spots—how do they feel about those things and what can be done about them?

> A child was so withdrawn that he would not speak to anyone. He would not go to the restroom because he would not raise his hand. He did not want to play with anyone or go to centers. By the end of the year he had playmates. He would go to centers and initiate play with others. He would come and tell me things. I would give him directions, and he would say, "I don't like that. How about I do this now and that later instead." This year he comes by and says, "Hello." He speaks to other people. It is amazing to watch him grow from an isolated person to one who contributes daily. The whole class supported the fact that we were going to get everyone involved and do this together.

> —Focus group of teachers
> from Hazelwood and Auburndale (Kentucky) Elementary Schools

---

Implications and Applications

Once SEL goals are specified, relevant activities are selected that can be implemented reasonably well in the contexts for which they are planned. For example, a peer counseling program designed to enhance students' ability to make healthy decisions and to resist negative peer pressure may be more appropriate for and work better at the middle and high school levels than in an elementary school. On the other hand, to accomplish the same goals at the elementary level, classroom-based video presentations with discussions may work best. Also relevant to examine is the individual school context. The community in which the school is located (e.g., To what extent does it value education? Are various educational options available?); the resources available (e.g., funding); the cultural and demographic composition of the student population (e.g., Is there little or much diversity?); and the short- and long-term goals of the school and the district influence the choice of SEL programs.

There are two basic ways in which SEL programs are introduced to schools. They may be integrated throughout the curriculum, or they may be presented as specific program activities. In either case, effective SEL programs are not introduced as add-on activities but become integrated compo-

EXAMPLE 19A
REINFORCING SOCIAL PROBLEM-SOLVING STEPS THROUGH ACADEMIC INSTRUCTION AND REAL-LIFE APPLICATION

The steps used in the Social Decision Making and Problem Solving Program's formal SEL lessons [outlined in Example 1E] may be reinforced in many ways. On the following pages, a similar structure is used in academic coursework [here, historical/current events] and in monitoring personal situations [here, the Personal Problem-Solving Record, which also has a computerized version].

—Elias and Tobias (1996)

History/Current Events Outline and Personal Problem-Solving Record

Worksheet 5-2. Creating a Newspaper Article

Directions: Imagine that you are a reporter for *The New York Times*. You have been asked to write an article on the social studies topic you have just finished studying in class.

Think about some part of the topic as an event or *problem*. Then, use the problem-solving outline to help write your article. Be sure your article starts with a headline and then answers the following questions:

1. What is the *problem* you are thinking about?
2. What *people* or *groups* of people are involved?
3. What *feelings* and *goals* does each person or group have?
4. What are some possible *solutions* to achieve each goal?
5. What are some of the *consequences*, both long- and short-term, for each possible solution?
6. What solution was chosen? Do you think a different choice should have been made? If so, why?
7. What could have been done to *improve* the chosen plan?
8. *Summarize* the information on the article and draw some conclusions.

HEADLINE: _____

Current Events

1. What event are you thinking about? When and where is it happening? Put the event into words as a problem.
2. What people or groups are involved in the problem? What are their different feelings and points of view about the problem? Try to put their goals into words.
3. For each group, name some different solutions to the problem that the members think might help them reach their goals.
4. For each solution, think of all the things that might happen next. Think about short- and long-term consequences.
5. What do you think the final decision should be? How should it be made? By whom? Why?
6. Think of a plan to help you carry out your solution. What could you do to make your solution work?
7. Make a final check. What might happen that could keep your solution from working? Who might disagree with you? Why? What else could you do?

EXAMPLE 19A—*continued*
REINFORCING SOCIAL PROBLEM-SOLVING STEPS THROUGH ACADEMIC INSTRUCTION AND REAL-LIFE APPLICATION

Worksheet 10-6

Personal Problem-Solving Record

Name: _____   Date: _____

Class: _____   Page No.: _____

1. I was feeling:

2. My problem was:

3. My goal was:

4. I tried to stop and think of as many solutions as I could, and I thought about their consequences.

   Solutions that I thought I might try: If I tried it, these things might happen next:
   _____   _____
   _____   _____
   _____   _____
   _____   _____

5. My plan for solving my problem was that I would:

6. After I tried it and rechecked it, I found that it worked:
   a. very well   b. OK   c. not so well   d. terribly

7. The next time something like this happens, I might:

Source: Elias, M.J., and S.E. Tobias. (1996). *Social Problem-Solving: Interventions in the Schools.* New York: Guilford.

EXAMPLE 19B
GROUP MEETINGS AND ACTIVITIES TO REINFORCE SEL INSTRUCTION

In Berkeley Heights, New Jersey, Social Decision Making Clubs are used to build upon and extend classroom-based SEL instruction. Teachers refer students to the "Club" who need extra practice in developing their interpersonal and problem-solving skills. At the middle school level, a resource room teacher runs the group as a class period during the school day, while on the elementary level, teachers are paid to run before- or after-school Clubs. Teachers make Clubs fun by having kids bring their problems to the Club and creating a real group effort to come up with solutions. Then, the kids check back with one another to see how their solutions are going. In one of many success stories, a mildly autistic boy attended the Club as part of a social problem solving-based school-home program to keep him from being placed out of district. He is now counted as one of the district's college graduates.

In another example, children who have trouble making friends meet once weekly for six to eight times with Guidance Counselor Marge Delaney in a North Brunswick, New Jersey, elementary school for a "Lunchtime Group." At the group, students watch episodes from the acclaimed "Talking with TJ" video series and carry out the program activities to build their teamwork and conflict resolution skills (cf. Elias and Tobias 1996). The groups are not at all stigmatizing. They are fun, and the students prefer them to the torture of sitting through lunch and recess without the skills to interact effectively.

Finally, an interview with a student at North Country School, Lake Placid, New York, highlights how group decision making is applied to a charitable cause:

> We save money from Wednesday lunches by just having soup, and we donate it to people with real problems. The people who decide where it goes are a representative from each house and each level. They discuss who to give the money to that year. Last year we gave it to an AIDS research foundation and to "The Hunger."[1]

[1] The kids' name for a group that distributes food to those in need.

---

nents of the school improvement plan. All stages in the process of program adoption—including identification, review, planning, goal setting, orientation, implementation, and evaluation—should be conducted collaboratively and should involve staff, students, and parents as well as community representatives. This process is best accomplished if a representative committee or subcommittee of the school planning and management team (school improvement team) representing all four constituent groups—staff, students, parents, and community—is formed and assigned the responsibility of coordi-

nating and shepherding the stages in the adoption process. It would appear that a combination of both approaches works best, as one reinforces the other.

The following example demonstrates how schools that use programs with a problem-solving and decision-making orientation have successfully coordinated and integrated their SEL programs into the general learning goals of the school:

> In elementary, middle, and high schools, higher-order thinking and problem-solving skills are interwoven throughout the curricu-

EXAMPLE 19C
INNOVATIVE STUDENT SUPPORT SERVICES THAT REINFORCE SEL

After a while, principals recognize that some students need an additional service beyond what formal classroom SEL lessons provide, one that is flexible enough to deal with real-life issues as they happen. Using a variety of programs, they have created variations on a problem-solving room (e.g., a crisis room) as preventive or remedial parts of school discipline systems. Here are some examples:

The Solution Room: "A safety net for kids is being able to go there when they are in trouble to work out their problems. Kids even come to the room on their own—they are taking responsibility and want to fix up what they have done wrong."

The Reading Room: "The Reading Room is run by the principal every day as part of her commitment to developing relationships with students who have problems regulating their behavior. Because students often come to the room upset, children read first to distract them, calm themselves down, and get them ready to problem solve. They are required to stay in the room for three recess periods, so that they will feel the weight of the problem. The time also allows the principal to develop a rapport with the students who need her help the most."

The Thinking Corner: "Books on social skills are available for students to read and reflect on. A 3rd grade boy about to fight goes into the Thinking Room and reads the book, *I'm Always in Trouble* (developed by the Raising Healthy Children program). He tells Carol (a staff member visiting the room) that the book says how to "use my words and not my fists." Next he takes Carol though the book to show the points that he thought were important. Then he returns to his group—he was able to manage his mood!"

Social Problem-Solving (SPS) Computer Lab: "Kids go to the SPS Lab when they are referred by a teacher or counselor or if they want a place to work out trouble they have gotten into or to think about a problem or decision in their life. Using the Student Conflict Manager/Personal Problem-Solving Guide computer program, they go through the same SPS steps as they are learning in class. They make an action plan, and we do some role playing. For tougher problems or more resistant kids, we spend time first on feelings, using drawing materials as well as the computer."

Other variations include the "Problem-Solving Lunch" and the Problem-Solving Room at the Children's Institute (where out-of-control children with severe social and emotional problems can go to use the social problem-solving method to understand what happened to them, manage their strong feelings, solve whatever problems have been created, and plan to keep out of similar trouble in the future). At the Primary Mental Health Project, Child Associates who usually see children as part of the program also take on kids in crisis, to give them someone to talk to who is not involved. Some Associates go to classrooms first thing in the morning after kids have been disruptive the prior day, to check in and help them get off to a good start. Common features include having students stay for more than one visit and having adults other than teachers (such as college students, aides, trained volunteers) work with the students (except those with pre-existing SEL deficits).

—Based on interviews with those implementing the Social Development Program/Raising Healthy Children in Washington, the Social Decision Making and Problem Solving Program in New Jersey, and the Primary Mental Health Project in New York.

lum. Students are taught how to monitor their thinking, and how they make choices in solving academic problems in various subject areas such as math, science, and language arts. Students are then taught to transfer the skills they learn and employ them in solving academic problems and solving social problems. This transfer of learning is supplemented and reinforced through specially designed social problem-solving group activities, including different types of cooperative learning. Teachers also receive training in teaching higher-order and critical thinking skills and in helping students transfer these skills to social situations.

Students are given assignments to use their critical-thinking and problem-solving skills in social situations within and outside of the school setting. They record notes about the situations in which they problem solve, and are asked to describe the critical thinking and problem-solving skills they use to solve the social dilemmas they face. They report back to class on their experiences and receive feedback from their teachers and peers.

The link between academic learning and SEL is one of the more important aspects of coordinating and integrating SEL into the life of the school. Programs should be selected that can be implemented in ways that enhance students' overall performance in school, including their academic achievement. Time devoted to SEL programs may in fact reinforce and enhance academic learning, and therefore should not be perceived as detracting from academic attention and focus. The reverse is also true. Academic focus is not perceived as undermining or negating the importance of SEL, but as embracing, reinforcing, and validating it. The extent to which this reciprocity and synergy is achieved has much to do with how well SEL programs are conceptualized, coordinated, and integrated with academic activities.

SEL activities and information that are fully integrated into regular classroom activities are taught primarily during the regular school day. Other SEL activities that are very much a part of the school improvement plan, although not taught as part of regular classroom lessons, add important learning experiences. These instructions are presented at special periods during the school day, or before or after school hours. After-school programs or class field trips offer opportunities to both introduce and reinforce SEL skills and to experiment with methods (such as adventure-based learning exercises) not suited to the classroom or school yard. In these settings, students may also have the opportunity to practice SEL skills with a different group of peers or with mixed ages that broaden their experience and confidence in SEL applications. Evening programs that bring together parents and students are also effective ways to reinforce SEL instruction. The goals and objectives of these after-school activities should be clearly articulated and in agreement with the goals of the school improvement plan. As much as possible, the most effective after-school SEL activities are linked to in-school activities so that students are able to connect them with the important learning that occurs during regular school hours.

Aligning with District Goals

G U I D E L I N E   2 0   ▼

SEL programs that are most clearly aligned with district goals and that have the support of the district administration are most likely to succeed.

Rationale

Although it is desirable for schools to have some autonomy in identifying and developing SEL programs, it is also important for the programs they select to be consistent with district goals, policies, and overall school improvement strategies. Increasingly, state core curriculum standards also must be consulted (see Figure 1.4 in Chapter 1). Such alignments reduce the probability of political, legal, and ethical conflicts, while increasing the probability of central office support.

EXAMPLE 20A
DISTRICTWIDE SUPPORT STRENGTHENS SEL PROGRAMS

In the School Development Program, participating schools learn a process for school management and reform, but the specific actions and steps are left to the school teams to define. Each of the schools must develop a plan, and the process of developing this plan helps the staff realize their school's critical needs. We structure our training and meetings so that each site can learn about other schools' programs and activities. Doing so encourages freedom and flexibility among participants to make decisions based on what is best for a particular school. We want them to have the kinds of experiences that will enable them to get started once we give them the tools.

—Lystra Richardson, School Development Program

Each school must send representatives to a workshop. The first week is a "101" training experience explaining what the program is and how to try things out at home. Usually schools send the principal. In February, the "102" training occurs. That is when we talk about the process—how did it work and how did it feel? The schools will send other people, like school psychologists, parents, community members, board members, or mental health professionals, depending on their needs. The school teams are from 10 to 15 different areas. The teams, representing a diversity of experience, are put into adult learning teams. We use the week to share ideas, solve problems together, and experience consensus, collaboration, and enthusiasm. Participants concentrate on teaching the community, students, parents, and school staff when they get back home. We do a lot of follow-up: post-training discussions, retreats, site visits to other districts, and special kick-off events. We also have a Web page and a video series and send out a newsletter three to four times a year to share the schools' stories.

—Valerie Maholmes
School Development Program

Implications and Applications

When planning to introduce an SEL program to a school, it is a good idea for the staff to check with the central office to see what, if any, SEL initiatives are planned for the district or exist in other schools in the district. Likewise, staff should investigate any new state or federal initiatives (e.g., Safe and Drug Free Schools). Local policy guidelines relevant to SEL programs also need to be examined. This information guides decisions about which programs to select or modify and how best to prepare and engage students, parents, and the community in planning and introducing a program.

Not surprisingly, the more aligned an SEL program is with district goals, the more likely the program is to receive needed resources. For example, many districts support nonviolent conflict resolution programs but may not identify nonviolent conflict resolution among its priorities for a given year. There may be no funding available for special speakers, staff development, and materials to support a conflict resolution program, especially one that is integrated with classroom procedures. On the other hand, a "tele-mentoring" program may fit better with a district's goals, and though it may require installation of more computers, purchase of expensive software, special training, and allocation of additional computer time beyond the regular school day, the central office may be more supportive of this program. Of course, costly programs that require significant expenditures, though in line with the district's goals, may not be supported due to limited funds.

The alignment of an SEL program with the school district's policies, goals, and priorities is important also from the perspective of longevity and survival. The more aligned the SEL program is with the district's priorities, the more likely it is to be sustained during times of budget and program cuts, and during staff reassignments and turnover.

How is SEL alignment achieved? First, review district goals in the areas of student academic and psychosocial development, and select programs that at least do not contradict or conflict with those goals. Second, develop program goals that match or complement district goals. Third, in implementing SEL programs, draw upon training resources provided by the central office, including staff development and student development opportunities.

The Role of Home and School Collaboration

G U I D E L I N E   2 1   ▼

When home and school collaborate closely to implement SEL programs, students gain more and the SEL program's effects are most enduring and pervasive.

Rationale

The most important part of a young person's community is the family. There is strong evidence to suggest that when home and school collaborate, programs tend to have many more positive outcomes that last for longer periods of time (Haynes and Comer 1996, Walberg 1984). Students are more likely to adopt positive standards if the standards of school, home, and community are clear and consistent (Gottfredson, Gottfredson, and Hybl 1993; Hawkins, Catalano, et al. 1992). Therefore, many educators have discovered the benefits of bringing family members into the process of social and emo-

tional skill building with family homework assignments, letters describing current topics, invitations to observe class lessons, and actual instruction on how parents can use the techniques with their children. The impact is even greater if the same framework is used by family members, daycare providers, clergy, local police officers, and recreational supervisors.

EXAMPLE 21A
PARENTS' NIGHT

In Kentucky, a visit to the Child Development Project (CDP) showed us how the project incorporates parent involvement through workshops. Tickets are donated from a local show and given away to parents who attend. On Family Science Nights interactive displays in every classroom, developed by the children, engage their parents' interest. Another example is Read Aloud Nights. A CDP book is chosen, and after it is read to the whole group, there is a dialogue between the kids and parents in small groups. After one of these nights, a dad told his child's 4th grade teacher that he "had not been read to in 20 years." Mary Beth Lykins gives her kindergarten students a take-home activity: "Ask your parents, What is the story of how I got my name?" She sends home a worksheet, and then each child presents his or her story to the class. The class applauds after each one.

Implications and Applications

Parents and guardians are often eager and willing to participate in efforts which they perceive to be in their children's best interests. In selecting, introducing, and implementing SEL programs, parents and guardians should be informed of program goals and program components as well as how these elements are to be implemented. There should also be clearly defined roles for parents. Involving parents in supportive roles, as well as making them active participants in planning and implementing some SEL activities, is often helpful in bridging the gap that sometimes exists between the expectations of home and the demands of school (Meadows 1993). Specifically, parents and guardians may

- Serve with staff and students as members of planning and management teams to help identify, select, and develop SEL programs.
- Actively participate in programs designed to encourage parents and students to work together on specific projects.
- Serve as instructors or co-instructors with teachers and other parents for specific SEL curricular components and activities.
- Provide logistical and material support in the form of fund-raising efforts and other material contributions that make SEL activities possible.
- Mentor individual students or groups of students.
- Act as SEL liaisons to community groups and agencies, representing the interests of the school and students, and gaining community support for SEL activities through creating newsletters and sponsoring SEL-related events.

Second Step, a popular prevention program, includes take-home videotapes about the curriculum that can be circulated among families. They demonstrate the program elements their children are learning at school and show how the principles can be used by parents at home. Teachers have been enthusiastic about this method of communicating with families who may not typically attend curriculum nights (Ramsey and Beland, 1996).

Evening programs that bring together students and parents are also effective methods for expanding and reinforcing SEL instruction. The middle school at Crossroads School for the Arts and Sciences in Santa Monica, California, invites parents for a "Life Skills Evening" early in the semester.

Parents meet with their child's teacher for some introductory remarks about the curriculum and methodology, and are then given an opportunity to experience some of the same SEL methods their children participate in. The teacher takes them through a playful warm-up exercise designed to help them feel comfortable and attentive. Then, they sample an approach their children are experiencing: a sharing circle. Parents are asked: "What do you find challenging about raising an 8th grader, and what do you find is working well for you?" They are given the right to pass, just as their children are in their classrooms. Parents appreciate being able to both speak about and listen to answers to such questions—and learn that the same is true for their children in SEL activities.

An added benefit of parent outreach is that it reduces parental opposition that sometimes arises when parents are not aware of the content of SEL programs. A program with devoutly religious parents and educators showed that some had negative reactions to specific lesson titles; their reservations disappeared when they read the entire lesson. One parent, for example, was concerned by a lesson titled "Self-Talk." The lesson instructs students to gather their resources in challenging circumstances by telling themselves, "Calm down. I can handle this." After reading the lesson, the parent commented that he actually agreed with everything in the lesson. "As a religious person, I would take it one step further in our school, and suggest that children think of relevant scripture for inspiration." Many parents are gratified to learn that SEL programs encourage students to consider family rules and expectations when evaluating possible solutions to a problem. The way SEL programs improve academic learning is also of interest to most parents (see Guideline 10).

Overall, benefits accrue when parents let their children know through words and actions that they support an SEL program. In addition, the home and school connection is strengthened through the careful planning of SEL activities that students can practice at home with siblings and parents. The Social Development Research Project fosters this aspect by having a Home-School Coordinator in its Seattle sites, serving as a bridge between parents and teachers and between classroom SEL lessons and desired home follow-through.

The Value of Securing Community Involvement and Support

G *UIDELINE* 2 2 ▼

Adequate community involvement in and support for SEL programs enhances their effects.

Rationale

The school is part of the community in which it is located and should be connected to the rest of the community in meaningful and helpful ways. It is widely acknowledged that community involvement in, and support for, SEL programs is essential for these programs to be maximally successful. The actions of the school are enhanced when it engages the wider community in its work of educating and developing the community's children.

Implications and Applications

A fundamental premise of the School Development Program and the "Comer Process" is that schools must have some organized link to the rest of the community. Ideally, these links include a parent-teacher organization, a school improvement team that includes representation from the wider community, a representative on the school board, a mental health team to address both normative and event-triggered social and emotional issues, and membership on a communitywide steering committee. These various linkages provide the synergy necessary to ensure that SEL programs reflect the

skills, attitudes, and values that are priorities in the community. Other means to engage the community include school newsletters and newspapers, mailed notices, public service announcements in the media, public testimonies at meetings and public hearings, and openness to visits from community members.

The community can be involved in supporting the school's SEL program in several ways:

• Community agencies, businesses, and organizations can provide opportunities for students to participate in community-based projects in which students learn and develop civic responsibility and altruistic attitudes in providing service to others.

• Organizations can make financial and other material resources available in sponsorship or support of SEL programs.

• Community organizations may provide guest presenters to give special talks and lectures, and have mentors work with students and staff on SEL projects.

• Individuals in the community may volunteer time to assist with or complement the implementation of SEL activities.

The Peacebuilders Program, based in Tucson, Arizona, arranges with the local news station to have a two- to three-minute spot each week to publicly congratulate the district's "Peacebuilders of the Week." Also, the local cable access station publishes their names, and local papers regularly cover program activities. For decades, the Primary Mental Health Project has used volunteers from the communities in its hundreds of sites to serve as tutors and companions to young elementary-school students at risk for poor socialization and academic skills. Efforts at whole-community involvement can be assisted by including adult stakeholders in training opportunities. Daycare providers, volunteer coaches, recreation workers, police officers, and parents have been trained in the same social problem-solving approach that is used in schools in Somerville, Summit, and Berkeley Heights, New Jersey.

Summary

Schools are not mere buildings. They are contexts that impart important socialization messages to children. If they are inviting, empowering, nurturing, and competence-enhancing, then the students in them will see themselves as important and believe that their future matters. But that isn't sufficient. Students also need the social and emotional skills to handle the challenges of learning and living in modern society. When SEL programs impart those skills in a context that's supportive, in which SEL programs are well coordinated and integrated into the academic and social life of the school, students understand that these skills matter and can help them in all facets of life. The approach to SEL selection, planning, and implementation should be informed by the awareness that student empowerment, school district support, home and school collaboration, and community support and involvement increase the durability, longevity, and probability of success for school programs in general and SEL programs in particular.

EXAMPLE 22A
BUILDING OUR FUTURE TOGETHER: SENIOR CITIZENS FILL AN EMOTIONAL VOID

Dr. John Conyers, Superintendent of Community Consolidated School District #15, serving eight municipalities in Northwestern Cook County (Illinois), encourages a number of initiatives in his schools that build social and emotional learning. But perhaps the most special of these involves senior citizens.

> *Senior Exchange* gives residents over age 55 an opportunity to help the schools while also earning money to pay the portion of their property tax that supports District 15. . . . They work in computer labs, resource centers, lunchrooms, school offices, and classrooms. . . . More than one participant has told us that the opportunity to contribute has "saved my life."

The *Generations Exchange* program finds more informal ways to bring senior citizens into the schools. A "Foster Grandparents program," says Conyers, links unrelated children and seniors in a simulated grandparent-grandchild relationship." The idea came up when, on a Grandparents' Day, educators realized how few grandparents the students had contact with. "Over the years," Conyers continues, "this program has proven to be a wonderful experience of love, sharing, and compassion for both kids and seniors."

Other programs, like *Computer Friends*, have direct academic benefits. During a computer project involving a simulated trek on the Oregon Trail, students wondered why their senior volunteer was giving them so many detailed suggestions. "One boy turned to her and demanded, "How do you know so much?" "My great-grandmother was on the Oregon Trail. . . . I have her letters about experiences during the trip." Later she shared the letters with the students.

—cf. Conyers (1996)

6 Introducing and Sustaining Social and Emotional Education

Starting a new program—whether it is a language program, science program, or SEL program—can be exciting, but it is also difficult. The same is true when we change some procedures and approaches from those traditionally used in our classroom or school. We wonder, what exactly is this "innovation" supposed to look like? How will the students react? How will I or the other people carrying it out feel about it? How will it fit with other things being done?

There are many ways to think about these questions. We have tried, throughout this book, to give real, tangible examples, based on recent feedback and experiences, to help readers get a sense of the look and feel of social and emotional skill-building activities. And in Appendix C, we provide contact information about sites that readers can call and visit if they want to talk with people who are actively implementing high-quality SEL programs or if they want to see them in action.[1]

In this chapter, we present the most important considerations in carrying out SEL programs in three stages: selecting and piloting a program, expanding the program, and creating conditions that ensure long-term success.[2] Later we also describe roadblocks and obstacles at each of these stages, along with specific examples of how to overcome them.

Selecting and Starting a Pilot Program

GUIDELINE 23 ▼

In selecting a specific SEL program, educators must consider identified local needs, goals, interests, and mandates; staff skills; preexisting efforts; the nature of instructional procedures; the quality of materials; the developmental appropriateness of the program; and its respect for diversity.

---

[1]Through CASEL, resource materials and, where available, video resources may be obtained that provide examples of programs in action or of techniques being used.

[2]We have focused on information derived from programs that have demonstrated their effects through research, and especially those operating for at least several years outside of a demonstration project context. For specific, detailed elaboration on the ideas in this chapter, see Huberman and Miles (1984); Lippit et al. (1985); Hord et al. (1987); Zins (1992); Elias and Clabby (1992); Hawkins, Catalano, et al. (1993); Consortium on the School-Based Promotion of Social Competence (1994); McElhaney (1995); and Miller, Brodine, and Miller (1996).

Rationale

You should feel comfortable asking certain questions about SEL approaches, whether they are procedures for use in individual classrooms such as The Responsive Classroom, programs targeted for specific grade levels such as PATHS, or school-wide models such as the Child Development Project. It will be increasingly necessary to ask these questions because we anticipate a growing number of slickly packaged, well-marketed efforts at building students' "emotional intelligence." Most of these will be untested and provide inadequate guidance for clear implementation. Such programs are unlikely to endure or to produce genuine and generalizable skills gains, especially for students who are disadvantaged and may have learning difficulties.

Implications and Applications

With the considerations just noted in mind, here is a set of questions to help guide your program selection:

• What is out there, and how does it match up with what you already do, needs you have identified, your goals, and staff skills needed to carry it out? Any program carried out only during a designated "program time" is unlikely to have long-lasting or far-reaching effects.

• How does the program or approach assume children learn and change? A theoretical framework gives educators a way of addressing particular situations and needs not explicitly addressed by the program materials.

• How well targeted is it to the appropriate developmental period(s)? Although it may seem obvious that SEL efforts are more likely to be successful when characterized by instruction that is appropriate to students' developmental levels, too many programs overlook this consideration.

• What is the quality of the materials? The most effective materials are clear, up-to-date, engaging, user-friendly, fun, and adequate in supply or accessibility.

• How does the program address diversity, including cultural and learning differences? Diversity requires explicit consideration because of the increasing heterogeneity of today's classrooms. A diverse SEL program is one that is sensitive, relevant, appropriate, and responsive with regard not only to cultural matters, but also the ethnicity, gender, physical challenges, and socioeconomics of students served, as well as of the faculty and staff carrying out the program. Its procedures go beyond awareness to include an embracing and appreciation of differences (Banks 1992; Gager, Kress, and Elias 1996).

A special word should be said about preexisting SEL efforts. The most potent are current classroom and school rules and discipline systems. Others include the health/family life education curriculum and any other SEL programs in place (or those recently tried and discarded). These are all powerful forms of SEL instruction. Their implications for selecting new SEL programs and planning their implementation must be given extensive thought. There is no evidence of an SEL program that has endured where it has not "fit" within its school or district, even if piloted successfully on a short-term, limited basis.

GUIDELINE 24 ▼

SEL activities and programs are best introduced as pilot programs.

Rationale

Getting started is exciting, but it is also hard, even when enthusiasm and inspiration are our allies. A pilot program allows a school to start small. Veteran principal Tom Schuyler of New Jersey says it best: "If a pilot works out well, great! You now can continue into a larger program. If the pilot doesn't work, it doesn't mean the entire SEL idea has to be thrown out. After all, it is just a pilot.

Who would expect a great success the first time out? We can learn from a pilot, and then we can pilot again." Tom also points out that a pilot allows implementers to place less pressure on themselves. They have some room for miscues, false starts, and finding their style.

Implications and Applications

Piloting doesn't mean just getting started. Planning is essential, because the seeds of future SEL efforts are being sown by what one does in the present. Veterans of successful pilots recommend the following:

- *Be focused* on the positives, on what you have to gain from doing this activity and the benefits that your efforts can bring to the children you care about so much.
- *Be clear* about what you want to do. Articulate a set of goals that are specific, reasonable, and measurable, using indicators that make sense to you and your colleagues.
- *Be prepared.* Don't jump into this effort lightly. Make sure you have the needed resources (financial and otherwise), that you have done your homework in planning for this effort, and that everyone who needs to be on board is, in fact, on board. Clearly, an increasing amount of preparation is needed as one's efforts involve a larger number of classrooms or schools.
- *Be predictable.* The importance of regularity and predictability for students cannot be overestimated. Students tend to feel most comfortable when there is a regularly scheduled and adhered-to time for SEL activities. During periods in which no formal instruction is planned, students benefit from regular reviews of SEL principles so they know that SEL ideas and skills still apply and are relevant to their behavior.
- *Be integrative* and link the SEL effort with other subject areas, including at least one basic academic subject. This effort will help ensure that SEL is not perceived as an add-on.
- *Be ready to reinforce.* Plan ways for specific activities or lessons to get extended and reinforced beyond their specific presentation. To enhance generalization, incorporate strategies to change the environment in which children function so that the culture encourages and rewards the use of new skills and promotes their generalization; this outcome is much more likely to happen with efforts that occur during all or much of the school year.

Beyond these guidelines, there is great consensus that it is advantageous to have access to tangible examples of successful efforts at building SEL skills. Throughout this book and in Appendix C, we have tried to provide as many of these as possible. In this section, the applications are largely cross-references to earlier examples. While far from exhaustive, they provide starting and comparison points for examining the ever-increasing volume of materials being produced in this area.

Expanding the Pilot Program

Once you have shepherded a pilot project through its initial run-through, you may well want to repeat what you have done, just to get a better sense of it, improve it further, or tailor it to some population that you feel could have learned more.

This stage is one that relatively few programs reach. There are many reasons for this reality, including changes in key personnel, shifts in district goals, and failures to keep programs responsive to changing student, educator, and community needs. Time and again, program expansion has appeared easier than it actually is. Difficulties at this stage may sabotage a promising beginning. Therefore, the guidelines for this section are strong statements designed to prevent truly promising efforts from self-destructing.

GUIDELINE 25 ▼

Professional development and supervision are important at all levels.

Rationale

Preparation and ongoing support for carrying out the program are best provided by well-prepared instructors who receive high-quality supervision and engage in ongoing staff development (e.g., coaching, supervision, mentoring, collaboration, planning). Of special importance is professional development in the area of providing a safe environment in which children can express their feelings. Administrators must be prepared to understand the program at all levels: to provide support, coaching, and supervision; to participate in planning; and to seek out appropriate outside guidance for the program.

GUIDELINE 26 ▼

Be clear about your planning process and your view of how programs expand successfully in your setting.

Rationale

Expanding the program is easier when it is guided by a clear approach to planning, implementation, management, and evaluation based on an underlying theory or model of change, and when adequate and ongoing administrative support is available. Identifying expectations and responsibilities for everyone involved, from parents and teachers' aides to the superintendent and other administrators to community members is important. The school board has a role as program supporter and, perhaps, funds provider; cultivating its support should be a proactive task. Calhoun (1993) provides an excellent overview of an action research model that teachers, principals, or district administrators can use to plan, monitor, and continuously improve SEL efforts (see also Elias and Clabby 1992, Kelly 1987, Kusche and Greenberg 1994).

GUIDELINE 27 ▼

An SEL program or approach that addresses a wide range of life skills and problem prevention areas tends to have the most impact.

Rationale

For a program to take hold beyond the pilot stage, it must be linked with an array of skills, concerns, and specific topics that educators believe students must master. An SEL approach that serves as an umbrella for related issues within a common framework is most likely to be seen as useful and therefore accepted more broadly. Comprehensive SEL efforts

- Integrate and incorporate cognitive, affective, and behavioral skills.
- Reflect a coherent set of attitudes and values applicable to a variety of situations.
- Address *specific* topics, such as alcohol, tobacco, drugs, violence, and AIDS.
- Address *generic* topics, such as problem solving, social skills, stress management, and communication skills.

GUIDELINE 28 ▼

Allow the necessary time and support for the program to strengthen and grow.

Rationale

People tend to rush into implementation or to try to share materials or in other ways cut corners

EXAMPLE 25A
THE IMPORTANCE OF ONGOING PROFESSIONAL DEVELOPMENT AND SUPPORT: ADVICE FROM LEADERS OF SITE-VISITED PROGRAMS

The teachers are quick to say that the students' problems are from the parents—but they really have to realize that they make such a difference in just being a good teacher to these kids—it is almost like being a surrogate parent. We want to make sure the teachers are teaching in the very best ways with the very best skills in order to effectively build that protective environment for kids. That protective environment can prevent those things leading to delinquency and drop out.

—Kevin Haggerty
Social Development Research Group

An SEL program like PMHP [Primary Mental Health Program] is a constant growth cycle for everyone involved. You constantly have to nurture and validate. If you don't do that, the effectiveness will slip away.

—William Haffey
Monroe County, New York,
Board of Cooperative Services
Primary Mental Health Program

The challenge of institutionalizing SEL programs in the schools is that there is the problem of adult learners, where it is difficult for them to immediately embrace the new teaching methods of SEL. The administration has to motivate the whole staff over a long period of time. They have to talk with the teachers, [show] that it is a developmental process to take some risks and let down some control in the classroom.

—Darlene DeMattia, Principal
Watsessing School, Bloomfield, New Jersey,
Social Decision Making and Problem Solving

An SEL program needs to grow with the changes of the society around it. It is good to provide ongoing education in order to promote constant development. It is not necessary to change the program, but the people involved in implementing the program need to adjust to new problems that develop. You have to keep progressing.

—Karen Bachelder, Executive Director
Committee for Children
Seattle, Washington

as a program expands. These actions are the equivalent of withholding water from a newly sodded lawn. For programs to take hold, a few conditions are essential:

• Sufficient time must be allocated to deliver the program on a consistent and frequent basis and to coordinate efforts.

• Adequate materials must be available.

• Organizational support must be provided.

• The teaching of the program must cover all or much of the school year.

• Implementation must span multiple years without gaps in instruction.

GUIDELINE 29 ▼

Systematically involving students who are receiving special education helps build a cohesive program climate and increases generalization of learned skills to situations students encounter in daily living.

EXAMPLE 25B
HAVING REGARD FOR ONE'S PROFESSIONAL INTEGRITY

On the wall in a staff lounge in a Jewish Day School where SEL is taught:

> Rabbi Elazar ben Shamua taught: The dignity of your student should be as precious to you as your own. The dignity of your colleague should be as precious to you as your reverence for your teacher. The reverence for your teacher should be as great as your reverence for God.

> —Pirke Avot, "Ethics of the Fathers," Chapter 4, Verse 15

This wisdom dates back many centuries and shows that from a high regard for one's own professional integrity, benefits flow to one's colleagues, mentors, and students—and to oneself.

EXAMPLE 26A
PRINCIPLES TO GUIDE SEL PROGRAM DEVELOPMENT

James Kelly's (1987) social-ecological approach has been used by many schools to implement programs to improve students' social and emotional well-being. Here are Kelly's principles to guide program development:

1. People, settings, and events are resources for program development.
2. Resources must be identified and carefully used.
3. Emphasize the activating qualities of people, settings, and events.
4. Coping and adaptation are the dominant means of growth and change.
5. Systemic events and processes must be understood.
6. Consider how people and settings are in dynamic interaction.
7. Assess people, settings, and events over time.
8. Programs succeed as relationships are formed.
9. Attend to any side effects of establishing a program.
10. Program development is a flexible, improvisational process.

Rationale

A classroom or a school is a community. When individuals are excluded, intentionally or not, the community is diminished. On the other hand, when ways can be found to involve all members of a community, everyone gains. In essence, the group's "emotional quotient"—its EQ—rises dramatically.

Students who are disadvantaged are the least well equipped to navigate and somehow reconcile loopholes and gaps in the instruction they receive. Continuity is important. Therefore, SEL should be provided consistently to students in special education, either in inclusive or self-contained classrooms, as is most appropriate. Where needed, additional skill development opportunities can be provided (see Guidelines 11 and 12).

Relevance for Long-Term Implementation

How long is "long-term implementation" of a particular program? The answer is something less than a lifetime but greater than two or three years. It is well recognized that once an innovation is introduced, it typically requires 18 months to three years (depending on the innovation's complexity) for all parties to understand, adapt, and own it (Hord, Rutherford, Huling-Austin, and Hall 1987).

The following guidelines apply in particular to creating enduring efforts to promote SEL. They build on successful attainment of the guidelines presented up to this point. But the concept here is dynamic, rather than static. What a program is accomplishing, what its goals are, and what exactly the program needs to consist of are matters that merit frequent reconsideration, in what we call *a spirit of continuous improvement*. Sometimes this means that an innovation can no longer be modified sufficiently to reach desired goals. In that case, another innovation may be needed.

G U I D E L I N E 30 ▼

To foster long-term commitment, it is helpful to have a designated program coordinator, social development facilitator, or a social and emotional development committee. Committees typically are responsible for seeing that the various activities needed to effectively meet program goals are carried out. They monitor SEL-related efforts inside and outside the school.

G U I D E L I N E 31 ▼

Long-lasting SEL programs are highly visible and recognized. These programs "act proud" and are not "snuck in" or carried out on unofficially "borrowed" time. They do not act in opposition to school or district goals, but rather are integral to these goals.

G U I D E L I N E 32 ▼

Effective SEL approaches use portfolios, exhibitions, fairs, group presentations, and print and electronic media both inside and outside of school to invite participation and encourage the involvement and commitment of the larger community. By using a variety of approaches, SEL programs extend the reach of the program beyond formal school and classroom settings, and reach out to bring others in.

G U I D E L I N E 33 ▼

The longer a program is in place, the more it will have to be adapted to changing circumstances. Implementation must be monitored and the program's outcomes evaluated regularly.

Rationale, Implications, and Applications for Guidelines 30–33

In the school, coordination requires that SEL efforts be linked explicitly to any school health/family life education program; to special services, whether for at-risk or classified youngsters; and to any relevant local, state, and federal policies (such as Family Life Education, Safe and Drug Free Schools and Communities, or Workplace Readiness legislation). An individual or group needs to have clear responsibility and authority for ensur-

ing that this coordination takes place.

Another responsibility includes any gradual but systematic plans to expand SEL efforts and inform others about them, an activity associated with program longevity. Typically, this endeavor first involves sharing and discussion within a grade level, then with adjacent grade levels, next with other schools, and finally at the district level. At the same time, parallel discussions are held with parents and the community to ensure that they understand the nature of the social and emotional learning that is occurring. The key concept is that

---

EXAMPLE 30A
THE RESPONSIBILITIES OF A SOCIAL DEVELOPMENT COORDINATOR

At the Children's Institute—a private school in Livingston, New Jersey, that specializes in working with students who are emotionally disturbed and display conduct disordered behavior—the role of Social Development Coordinator was created to bring together SEL efforts in the school. These included Social Decision Making and Problem Solving, Skillstreaming, a problem solving/crisis intervention room, infusion of social decision making into academics, and social skills groups run by the social work staff. The Coordinator provided this summary of her role:

1. Organize and implement structural framework of the schoolwide program:
   - convene, organize Social Development Committee
   - schedule and chair staff sharing meetings
   - coordinate and share classroom schedules
   - maintain chart of skills being worked on across classes
   - maintain lesson binders
   - encourage schoolwide use of posters with terminology

2. Train new and current staff members:
   - orientation and follow-up
   - learn from one another
   - advanced SPS workshops and collaborations

3. Extend the program into the children's homes:
   - parent workshops
   - information booklets
   - host a Social Development Day
   - learn-a-thon
   - Children's Institute Social Development newspapers (staff, students)

4. Motivate staff:
   - minimize paperwork
   - keep exciting materials available
   - implement program in existing curriculum areas
   - get them involved

EXAMPLE 31A
INSTITUTIONALIZING SEL PROGRAMS

Many programs focus exclusively on academic achievement. We attempt first to create a school climate that permits parents and staff to support the overall development of all children in a way that makes academic achievement and desirable social behavior at an acceptable level both possible and expected. We believe that such an approach has a much greater potential for improving students' chances of achieving school success, decreasing their likelihood of being involved in problem behaviors, and increasing their chances for life success.

The School Development Program is not a "quick fix," nor is it an "add on." It is not just another new activity to be carried out along with the other experiments and activities already under way in a school. It is a nine-element process model—three mechanisms, three operations, three guiding principles—that takes significant time, commitment, and energy to implement. It is a different way of conceptualizing and working in schools and completely replaces traditional organization and management. All of the activities in a school are managed through the school development process. And most important, the SDP produces desirable outcomes only after a cooperative and collaborative spirit exists throughout a school.

—James Comer
School Development Program
New Haven, Connecticut

There is another issue—time. People want to see change within a two- to three-year period because that is how long board members at the top hold their positions. Administrators should have a much longer perspective. It might actually take seven to ten years to integrate programs.

—A. Dirk Hightower, Director
Primary Mental Health Project

You can have the best program in the world, but if teachers cannot teach it well, then what do you have? There is a need for constant revision, and the capacity as an organization to do so involves ongoing expense and commitment to better the program. You must support it, revise it, and pay attention to ongoing quality, to evaluate and change the program. People overestimate the simplicity of this.

—Karen Bachelder, Executive Director
Committee for Children
Seattle, Washington

---

of a gradual but systematic sharing of information and opportunities to become involved in the effort. It includes providing tangible examples of SEL activities and applications for school personnel, school board members, parents, and other community members to see. Increasingly, print and electronic newsletters and Web sites will contribute to these efforts.

A retired school principal in New Jersey with nearly two decades of experience implementing so-cial and emotional learning programs was initially resistant to any kind of program evaluation. He eventually embraced it, stating that we have an ethical responsibility to be clear about the indicators we believe will reflect the impact of programs, expected implementation actions, and boundaries, past which program tampering, bending, and erosion will undermine its integrity. He believes that these considerations are as vital for the individual classroom teacher as they are for grade-level, building, or districtwide program implementation. (See Chapter 7 for a full discussion of the importance of evaluation.)

Anticipating and Overcoming Obstacles and Roadblocks

That same New Jersey principal, like so many effective administrators and teachers, spoke of the need to "always have your antennae out there, so you can find out about the early signs of trouble. You also need people whom you can trust who will let you know what is really going on." To formalize this concern, we introduce Guideline 34.

G U I D E L I N E   3 4   ▼

Persistence and commitment are essential to overcoming obstacles that may hinder start-up of the SEL program and snarl the implementation. Because problem solving involves the modeling of the skills that educators are trying to teach students, the process of resolving issues contributes greatly to the effectiveness of SEL efforts.

Rationale

There is no innovation without bumps in the road. Likewise, there is no learning without a bit of challenge and struggle. All of the programs drawn upon in this book have been modified in the light of experience. Programs are always adapted to fit local conditions—usually in response to a particular problem or shortcoming.

Nevertheless, the process of encountering and handling these difficulties can be daunting. One might be tempted to wonder if the cure is actually worse than the sickness. Keep in mind that you will not be the first to travel this challenging road. To the extent possible, we provide here a bit of a road map to help you see the twists and turns and roadblocks likely to appear on your journey. For

this purpose, we draw upon a list of obstacles from two recent surveys of practitioners of SEL programs, both of which are available elsewhere for more in-depth study. The first (Elias 1993) included teachers, administrators, school psychologists, guidance counselors, special educators, parent educators, and mental health professionals with years of experience implementing SEL programs. The second was the result of a series of ethnographic on-site visits of established SEL programs, carried out by three on-site visitors and a support team at Rutgers University from September to December 1996 (Elias, Bruene-Butler, Blum, and Schuyler 1997; Appendix C lists the programs visited).

Many concerns about carrying out SEL activities were raised. Some questions were of a skeptical nature; others reflected hesitation about taking on this type of work. Some questions addressed nuances in instruction or program administration; others reflected the need to constantly refine and improve procedures for reaching the students most at-risk of failure. In all cases, the message was clear: Once one is committed to the idea that schools must provide, as part of their mission, the conditions that will promote knowledgeable, responsible, and caring children—with the social and emotional intelligence needed to fill a variety of critical life roles—then addressing obstacles becomes a question of not "if" but "how."

Implications and Applications

The guidelines, of course, have been developed to anticipate many obstacles. Anticipate, however, does not mean, eliminate. In walking the path to implementing long-term efforts for building students' social and emotional skills, we will inevitably encounter rough weather, bumpy roads, and confusing signs. The obstacles and roadblocks that one is likely to encounter, however, have been fairly well mapped and can be organized into several categories. Within each, we have grouped the main concerns that emerged in the two surveys.

1. Those concerns most likely to arise, especially in the beginning, and which most SEL programs have dealt with effectively.

- "This is no different from character education. Why do we need this?"
- "Won't this take time away from important academics?"
- "Schools shouldn't be doing this."
- "We already have plenty of programs in self-esteem, drug prevention, smoking prevention, and more. We don't need anything else."
- "How does SEL fit in with block scheduling?"
- "We need decent materials, and they are too expensive; we will have to cut back or share."
- "I would rather not do this; this is what school psychologists, counselors, or therapists do."
- "This will take time away from activities that will boost test scores."

The key to dealing with these obstacles is to address them openly but intelligently. These make up the most basic set of concerns, and numerous teachers and administrators have worked past them. None is insurmountable. For example, SEL clearly complements academics; the thousands of educators who implement SEL in the school are neither crazed nor professionally suicidal. They work in public and private schools and are cognizant of the need to have children develop their intellectual skills. Intelligent preparation means that those embarking on SEL efforts need to have contact with those who have been through the stormy weather and survived. How did they do it? The closer their situation is to yours, the more comfortable you can feel with the solutions. But do not try to pilot without addressing these obstacles, or you invite sabotage.

2. The questions that seemed difficult or most feared at the beginning, but that rarely emerge in reality and, when they do, can be handled with minimal difficulty.

- "This is a way of inculcating the child with new-age values."
- "Teaching values belongs in the home."
- "We shouldn't devote time to building self-esteem."
- "This will compromise family privacy."
- "This cannot work because of increasing numbers of students exhibiting aggression, unkindness, and other troublesome behavior patterns."
- "Some kids just will not get it—then what will we do?"
- "There is a lack of parent follow-up at home to support in-school learning, so it cannot work."
- "What do I do when a student brings up sensitive personal or family material in a classroom or group discussion?"

Here, the words of Franklin Roosevelt and Harry Truman are useful: "We have nothing to fear but fear itself" and "The buck stops here." Fear of these obstacles has paralyzed many educators. SEL must work in the context of shared values and be visibly focused on the goals of promoting children's social and emotional skills, ensuring healthy development, and preparing students for life as family and community members, active citizens, and productive members of workplaces—including the school. Educators must work toward these goals. There is room for dialogue about how to do so. Beginning a pilot program and making modifications often provide a concrete, action-oriented focus for such dialogues.

Here again, intelligent preparation will help. SEL loses ground whenever any poorly constructed and inadequately implemented program without a theoretical and empirical base is carried out and fails. The bandwagon for building emotional intelligence is still gathering momentum, and much of the force behind it is economic. The SEL programs in this book hold family values and privacy in a cherished position (but not an isolated one); they are committed, in Robert Slavin's terms, to find "success for all"; and they recognize that in certain circumstances SEL will need to be taught effectively without active home collaboration. Sadly, for some students home collaboration is not even an option. When the subject is SEL, not reaching a student means that the student is at high risk for dangerous interpersonal consequences. In a spirit of continuous improvement, there must be a commitment to using the problem-solving skills of SEL to address these obstacles if and when they occur. Others have done so successfully. Sometimes dangerous curves are not so bad when one drives slowly, uses caution, and chooses a safe and well-maintained vehicle.

3. Questions or comments that pose the greatest problems and require continuous commitment to overcome include the following:

• Unrealistic expectations—for the time needed for student skill development; for institutionalizing SEL; for the existence of a magic bullet or inoculationist approach; for the need to adapt to ongoing change in students, staff, the community, and therefore in SEL efforts.

• Turnover in both teaching staff and administration, and concerns about how to continue to train everyone who needs to be trained, especially after the initial kickoff.

• Fears that the program won't continue when external support is withdrawn or the political winds change.

• The current mandated curriculum exceeds classroom time.

• Problems with current staff development models, how to provide ongoing support to implementers, lack of educator training in areas of prevention and SEL.

• Rushing to judgment about a program, cutting corners, not documenting.

These complex issues are the lot of those committed to building students' social and emotional skills. The best solution is to network with other implementers and mutually solve problems. Although these are not problems for which "set" solutions can be reached, *they are not uncommon for anyone working with a comprehensive or schoolwide program.* Once education becomes explicitly inter-dependent across grade levels and buildings, obstacles become magnified, and good emotional regulation, self-calming, stress management, and creative problem-solving skills—the skills we want our children to develop—become essential. In many SEL training programs, these issues would be treated as part of "advanced" training. Indeed, they may look a bit difficult. Once you have gotten far enough down the road to encounter them, you are likely to have accumulated the savvy to navigate past them.

Summary

As you embark on the implementation process, it is important to remember that you are not the first classroom, school, or district to make this journey. Learn from other implementation sites. Implementation issues tend to be similar across different programs, so there are a wide variety of sites to consult. Appendix C contains a list of some that are willing to be contacted. CASEL maintains a cumulative database of new programs and sites as well as those that no longer function actively. Look for a site that is geographically close and that has goals and implementation conditions similar to your own.

During these difficult times, it may be helpful to draw on the perspective of a school that adopted the SEL-related school theme "To Be or Not To Be." Staff and students emphasized having the courage to pursue cherished goals for oneself and others and the competence to do so effectively. The school's motto embodied this theme: "If I am not for me, who will be? If I am for myself alone, what am I? And if not now, when?" This wisdom from the ancient sage, Hillel, and the idea of courage emphasized as a goal can help propel us past barriers large and small. We must have the courage and commitment to work continuously and act to meet the developmental needs of all children.

7 Evaluating the Success of Social and Emotional Learning

WHETHER YOUR SEL PROGRAM INVOLVES ONE CLASS-room or several schools, you must determine from the start how you will evaluate the program. When the program is carefully planned, evaluation typically isn't a problem, but schools that are directed to set up programs on short notice may, in their haste to show they have a program, neglect to plan for evaluation. Nevertheless, the public will want to know how the program is working. Public concern about accountability is growing; everyone recognizes that resources are too limited to apply to programs that do not produce good results. You must carefully specify the outcomes you want from your activities, and then examine the relationship between the desired outcomes and those actually attained. By making needed adjustments along the way, you can be confident the program really is effective.

Evaluation begins when a program is initially being developed, with identification of goals and methods for documenting program activities. It continues as long as the program is in use. Each of the authors of this book has had the experience of being asked to help evaluate an SEL program as it was winding down because the school needed an evaluation report. This sort of evaluation rarely results in learning how to maximize what a program can do to benefit children (Linney and Wandersman 1996). Rather, evaluation begins with a commitment to being reflective.

The Reflective Educator

More and more educators are embracing the idea of the "reflective educator" (Brubacher, Case, and Reagan 1994) or the "scientist practitioner" (Barlow, Hayes, and Nelson 1984). Reflective educators carefully examine their own and others' professional practice, and engage in school-based action research with fellow "researcher-teachers" (Calhoun 1993, Johnson 1993). Essentially, what this means is that if we want to improve our professional practices, we must think carefully about what is taking place in a given situation, correctly identify the options available through an analytical process, and make conscious choices about how to act. "Reflective educators are constantly testing the assumptions and inferences they have made about their work as teachers" (Brubacher et al. 1994, p. 131). As educators, we are required to make numerous decisions every day about how to act. Our skills in simultaneously reflecting, analyzing situations, making judgments, and acting determine how successfully we handle the challenges associated with educating young people.

Many studies have found educators to be more reactive than reflective, however (Brubacher et al. 1994). Our experience is that educators and schools caught up in a reactive cycle rarely escape and seem to always be playing what a New Jersey principal colorfully calls "catch-up," "putting out fires," and "being on roller skates trying to plug up leaks in the dike." These are not the reasons why most of us went into the education field. Reflective practice and a commitment to knowing genuinely and continuously the effects of our actions can break the reactive cycle.

Most effective educators take pride in being able to justify their decisions and actions in the classroom—that is, providing solid and defensible reasons for their course of action (Calhoun 1993, Hamm 1989). Such reasons are based on well-conceived frameworks (as discussed in Chapter 4), ideas from research, and the collective experience of the teachers in that school or district. Indeed, evaluation data from a school's SEL program can provide focused direction about the next appropriate course of action. Efforts to improve SEL and other aspects of schooling will benefit from our adopting reflective approaches to professional practice.

Creating a Culture That Supports Reflection and Inquiry

Chapter 5 emphasized the importance of school culture in promoting SEL. Similarly, this culture also significantly influences the value placed on reflection and inquiry (Zins, Travis, and Freppon 1997). Schools that exemplify a culture of inquiry have teachers, administrators, and others who collaboratively seek to better understand and thereby improve the educational experience (Brubacher et al. 1994, Johnson 1993). In such settings, ideas such as SEL are emphasized, and the evaluation of programs is considered important.

Administrative support is a key to establishing such a culture. Words must be backed up by actions. Administrators must encourage teachers to trust, to be intellectually curious, to share, to raise questions, to be open to challenge, to provide mutual support, and to express doubt—and they must give teachers the time to do so, and ample

freedom to try new actions based on these efforts. Administrators should also model such behaviors themselves. Establishing and maintaining productive working relationships is critical if educators are to examine current practices, modify them as necessary, and discard less effective ones. Unfortunately, the organizational structure of most schools tends to keep staff isolated from one another, which in turn limits their opportunities for mutual support, reflection, and collaboration.

There are a number of ways for schools to encourage collegial support. Most involve changing school culture and organizational structures so that more interactions occur within and across grades and schools. Approaches that give teachers opportunities to discuss, think about, and try new practices allow them to enter new roles like peer coach or teacher researcher, or use new organizational structures like decision-making teams or site-based management (Lieberman 1995). For example, peer support groups involve having a small number of professionals with similar areas of interest meet regularly to learn from one another, solve problems, and provide support for professional development activities. An atmosphere of trust and support is established so that members help one another with professional problems, learn new ideas, and deal with stress, isolation, and burnout (Zins, Maher, Murphy, and Wess 1988). They likewise promote a culture of inquiry and reflective practice. Consequently, these teachers "are never satisfied that they have all the answers. By continually seeking new information, participants constantly challenge their own practices and assumptions. In the process, new dilemmas surface and teachers initiate a new cycle of planning, acting, observing, and reflecting" (Ross, Bondy, and Kyle 1993, p. 337).

A culture that supports reflection and inquiry doesn't necessarily require new resources; it requires staff and administration to look at the current resources in a new light and redirect them to meet new goals.

First Steps

Where do we begin? It is this question that paralyzes many educators and keeps them from taking the first step in deciding how to evaluate their SEL programs. Educators are very familiar with establishing immediate and long-term objectives for academic programs and can use this knowledge to help them do the same for SEL programs, which do have specific long-term goals, such as the development of citizens who are productive, knowledgeable, responsible, caring, contributing, nonviolent, and healthy members of society. It is usually necessary, however, to focus on intermediate objectives, such as learning skills for social problem solving, conflict resolution, self-control, and respect for others, to document that an SEL program is on the right track. By so doing, we learn ways to modify the procedures as the program continues, as even the best program will likely need some fine-tuning to meet the needs of the community.

G U I D E L I N E   3 5   ▼

SEL programs have clear implementation criteria and are monitored to ensure that the programs are carried out as planned.

Rationale

After an SEL program has been selected, the next step is to monitor the implementation process to track how it is actually carried out: Is the SEL program really being taught? By how many teachers? In how many schools? Are nonteaching staff using SEL program strategies? All of us are familiar with well-designed programs that never begin or that, once started, look a lot different than everyone thought they would.

The next question is whether instruction is being carried out in the manner planned. Too often, we have observed, people conclude that a program is not working, when in fact its shortcomings stem from how the program is being presented by teachers and other staff. Too often, the effective instructional methods described in Chapter 4 are omitted or deemphasized in the interests of time.

There are many legitimate reasons why teachers may make significant changes in program content; however, when carefully planned activities are modified to such an extent that they no longer resemble the original program, the goals and objectives of the program should be reexamined to see if they are still relevant.

Implications and Applications

Instead of dropping programs when they do not meet expectations, it might be preferable to investigate *why*. For instance, we may find that program activities are unclear, teachers are uncomfortable with the teaching methods, insufficient time has been allotted, or insufficient supervision or coaching has been provided. The program itself may not be at fault.

When program implementation is separated into the following steps, it can be made quite manageable: (a) identify the core elements of the instructional program and (b) develop a mechanism for determining that they are being carried out correctly. To illustrate, a specific lesson on using self-control as an alternative to aggression may consist of the following steps (McGinnis and Goldstein 1984, p. 145):

1. Stop and count to 10.
2. Think of how your body feels.
3. Think about your choices:
   a. Walk away for now.
   b. Do a relaxation exercise.
   c. Write about how you feel.
   d. Talk to someone about it.
4. Act out your best choice.

A teacher could easily check off these steps as they are taught. As a result, we would have some evidence that these specific skills were covered. If one or more steps are skipped, we can determine whether additional needs like time, resources, training, or support teachers might help. A similar approach can be used with other skills. Relatedly, notations can be made to indicate the extent to which students appear to have *learned* the skills being taught.

On a broader level, a questionnaire can be constructed regarding the overall implementation process. For example, one form used as a vehicle for reflecting on social problem-solving instruction follows this outline (Elias and Tobias 1996):

• What reactions did students have to this session (for whom was it most/least effective)?
• What were the most effective or favorable aspects of this session?
• What were the least effective or favorable aspects of this session?
• Describe implementation issues that required your attention.
• List the points that need to be followed up in the next class meeting.
• What are some suggested changes in this lesson/activity for the future?

Such information is gathered after each activity or instructional unit. Outcomes of programs can be assessed meaningfully once we know what instruction was provided, and its nuances.

G U I D E L I N E   3 6 ▼

Effective SEL programs are monitored and evaluated regularly using systematic procedures and multiple indicators.

Rationale

Evaluation must be seen as an essential component of the program, not an add-on. It is most helpful when it proceeds in a step-by-step manner. Therefore, after documenting that the planned SEL activities took place, the next step is to determine their effects or outcomes. Contrary to the fears of

some, the purpose here is not to assess an individual teacher's competence or personal performance. Rather, the intent is to answer questions about SEL instructional outcomes based on more than just intuition and anecdotal reports.

Implications and Applications

In conducting an evaluation of your SEL program, a number of questions can be raised (which of course may vary depending on whether you are a teacher, principal, or superintendent):

• What are the goals for SEL in my classroom, school, or district? Are they clearly specified?
• What evidence do we have that we are making progress toward reaching our SEL goals?
• In what way are parents involved in SEL in my classroom, school, or district?
• Are lessons presented with enthusiasm and clarity?
• How does the teacher model the skills outside the lesson?

More specifically, teachers may want to know how well individual students are mastering specific knowledge, skills, and attitudes. Or they may want to know whether students are applying what they learn in the classroom in other settings, such as hallways, assemblies, and the playground.

For a principal, it may be important to know what is being done outside the classroom to promote SEL, such as in clubs, on the playground, and through sports. How well are staff prepared for building students' SEL? Is there adequate administrative support for teachers? Superintendents may ask how SEL efforts are coordinated within the curriculum, across grades, and across schools, or about the long-term effects of SEL activities. They will also want to examine school policies and state curriculum standards to see how they are compatible with and supportive of the program. And they will want to know if the SEL efforts are comprehensive, coordinated, and integrated (characteristics associated with effectiveness, as noted in Chapters 3 and 4). Each of these issues illustrates, from different perspectives, how to determine whether a program is working.

An example of a user-friendly approach that addresses the issues raised above was developed by Linney and Wandersman (1991) in their Prevention Plus III model. Their manual describes the procedures to follow in a straightforward manner. Example 36A illustrates the four steps using a program directed toward the development of peer and social relationships. As you can see, the systematic process outlined helped ensure that important program components were examined.

EXAMPLE 36A
PREVENTION PLUS III MODEL

Step 1. Identify Goals and Desired Outcomes

A. What are the primary goals of the program?

Example: Learning to choose friends, develop peer leadership skills, deal with conflict among friends, recognize and accept alternatives to aggression and violence.

B. What groups were you trying to reach?

Example: All students in middle/junior high school.

C. What outcomes were desired or what did you hope to accomplish?

Example: Increased interpersonal interactions, greater confidence in one's decision-making skills, more prosocial caring behaviors, and less interpersonal conflict.

Step 2. Assess What Was Done During the Program

A. What activities were planned?

Example: Role-playing exercises involving asking a friend to go to a football game.

B. When was the program actually implemented and who were the participants?

Example: Taught during the group guidance period at the beginning of each day during the third and fourth weeks of the first quarter.

C. How did participants evaluate the activities?

Example: Reported that the exercise was realistic and easy to follow.

D. What feedback can be used to improve the program for the future?

Example: More time should be devoted to the activity so other situations can be discussed.

Step 3. Assess Immediate Effects of the Program

Describe what changes have occurred based on the desired outcomes, evidence that the outcome was accomplished (using before and after scores), and amount of change.

Example: Students mastered the eight steps of the role-playing activity with an average of 95 percent accuracy.

Step 4. Assess Ultimate Program Effects

Describe whether the ultimate goals and outcomes have been attained.

Example: Student logs indicated that there was an increase since the second week of school until the present in the average number of student interactions outside the school from 1.3 to 1.8 per week.

GUIDELINE 37 ▼

SEL programs have clear outcome criteria with specific indicators of impact identified and outcome information gathered from multiple sources.

Rationale

Vague goals are nearly impossible to quantify (or to reach). When outcome criteria are specified clearly, however, it is usually easy to determine whether they have been attained. Because a major focus of SEL is the application of skills in a variety of settings, it is important to gather outcome data from different people and contexts.

Assessing the effects of SEL can be challenging, involving as they do unaccustomed outcomes such as social problem solving, interpersonal interactions, and cooperation. Moreover, these skills are to be demonstrated in the real world in various settings. Changes in student behavior must be observed and factors affecting their learning examined. Usually, observable results don't appear for quite some time, as research consistently indicates that, despite our impatience, it usually takes two to three years for a curriculum innovation to begin to be implemented in a reliably impactful manner (Hord et al. 1987).

Implications and Applications

As noted earlier, outcome evaluation begins by clarifying the goals of a program. What do we want students to get from the SEL instruction? The most effective programs specify cognitive, affective, and behavioral skills, attitudes, and values that they want students to attain. As you will recall from Chapter 3, essential components of a comprehensive SEL program include an awareness of feelings (self-control, knowing the relationship between feelings and reactions); decision making (problem awareness, planning, considering consequences); character (honesty, motivation, persistence); management of feelings (anger management, self-calming); self-concept (feeling likable, self-confidence); communications (listening, following directions); group dynamics (peer resistance, leadership skills); and relationship skills (sensitivity to others, caring). The ultimate success might be defined as helping students become productive, contributing, nonviolent, healthy citizens. They are involved community members, effective workers, responsible family members, and lifelong learners who exhibit intrapersonal intelligence, generosity, mastery, belonging, and independence.

You will also want to examine the school climate (discussed in Chapter 5) to ensure that it is a safe and caring environment where children trust their peers and teachers. As these goals become clearly identified, specific, and measurable, they will be more useful. A detailed listing of SEL Curriculum, Instructional, Implementation, and Evaluation Issues is shown in Example 37A.

Information about the program can be gathered from a number of relevant constituencies. For example, using the approach used to assess social problem solving, information about implementation could be obtained by observers or implementers (teachers). We have asked students for their opinions about activities (e.g., whether they liked them, what was best about them, what should be changed, whether they use the skills learned in the lessons, etc.), and likewise have surveyed parents for their reactions to our programs. Such information about consumer satisfaction gathered from multiple sources is important because research indicates that participants are less likely to use a program they do not like, regardless of its potential effectiveness (Reimers, Wacker, and Koeppl 1987). In addition, this information tells how skills learned in the programs are applied in multiple settings with other people. This is often called the "spread of effects" or generalization—critical because we cannot teach skills for every circumstance in which students might find themselves.

Effective methods of measuring SEL outcomes can be found in many different sources, including Alessi (1988), Elias and Tobias (1996), Furlong and

EXAMPLE 37A
KEY STRUCTURAL ELEMENTS OF SOCIAL AND EMOTIONAL LEARNING PROGRAMS

Curriculum and Instructional Issues
• *Theory-based:* A clear theoretical framework guides program strategies and practices.

• *Developmental:* The SEL instructional methods and content provided are developmentally appropriate for the ages and grades at which the program is delivered.

• *Culturally appropriate:* These programs foster appreciation of diversity and respect for the demands of growing up in a pluralistic society. They are sensitive, relevant, and responsive with regard to the ethnic, gender, and socioeconomic composition of students served as well as of faculty and staff delivering the instruction and services.

• *Comprehensive:* The most beneficial programs integrate and incorporate cognitive, affective, and behavioral skills (e.g., problem-solving, stress-management, decision-making, and communication skills), and convey prosocial attitudes and values applicable to a variety of specific topics such as alcohol, tobacco, drugs, AIDS, violence, nutrition, peer and family relationships, coping with transitions and crises, performance at school, and community service. These programs address specific factors that place children at risk for developing maladaptive behaviors and that serve to buffer them from negative influences; support children's total development and empowerment; provide a balance between preventing children from risk factors that may lead to negative behaviors, and giving them access to protective factors that enhance their ability to resist these negative influences.

• *Integrated:* They are immersed and reinforced within the general curriculum, complementing other existing subject areas, including some basic academic subjects as well as health or family-life education; in other words, SEL becomes an integral part of the school's program and not an add on, and the programs are provided over multiple years.

• *Coordinated:* These programs involve partnerships among students, parents, educators, and community members; linkage to comprehensive school health program and special services; and connections with other SEL programs within and outside the school. In addition, classroom instruction and activities are connected to other school-community SEL efforts as well as to local, state, and federal policies for drug, AIDS, and health education.

• *Active instructional techniques:* Educators use skill-based, experiential, or cognitive approaches to engage learners through methods such as modeling, role-playing, performance feedback, dialoguing, positive reinforcement, portfolios, expressive arts, play, community-building skills, exhibitions, projects, and individual goal setting (opportunities for practice). Application of skills in the real-world of the playground, lunchroom, and neighborhood are central. Peer leadership components are included, especially at the upper grades.

• *Generalization:* SEL strategies emphasize environmental change so that a culture is created that encourages and rewards the use of new skills and promotes their generalization. Part of this effort involves evaluating the nature of norms for responding to misbehavior, victimization, and related violations of school rules, and the degree to which these are shared by school staff, parents, and students.

—Based primarily on Consortium on the School-Based Promotion of Social Competence (1994)

EXAMPLE 37A—*continued*
KEY STRUCTURAL ELEMENTS OF SOCIAL AND EMOTIONAL LEARNING PROGRAMS

- *Supportive Climate:* They create a climate where it is safe and possible for children to bond (feel trust, connection, even affection) with their teachers and classmates and where their vulnerability is protected.

- *Materials:* The instructional and training aids are clear, up-to-date, engaging, user-friendly, and fun.

Implementation and Evaluation Issues

- *Program selection:* Particular approaches to SEL and specific SEL programs are selected based on identified local needs, concerns, interests, skills, and preexisting efforts.

- *Planning and management:* Program efforts are guided by a clear planning, implementation, and management plan based on an underlying theory or model of change. Adequate and ongoing administrative support is available.

- *Contexts:* They involve key environments of children and occur within an organizational, community, and family culture that is supportive. They include after-school and extracurricular initiatives such as peer leadership and mediation that are coordinated with other instruction.

- *Personnel roles:* There are clear roles and explicit responsibilities for teachers, special services staff, parents, principals, superintendents, and even school board members.

- *Preparation and ongoing support:* Programming is provided by well-prepared instructors who receive high-quality supervision and engage in ongoing staff development (e.g., coaching, supervision, mentoring, collaboration, planning). This element emphasizes the development of knowledge to enable them to provide a safe environment in which children can express their feelings. In addition, it prepares administrators to understand the program; provide support, coaching, and supervision; and participate in planning.

- *Resources and time:* Sufficient time is allocated to deliver the program on a consistent and frequent basis and to coordinate efforts. Adequate materials are available. Organizational support is provided. Programming covers all or much of the school year and occurs across multiple years (e.g., pre-K–12). A school-level program phase-in period usually takes three to five years for full implementation.

- *Evaluation:* These efforts are monitored and evaluated regularly using systematic procedures and multiple sources for ongoing program development, assurance of integrity, and identification of indicators of impact on specific outcomes. They articulate clear implementation, process, and outcome criteria. Evaluation summaries give examples of indicators of success and provide anecdotes of positive effects on students, school staff, parents, and the community.

- *Dissemination:* SEL efforts are shared and discussed within a grade level, with adjacent grade levels, with other schools, within the district, and with parents and the community to ensure that individuals within these groups understand what SEL is occurring and are encouraged to contribute to its success.

Smith (1994), and the Skillstreaming series (Goldstein, Sprafkin, Gershaw, and Klein 1980; McGinnis and Goldstein 1984). Measures also may be constructed locally based on the specific needs of your setting (see Examples 37B and 37C). In deciding on measures and the evaluation process, do not overlook the potential contributions of your school psychologist, guidance counselor, social worker, nurse, and other noninstructional staff members. Some have particular expertise in SEL and would welcome the opportunity to contribute to SEL efforts.

G U I D E L I N E   3 8   ▼

To maximize the benefits of the evaluation process, SEL efforts are shared and discussed within a *grade level, with adjacent grade levels, with other schools in the district, and with parents and the community to ensure that members of these groups understand and contribute to the social and emotional learning that is taking place.*

Rationale

Everyone who participates directly or indirectly in the SEL program has a stake in learning about the effectiveness of these efforts. Armed with such information, they are much more likely to continue their support and involvement, and therefore expend the energy necessary to keep the program operating.

EXAMPLE 37B
A PRINCIPAL'S EVALUATION CRITERIA AND OBSERVATIONS

Many SEL programs are extensively evaluated, and many have formal and informal tools that can be widely used. At the individual building level, principals like Darlene Mattia of Bloomfield (New Jersey) use a variety of salient indicators to monitor the impact of SEL programs like Social Decision Making and Problem Solving:

> I'm not spending all my time dealing with uncomfortable situations, but instead spend more time working on improving the school, improving communications with parents by explaining what the child is doing in SEL, and teaching them the program's language. Detention used to contain 20 kids before the program; now there are about 2. It used to take 15 to 20 minutes to calm everyone down enough after lunch to start class. Now, any bickering stops once they walk in the door. My Peer Peacemakers tell me there are fewer physical fights, not as many arguments, and the students are more calm.

> I can see a difference in self-esteem. Children aren't easily able to fall to peer pressure. They aren't afraid to speak out. There is better behavior at home. Children understand the common language and the expectations [confirmed through objective testing in program concepts, content, and strategies]. The students use it every day in situations not just at school but on the playground and at home with siblings. They try to live up to it, and though they may not always do it, you can tell they are trying. They feel a sense of responsibility. They feel a sense of community and pride for the school, the teachers, and the other students. They even use it to help out the teachers. A teacher reported to me, "I was getting upset and one of the kids told ME to 'Keep Calm.' It does come back to you!"

EXAMPLE 37C
STUDENT ANECDOTES ABOUT PROGRAM EFFECTS

Student anecdotes tell evaluators a great deal about children's understanding of SEL programs and the use to which they put their learning. Here are examples from site visits:

> Primary Project has made me aware of a button that I have. When you press that button feelings are released. Others just leak out. Through Primary Project I have learned how to deal with these feelings, and I know that when I am with my Primary Project teacher I can push that button.

* * *

> I've wanted to get revenge on kids because they pick on me because I have ADHD. I would go to Primary Project and talk about things, and the next time that someone would pick on me I would tell someone instead of wanting to beat them up. I have so many friends now since I have been in Primary Project.

—Elementary students
Primary Mental Health Project
Rochester, New York

> I wish every grade had Morning Meetings (MM), but I also feel that if junior high doesn't have MM, that having MM over the years is really going to help me through the day. It teaches you how to act around people and how to meet new people. Once you have had MM for a few years, you don't need MM to guide you along. You can start a conversation with someone, start a game of tic tac toe. MM's are great, and I would love to have them in junior high, but I feel that I really don't need it because it's just, like, shown me the way.

* * *

> MM and group activities really help socially and to meet new people, but for me, it helped me to know people. There are some kids in my class who have just been there, sitting in a corner since kindergarten, and all of a sudden, I'm working with them and solving a problem and it's like, "Wow! I never knew you were nice."

* * *

> If something really good happens to you, it is a time to share. It is the one part of the day that I know I have attention. I might go home and try to talk to my dad, and I won't have his full attention, but at MM, everyone is looking at me and everyone wants to hear, and the teachers make sure of that.

* * *

EXAMPLE 37C—*continued*
STUDENT ANECDOTES ABOUT PROGRAM EFFECTS

I think it helps everything. If you are socially happy, then everything is sort of happy for you. If you don't know anyone, it probably will affect your schoolwork and your family at home. But if you have a good MM and you are happy and you get that good sharing attention, it really lifts your spirits. You are nicer to everyone around you, you concentrate on your schoolwork, you are nicer to your family. I think being happy helps everything.

—5th and 6th graders
Responsive Classroom
Washington, D.C.

My brother went into my locker, and I wanted to hit him because I was mad. I used Keep Calm, and I was OK.

—3rd grader
Social Decision Making and Problem Solving
Bloomfield, New Jersey

Implications and Applications

Program evaluation information is best shared across a variety of implementers, so that appropriate links with other SEL programs in and outside the school are maintained. Evaluation results keep classrooms connected to one another, to other school-community SEL efforts, and to local, state, and federal requirements. Consequently, SEL will be seen more as an essential component of the overall curriculum rather than as an add-on.

G U I D E L I N E 39 ▼

The results of SEL program evaluations are used to refine programs and make decisions about their future course.

Rationale

SEL program evaluation is not an end in itself. And, as we have stressed elsewhere in this book,

SEL programs are not static. Rather, they must continually evolve in light of changing student populations and effective instructional practices. In addition, they must change to meet new demands (Who would have guessed in the early 1980s that AIDS or violence would become major concerns of schools and communities in the 1990s?). The model of the reflective, scientific practitioner suggests that we need to use evaluation data to refine programs and make decisions about their future.

Implications and Applications

Admittedly, evaluating your programs will take considerable time, and there can be some anxiety associated with the process because of the uncertainty about the outcomes. As emphasized earlier, however, evaluation is an essential component of all educational programs and of reflective, scientific practice. Evaluation shouldn't simply tell you a program is effective or ineffective; it should help you identify specific ways of improving what

---

EXAMPLE 38A
TEACHERS REFLECT ON WHAT THEY HAVE DONE TO IMPROVE SEL ACTIVITIES

Teachers of the PATHS program in Washington monitor the impact of their lessons and share this with other teachers, as well as share recommendations for changes they have made or will make:

> The biographies were great. I turned the one on Harriet Tubman into an entire unit, which was a valuable learning experience for all of us. As an extension to the lesson on Maya Lin and the Vietnam Memorial, I read my class a picture book called *Talking Walls,* by Margy Burs Knight, which is about famous walls around the world, such as the Vietnam Memorial, the Great Wall of China, and the Western Wall in Jerusalem. We learned about these famous walls from around the world and then created a wall in our own classrooms that was special to us.

> Two activities I did to extend lessons were an I Feel Calm Book and a Friendship Mobile. For the book, students completed the sentence, "I feel calm when . . . " and drew an illustration. The Friendship Mobile showed a picture of the student with pictures of his or her friends at home, at school, and in the community.

> Now that I have taught the 3rd grade curriculum for one year, I am going to make some changes in what lessons I teach where. First, I am going to teach lessons 40 on up more toward the beginning of the school year because they deal with goal setting. I included a mini-lesson on Time Management with the lesson on turning in your homework. We talked about activities that take away from their homework (i.e., baseball practice/games, parents' activities). I did a little graph with the hours listed between when they got out of school and when they went to bed. We estimated how long homework would take if they worked on it a little each night, and how many days it would take to complete it. We also discussed using their time effectively during class time. Personally, I loved the lesson on getting your homework turned in on time.

---

you are doing. Are there aspects of the program that should be maintained, modified, or eliminated? Without evaluative information, judgments about program operation are subjective and possibly misinformed. When this happens, the results usually are harmful to children.

Another overlooked aspect of program evaluation is an analysis of cost-effectiveness and cost-benefits (Weissberg and Greenberg 1997). Not only might you want to consider examining the relative costs of different programs to solve the same problem (e.g., compare two social skills curricula in terms of personnel, time, material costs, and out-

comes), but perhaps more important, the alternative of offering no program to address the issues (e.g., What is the cost to the school, as well as to society, of unwanted teen pregnancy?). The implications of such information can be significant.

Summary

To evaluate or not to evaluate: that is often seen as the question. But here, we have presented the case that evaluating SEL activities is essential. We have no choice. Information about program operation

---

EXAMPLE 39A
BONDING TO SCHOOL HELPS PREVENT DRUG ABUSE IN HIGH-RISK STUDENTS

Many teachers feel that parents are the influence and do not realize the powerful and protective factor of the school in the child's life. Our evaluation showed these findings: Students who are the children of drug addicts had an equal amount of bonding to both the parents and school, but they looked forward to going to school more than kids of drug-free parents and liked school more, but they didn't do as well—they looked to school as an escape. That strong protective role of liking school later showed results in whether the kids would go on to drinking and smoking.

—Kevin Haggerty
Social Development Research Group

---

from the perspective of the teacher, principal, administrator, parent, and program recipients must be gathered from the time of initial conceptualization. The results are used throughout the life of the program to monitor its delivery and its outcomes, and to determine whether it should be maintained, altered, or discontinued. In addition, school climate is critical in supporting SEL programs and establishing a culture that values inquiry and reflection, keystones to effective program operation and evaluation. With all of this knowledge in hand, we are best equipped to make student-centered and outcome-oriented decisions about programs' future directions.

8 Moving Forward: Assessing Strengths, Priorities, and Next Steps

AS YOU CONTINUE TO THINK ABOUT YOUR OWN SEL programming efforts, do not be surprised if a mixture of exhilaration and dread accompanies the start of your work, whether you're launching a new program or modifying current efforts. In our experience, once you are moving forward with a high-quality SEL program, the reaction of the children and your own enjoyment of the process will help keep you engaged in these activities. To get you started, we have included the following:

• *A structured series of questions linked to recommendations for practice.* These questions will help you and your colleagues examine in depth your current efforts to provide high-quality social and emotional education for your students. By looking at what you are already doing at the classroom, school, or district levels, you can identify areas of strength in your SEL efforts, as well as areas in need of improvement. The next step involves careful planning, with the goal of setting priorities that reflect and sustain your strengths and then gradually add components that will make your SEL program more comprehensive.

• *A list of school sites that are willing to be contacted or visited.* By visiting these schools you can see SEL programs in action and talk to those actually involved in implementing them. This activity is perhaps your most important source of assistance in carrying out an effective self-assessment, since we all tend to work best with guidance from

colleagues. The experienced SEL practitioners at these sites—some of which are in their second decade of SEL work, while others are relative newcomers with only a couple of years' experience—can provide rationales, implications, and implementation details useful beyond the specifics of their programs. They can also share informative "war stories" about how, in the face of obstacles, they have persisted and adapted to establish meaningful social and emotional education for their students. Appendix C presents a list of these sites. Note, too, that many programs have video resources that supplement the written materials.

A Challenge to Examine and Enhance SEL Practices

Now that you have gone through the guidelines for social and emotional education, we encourage you to revisit your own SEL efforts. First, you may want to return to the series of self-reflection questions raised in Chapter 2 and the responses you wrote. We hope that the information provided in Chapters 3 through 7 has stimulated you to develop fresh insights as you think about your SEL goals; your SEL activities at the classroom, school, and district level; implementation considerations; or program evaluation needs. In this chapter we build on the questions in Chapter 2, the 39 guidelines, and recommendations for effective practice offered by other sources (e.g., Consortium on the School-Based Promotion of Social Competence 1994, Westchester County Task Force on Social Competence Promotion Instruction 1990) to assist you in moving forward with your own SEL efforts.

Read this chapter at a quiet time, with a notebook or computer to record your observations, and a soothing beverage to sip while you reflect. You are about to look at an overview of the key elements that should be considered in comprehensive SEL program development, implementation, and evaluation—a comprehensiveness that is an aspiration, more than an observed or expected reality in any particular program. We caution you not to become overwhelmed by what has been described, but rather to dream about what could be, and to then realistically plan *what you can do* in a spirit of continuous improvement. Consider also how this process can be used by an SEL planning and management team or a grade-level meeting to lay the foundation for successful SEL programming.

Key Considerations for Planning, Implementing, and Evaluating SEL Programs

Educators who are committed to implementing high-quality SEL programs examine critically the programs they currently offer, build from their strengths, and weed out less effective aspects. As you will recall, in Chapter 2 we asked you to list all the activities going on in your classroom, school, or district that support SEL. Typically, we have found that schools implement a diverse array of discrete programs focusing on drug education, violence prevention, sex education, character education, health education, and so on. We propose that you build upon the strengths and efforts already in place in a coordinated, integrated fashion that makes more instructionally efficient use of precious school time, while eliminating less effective

activities that are not as likely to develop students who are knowledgeable, responsible, and caring. *Often, what is needed is not more time or resources, but a refocusing of what we are doing already, and a reallocation of available resources.*

Questions to Address in Establishing High-Quality SEL Programs

As you may recall from Chapter 7, the Consortium on the School-Based Promotion of Social Competence (1994) outlined key elements of SEL programs to aid both the planning and evaluation of SEL programs. These elements are summarized in Figure 8.1 so you can easily refer to them while reading this chapter.

Do not be dismayed if you perceive gaps between your current efforts and the elements highlighted in Figure 8.1 The list includes features of programs with long-term implementation histories, resulting from a number of years of focused effort, problem solving in the spirit of continuous improvement, and good fortune!

Now, how do you take the concepts presented and think through their implications? We have found it most useful to proceed by asking ourselves a series of questions within a problem-solving framework. The questions in this section are for your use in revisiting your SEL efforts based on the self-reflection you did in Chapter 2 and while reading the remainder of the book. These questions are designed to stimulate and support constructive, systematic planning. As you go through the questions, remember, this is not a final exam! In fact, do not feel compelled to answer all of these questions at one time or even during one year. Our goal is to raise issues and concerns that you and your colleagues will want to revisit from time to time as you design, implement, evaluate, and institutionalize your SEL efforts.

By the way, we anticipate that most educators

FIGURE 8.1
KEY ELEMENTS OF SEL PROGRAMS

Curriculum and Instructional Issues
- Built on clear theoretical framework
- Culturally and developmentally appropriate
- Uses a comprehensive approach with cognitive, affective, and behavioral dimensions
- Integrated within general curriculum
- Involves a coordinated partnership
- Active instructional techniques used
- Promotes generalization
- Creates a supportive climate
- Includes engaging instructional materials

Implementation and Evaluation Issues
- Program selected based on needs
- Guided by planning and management framework
- Focuses on key environments
- Clear roles for personnel
- Adequate preparation and ongoing support provided
- Sufficient resources and time allocated
- Systematically monitored and evaluated
- Disseminated to relevant constituents

Source: Consortium on the School-Based Promotion of Social Competence (1994)

will feel that they have satisfactory answers to many of these questions. That's OK! In our collective experience, efforts with which we once were satisfied became open to questions as we learned more about SEL, saw more examples of the work in action, and looked more carefully to see how well all students' SEL needs were being met. In the spirit of continuous improvement, you are likely to find, as we have, that even the best SEL programs, classrooms, and schools are not beyond examination.

In reality, however, we often find that educators don't know the answers to these questions.

That is also OK, because educators are typically given few tools to help them examine this critical area of social and emotional education with the care that they examine a language or a science program. This book is designed to serve as a corrective measure. Indeed, readers may well find that their self-reflection will lead to asking colleagues to reflect and then share aloud what they are actually doing. Finally, you will note that some of our questions could easily be placed under different headings or in a different sequence. Even though the problem-solving steps are listed sequentially, the process is fluid rather than prescribed.

1. Describe your needs, goals, and current practices. The best place to start is to examine your local needs, your SEL goals, and the efforts now being made to develop students' knowledge, responsibility, and caring. Here are some key questions to think about:

- *Goals.* What are the goals of your social and emotional education programming efforts? Do they emphasize the enhancement of students' knowledge, responsibility, and caring? What other behavioral outcomes do they address? Are they clearly articulated, specific, and measurable?
- *Organization.* How is your program organized? Does it provide sequenced, developmentally appropriate instruction in skills, values, and information at each grade level?
- *Instruction.* How does SEL instruction actually take place? Does it emphasize interrelated cognitive, affective, and behavioral skills as well as prosocial values and attitudes toward self, others, and tasks?
- *Theory.* Would you best describe your SEL activities as based on explicit theories of instruction and behavior change or more as a nonintegrated potpourri of games and exercises?
- *Clarity.* Have you adopted and implemented programs with clear goals and objectives? Are your lesson plans or approaches sufficiently structured and detailed?
- *Transfer of skills.* In what ways are students ex-

plicitly taught to apply acquired skills to real-life situations?

• *Social and health component.* Does your program include modules that present accurate and relevant social and health information (e.g., tobacco, AIDS) that build on core skills and values instruction?

• *Integrated curriculum.* How are your SEL practices integrated into other academic subjects and school activities—especially those that focus on social development, health, and the discipline system?

• *Climate changes.* How do you expect your SEL efforts to affect the classroom and school climate?

• *Parent education.* Does your program have a parent-education component that supports the goals and objectives of classroom instruction?

• *Community involvement.* How are various community groups, organizations, businesses, senior citizens, and so on, involved with your efforts to promote students' SEL?

• *Sensitivity.* Are your SEL program materials attractive, up-to-date, and easy to use? Are your program materials and content culturally sensitive?

• *Enjoyment.* Do students and teachers enjoy your program and perceive it to be beneficial?

• *State mandates.* Does your SEL programming meet instructional mandates already established by the state?

2. What are your options? When assessing programs to meet the needs and goals described above, examine them critically, measuring them against the characteristics in Figure 8.1. Here are some important questions to consider:

• *Preparation.* What process was used to investigate possible programs and approaches to use in your district? What implementers have been contacted regarding their experiences? What sites have been visited?

• *Knowledge.* How recently have you obtained reviews of the latest SEL initiatives from central sources such as CASEL or ASCD?

• *Expertise.* Do you have established relation-ships with program developers, distributors, external consultants, or master teachers with the capacity to provide excellent introductory training to large numbers of implementing teachers?

Figure 8.2 presents questions and issues considered by the Westchester County Task Force on Social Competence Promotion Instruction (1990) in evaluating the quality of SEL programs.

3. Getting started. Now that you have done the preliminary work and are ready to begin, it is essential to consider what specific practices will be implemented, including current ones that will be maintained, modified, and eliminated. Here are some questions to consider:

• *Interaction.* Is your program structured to affect positively how implementing teachers and staff communicate and interact throughout the day with students? What opportunities do teachers create for students to practice newly acquired skills and to reinforce them for effective skill application?

• *Administrators.* To what extent and in what ways do administrators show leadership, commitment, and involvement in fostering high-quality SEL in your school? What recommendations could you offer them about how they could do even more to foster high-quality programming?

• *Support staff.* Are support staff (e.g., psychologists, counselors, secretaries, lunchroom monitors) meaningfully involved in promoting or reinforcing skills and attitudes taught in classroom lessons?

• *Preparation time.* How much preparation time is required for teachers to teach lessons effectively? Do they have ample time and support to do the best possible job?

• *Diversity.* How do you effectively adapt your SEL program lessons and activities to meet the educational and social needs of students of diverse family backgrounds and ability levels? If you have adopted a nationally available program, how have you modified it to meet the needs of your school with regard to socioeconomic levels, cultural diversity, and at-risk/special education students?

EXAMPLE 8.2
PROGRAM REVIEW WORKSHEET

Name of Program: _____ _____   Name of Reviewer: _____

Basic facts about the program:
   Grade levels for which the program was designed: _____
   Year developed or revised: _____
   Cost of program materials per class: _____
   Ordering address and telephone: _____
   _____
   Is training required before purchasing the program? _____

What skills are taught or reinforced in the program?

sensitivity to others	awareness of self and others
how to self-monitor	awareness of adaptive response strategies
evaluation	productive thinking
self-control	stress management
self-reward	consequential thinking
emotion-focused coping	decision making
problem awareness	persistence
feelings awareness	planning
realistic and adaptive goal setting	other: _____ _____ ___

What attitudes or attributes are taught or reinforced in the program?

accepting individual differences	having motivation to contribute
being willing to work hard	having values that are prosocial
honesty	feeling capable and positive toward self
willingness to take care of oneself	feeling likable
working cooperatively with others	feeling respect for self and others
being motivated to solve problems	having concern or compassion for others
being aware of values	

   (circle) personal, family, community, societal
   other: _____
   _____
   _____
   _____

EXAMPLE 8.2—*continued*
PROGRAM REVIEW WORKSHEET

What content is taught in the program?
What are the unit titles? _____

_____

List topics covered in the following areas (see scope)
Self Care: _____
Peers: _____
Family: _____
School: _____
Community: _____

What are the features of the program?
Is the content accurate and up-to-date? _____
Is there a clear developmental sequence for each grade level?_____
Are the activities and materials developmentally appropriate for the given grade? _____
How are the materials culturally sensitive? _____
Is the material attractive and easy to understand?_____

What instructional methods are used? (circle)

audiotapes	outside activities	workbooks
brainstorming	posters	worksheets
community service	rehearsal and practice	other:
cooperative learning	role play	_____
direct instruction	scripts	_____
guest speakers	simulations	_____
modeling	videotapes	_____

How easy will the program be to implement?
At the classroom level:

How long is each lesson? _____
How many lessons per grade? _____
Are all the materials provided?_____ If not, what additional materials are needed? _____
How much preparation time will be needed per lesson? _____
Will the program mesh with existing programming? _____
Are materials included to evaluate student performance? _____
What are the parent involvement activities? _____

EXAMPLE 8.2—*continued*
PROGRAM REVIEW WORKSHEET

At the school level:

Who teaches the program to students?_____

Are additional staff required to implement the program? _____

How much specialization training is needed? _____

Can training be purchased? _____ Cost: _____

Will the program developers train school systems trainers? _____

Cost: _____

What type of follow-up support is needed? _____

_____

Is evaluation or monitoring of teaching integrity part of the program?

_____

How effective has the program proven to be?

Has a study been conducted? _____

What was the population for the study? _____

_____

What was the impact on skills? _____

_____

What was the impact on behavior? _____

_____

Has the curriculum been used in more than one type of setting? _____

Describe: _____

_____

Overall rating of the program:

Poor 1 2 3 4 5 6 7 8 9 10 Outstanding

Analysis of the strengths and weaknesses of the program:

Strengths: Weaknesses:

_____   _____

_____   _____

_____   _____

_____   _____

Comments:

_____

_____

_____

Source: Westchester County Task Force on Social Competence Promotion Instruction (1990)

• *Ongoing support.* Do you provide on-site coaching and ongoing consultation and problem-solving support to implementing teachers and other staff, so that sound instruction is ensured and programs may be adapted to meet school or district needs?

• *Long-term support.* Is there a planning team and administrative support at the school level and an organizational structure at the district level to nurture long-term efforts to implement and institutionalize high-quality social and emotional education?

4. Is it working? Once the program is in operation, it is important to closely monitor what is occurring as well as to evaluate the attainment of goals. This should take place in ways that allow useful information to be shared with those who are carrying out the program and those who are responsible for modifying the program to better reach its goals for more and more students. Here are some questions to consider:

• *Student evaluations.* Are those SEL programs, activities, and procedures brought into the school supported by well-designed evaluations that have documented positive effects on students' skills, attitudes, and behaviors?

• *Systemwide process evaluations.* What are the procedures for monitoring how SEL efforts are being carried out in classrooms, at specific grade levels, or across buildings and in the district as a whole?

• *Systematic tracking.* How do you keep track of the program's effects on student behavior? How systematic are these procedures? How might they be improved?

• *Feedback.* What assessments are in place to measure "consumer satisfaction" as reflected in the feedback of staff, students, and parents involved in SEL activities? How are these efforts reflected in the overall school climate?

• *Usability.* Is your program sufficiently intensive at each grade level to produce changes in attitude and behavior, but flexible and adaptable enough so that it is feasible to implement?

• *Cost.* How expensive is the SEL programming to implement in the initial year and in subsequent years? Are there sufficient resources to cover this expense? How do the costs compare to the benefits?

5. Letting others know about the program. The results of the evaluation should be communicated to relevant constituents first, and then it is beneficial if they can be shared with other interested parties. Here are some questions to consider:

• *Parents and community.* How are parents and community members informed about the program?

• *Evaluation results.* Are evaluation results shared with the school board, teachers and staff, parents, the community?

• *Visibility.* Are program activities and products visible enough so that parents and community groups can see what is happening in addition to learning about the official evaluation results?

• *Use of evaluations.* What use is made of the evaluation information within individual classrooms, the school, and the district?

Caution: Bumps Ahead!

The road to social and emotional learning is not likely to be a smooth one. All the programs described in this book have been modified in the light of experience, usually for the better. Again, we remind you to seek support from others who have been through or are currently going through this process. Why do it on your own? Others have valuable experiences that they can share so that every step does not have to be a trial-and-error learning experience—at the expense of children and staff. Because they have been there, they can provide moral support and encouragement when you need it the most. Reach out to others; you'll be glad you did.

Epilogue

THROUGHOUT THIS BOOK, WE HAVE PRESENTED numerous examples of social and emotional learning in action, drawn from educators all over the United States. What you might not know is that we had enough material from these individuals to fill several more books. Several sites that we could not include also have a great deal to contribute. Be inspired by these individuals and their accomplishments, and have the courage to know that you can achieve similar goals! They, like you, care about children's intellectual development. And they, like you, want children to emerge from school into adulthood as knowledgeable, responsible, and caring members of society. Perhaps their pathways took them more systematically into the area of social and emotional education than yours did up to now. But the road is not closed to you; through this book, the ongoing work of CASEL, and the living examples in the program sites, advances in social and emotional education can be widely shared and realistically carried out. CASEL is committed to collaborating with educators who want to explore: (a) what SEL practices are most educationally responsible and scientifically respectable, (b) what existing SEL curriculum and training materials are worth considering for adoption and implementation, and (c) which schools are implementing high-quality programs that you might contact to learn more about such models.

As we enter the 21st century, successful teachers and schools must go beyond the basics to help their students become contributing, productive citizens. The metaphor of "emotional intelligence" should not be taken literally, but rather to denote the reality that learning requires the engagement of all aspects of what makes us human. Social and emotional education is not nonacademic; rather, it integrates subject matter, cognition, emotion, and behavior using active learning techniques in ways that must become a standard part of schooling. This integration leads to learning that extends beyond the classroom, that is internalized by students and becomes part of them, rather than something they take on simply to pass a test. SEL is the missing piece of our education system, as one can see by visiting sites where SEL is well implemented.

In Chapter 1, we noted that educators working to prepare students for the challenges that await them require a new vision of what it means to be educated. Children need to grow into adults who are smart in many ways: in short, they need to become *knowledgeable, responsible, and caring*. The U.S. Declaration of Independence, a model throughout the world for its statements about democracy, freedom, and our common humanity, identifies three inalienable human rights: life, liberty, and the pursuit of happiness. To exercise these rights in a democracy requires the knowledge to understand and find one's role in the challenges and joys of life, the responsibility to safeguard and administer the machinery of our liberty, and the caring—for others and for oneself in relationship with others—that leads to lasting happiness.

Regardless of the specific words you might prefer, we hope you share our recognition that we cannot be satisfied to focus only on the transmission of knowledge. Our educational system, with its many resources and incredible and dedicated talent, will make extraordinary strides as we recognize the social and emotional components that are the keystones of learning. The words of the Declaration of Independence can then be a contract among our schools, our families, and our communities—a contract that guarantees the well-being of all our children.

References

Adams, D., and M. Hamm. (1994). *New Designs for Teaching and Learning*. San Francisco: Jossey-Bass.

Adler, A. (1930). *The Education of Children*. (1970 ed.). Chicago: Regnery.

Alessi, G.J. (1988). "Direct Observation Methods for Emotional/Behavioral Problems." In *Behavioral Assessment in Schools: Conceptual Foundations and Practical Applications*, edited by E.S. Shapiro and T.R. Kratochwill. New York: Guilford.

Amish, P.L., E.L. Gesten, J.K. Smith, H.B. Clark, et al. (1988). "Social Problem-Solving Training for Severely Emotionally and Behaviorally Disturbed Children." *Behavior Disorders* 13: 175–186.

Asher, S., and J. Coie. (1990). *Peer Relations in Childhood*. New York: Cambridge University Press.

Banks, J. (1992). "Multicultural Education: For Freedom's Sake." *Educational Leadership* 49, 4: 32–36.

Barlow, D.H., S.C. Hayes, and R.O. Nelson. (1984). *The Scientist Practitioner: Research and Accountability in Clinical and Educational Settings*. Elmsford, N.Y.: Pergamon.

Bartz, K. (1991). *Hallmark Child Development Philanthropy Program: Review and Theory*. Kansas City, Mo.: Hallmark Corporate Foundation.

Beane, J.A., and M.W. Apple. (1995). "The Case for Democratic Schools." In *Democratic Schools*, edited by M.W. Apple and J.A. Beane. Alexandria, Va.: ASCD.

Berk, L. (1989). *Child Development*. Boston: Allyn and Bacon.

Bierman, K., M.T. Greenberg, and the Conduct Problems Prevention Research Group. (1996). "Social Skills in the FAST Track Program." In *Prevention and Early Intervention: Childhood Disorders, Substance Abuse, and Delinquency*, edited by R. DeV. Peters and R.J. McMahon. Newbury Park, Calif.: Sage.

Blythe, T., and H. Gardner. (1990). "A School for All Intelligences." *Educational Leadership* 47, 7: 33–37.

Boyer, E.L. (1990). "Civic Education for Responsible Citizens." *Educational Leadership* 48, 3: 4–7.

Bramlett, R.K., B.L. Smith, and J. Edmonds. (1994). "A Comparison of Nonreferred, Learning-Disabled, and Mildly Mentally Retarded Students Utilizing the Social Skills Rating System." *Psychology in the Schools* 31: 13–19.

Brandt, R. (1991). "America's Challenge." *Educational Leadership* 49, 1: 3.

Brendtro, L., M. Brokenleg, and S. Van Bockern. (1990). *Reclaiming Youth at Risk: Our Hope for the Future*. Bloomington, Ind.: National Education Service.

Brick, P., and D.M. Roffman. (1993). "Response: 'Abstinence, No Buts' Is Simplistic." *Educational Leadership* 51, 3: 90–92.

Brooks, J. (1981). *The Process of Parenting*. 2nd ed. Palo Alto, Calif.: Mayfield.

Brubacher, J.W., C.W. Case, and T.G. Reagan. (1994). *Becoming a Reflective Educator: How to Build a Culture of Inquiry in the Schools*. Newbury Park, Calif.: Corwin.

Bullard, S. (1992). "Sorting Through the Multicultural Rhetoric." *Educational Leadership* 49, 4: 4–7.

Calhoun, E.F. (1993). "Action Research: Three Approaches." *Educational Leadership* 51, 2: 62–65.

Caplan, M., R.P. Weissberg, and T. Shriver. (1990). *Evaluation Summary for the 1989-1990 Social Development Project*. New Haven: New Haven Public Schools.

Carnegie Council on Adolescent Development. Report of the Task Force on Education of Young Adolescents. (1989). *Turning Points: Preparing American Youth for the 21st Century*. New York: Carnegie Corporation.

Carnegie Task Force on Meeting the Needs of Young People. (1994). *Starting Points: Meeting the Needs of Our Youngest Citizens*. New York: Carnegie Corporation.

Charney, R.S. (1992). *Teaching Children to Care: Management in the Responsive Classroom*. Greenfield, Mass.: Northeast Foundation for Children.

Comer, J.P., N.M. Haynes, E.T. Joyner, and M. Ben-Avie, eds. (1996). *Rallying the Whole Village: The Comer Process for Reforming Education*. New York: Teachers College Press.

Committee for Children. (1992). *Second Step: A Violence Prevention Curriculum, Grades 4–5*. Seattle, Wash.: Committee for Children.

Conduct Problems Prevention Research Group. (1992). "A Developmental and Clinical Model for the Prevention of Conduct Disorders: The FAST Track Program." *Development and Psychopathology* 4: 509–527.

Consortium on the School-Based Promotion of Social Competence. (1991). "Preparing Students for the Twenty-first Century: Contributions of the Prevention and Social Competence Promotion Fields." *Teachers College Record* 93: 297–305.

Consortium on the School-Based Promotion of Social Competence. (1994). "The School-Based Promotion of Social Competence: Theory, Research, Practice, and Policy." In *Stress, Risk, and Resilience in Children and Adolescents: Processes, Mechanisms, and Interaction*, edited by R.J. Haggerty, L. Sherrod, N. Garmezy, and M. Rutter. New York: Cambridge University Press.

Conyers, J. (1996). "Building Bridges Between Generations." *Educational Leadership* 53, 7: 14–16.

Copple, C., I. Sigel, and R. Saunders. (1979). *Educating the Young Thinker: Classroom Strategies for Cognitive Growth*. New York: Van Nostrand.

Craig, H.K. (1993). "Social Skills of Children with Specific Language Impairment: Peer Relationships." *Language, Speech, and Hearing Services in Schools* 24: 206–215.

Damasio, A.R. (1994). *Descartes' Error: Emotion, Reason, and the Human Brain*. New York: Grosset/Putnam.

Damon, W., and D. Hart. (1988). *Self-Understanding in Childhood and Adolescence*. New York: Cambridge University Press.

Dorman, G., and J. Lipsitz. (1984). "Early Adolescent Development." In *Middle Grades Assessment Program*, edited by G. Dorman. Carrboro, N.C.:

Center for Early Adolescence.

Drug Strategies. (1996). *Making the Grade: A Guide to School Drug Prevention Programs*. Washington, D.C.: Drug Strategies.

Dryfoos, J.G. (1994). *Full-Service Schools: A Revolution in Health and Social Services for Children, Youth, and Families*. San Francisco: Jossey-Bass.

Dusenbury, L.A., and M. Falco. (1997). "School-Based Drug Abuse Prevention Strategies: From Research to Policy to Practice. In *Healthy Children 2010: Enhancing Children's Wellness*, edited by R.P. Weissberg, T.P. Gullotta, R.L. Hampton, B.A. Ryan, and G.R. Adams. Newbury Park, Calif.: Sage.

Edelman, G.M. (1987). *Neural Darwinism: The Theory of Neuronal Group Selection*. New York: Basic Books.

Eisenberg, N., and P. Mussen. (1989). *The Roots of Prosocial Behavior in Children*. New York: Cambridge University Press.

Elias, M.J., ed. (1993). *Social Decision Making and Life Skills Development: Guidelines for Middle School Educators*. Gaithersburg, Md.: Aspen. (Now available from the author.)

Elias, M.J., and J. Clabby. (1992). *Building Social Problem Solving Skills: Guidelines from a School-Based Program*. San Francisco: Jossey-Bass.

Elias, M.J., and S.E. Tobias. (1996). *Social Problem-Solving: Interventions in the Schools*. New York: Guilford.

Elias, M.J., L. Bruene-Butler, L. Blum, and T. Schuyler. (1997). "How to Launch a Social and Emotional Learning Program." *Educational Leadership* 54, 8: 15–19.

Elias, M.J., R.P. Weissberg, K.A. Dodge, J. D. Hawkins, P.C. Kendall, L.A. Jason, C L. Perry, M.J. Rotheram-Borus, and J. E. Zins. (1994). "The School-based Promotion of Social Competence: Theory, Research, Practice, and Policy." In *Stress, Risk, and Resilience, in Children and Adolescents*, edited by R. Haggerty, L. Sherrod, N. Garmezy, and M. Rutter. New York: Cambridge University Press.

Epstein, T., and M.J. Elias. (1996). "To Reach for the Stars: How Social/affective Education Can Foster Truly Inclusive Environments." *Phi Delta Kappan* 78, 2: 157–162.

Erikson, E.H. (1954). *Childhood and Society*, 2nd ed. New York: Norton.

Forgas, J.P. (1994). "Sad and Guilty? Affective Influences in the Explanation of Conflicts in Close Relationships. *Journal of Personality and Social Psychology* 66: 56–68.

Fullan, M.G., and S. Stiegelbauer. (1991). *The New Meaning of Educational Change*. New York: Teachers College Press.

Furlong, M.J., and D.C. Smith. (1994). "Assessment of Youth's Anger, Hostility, and Aggression Using Self-Report and Rating Scales. In *Anger, Hostility, and Aggression*, edited by M.J. Furlong and D.C. Smith. Brandon, Vt.: Clinical Psychology Publishing Company.

Gager, P.J., J.S. Kress, and M.J. Elias. (1996). "Prevention Programs and Special Education: Considerations Related to Risk, Social Competence, and Multiculturalism. *Journal of Primary Prevention* 16, 4: 395–412.

Gardner, H. (1983). *Frames of Mind: The Theory of Multiple Intelligences*. New York: Basic Books.

Gardner, H. (1993). *The Multiple Intelligences: The Theory in Practice*. New York: Basic Books.

Garmezy, N. (1989). *Report on School Climate as a Variable Implicated in Student Achievement*. Chicago: MacArthur Foundation Research Program on Successful Adolescence.

Gilligan, C. (1987). "Adolescent Development Reconsidered." In *Adolescent Social Behavior and Health: New Directions in Child Development* (No. 37), pp. 63–92. San Francisco: Jossey-Bass.

Glasser, W. (1969). *Schools Without Failure*. New York: Harper and Row.

Goldstein, A.P., R. Sprafkin, N. Gershaw, and P. Klein. (1980). *Skillstreaming the Adolescent*. Champagne, Ill.: Research Press.

Goleman, D. (1995). *Emotional Intelligence*. New York: Bantam.

González, M. (1991). "School-Community Partnerships and the Homeless." *Educational Leadership* 49, 1: 23–24.

Gottfredson, D.C., G.D. Gottfredson, and L.G. Hybl. (1993). "Managing Adolescent Behavior: A Multiyear, Multischool Study." *American Educational Research Journal* 30: 179–215.

Greenberg, M.T., and C.A. Kusche. (1993). *Promoting Social and Emotional Development in Deaf Children: The PATHS Project*. Seattle: University of Washington Press.

Greenberg, M.T., and J. Snell. (1997). "The Neurological Basis of Emotional Development." In *Emotional Development and Emotional Intelligence: Implications for Educators*, edited by P. Salovey and D. Sluyter. New York: Basic Books.

Greenberg, M.T., C.A. Kusche, E.T. Cook, and J.P. Quamma. (1995). Promoting Emotional Competence in School-Aged Children: The Effects of the PATHS Curriculum." *Development and Psychopathology* 7: 117–136.

Guzzo, B. (Autumn 1995). "Second Step in the Principal's Office." *Prevention Update*, p. 5.

Hamm, C. (1989). *Philosophical Issues in Education: An Introduction*. New York: Falmer Press.

Hawkins, J.D., R.F. Catalano, and associates, eds. (1992). *Communities That Care: Action for Drug Abuse Prevention*. San Francisco: Jossey-Bass.

Haynes, N.M., and J.P. Comer. (1996). "Integrating Schools, Families, and Communities Through Successful School Reform." *School Psychology Review* 25: 4.

Haynes, N.M., and B. Perkins. (1996). *School Climate Reports on the ATLAS Schools in Norfolk*. New Haven, Conn.: Yale Child Study Center School Development Program.

Haynes, N.M, C.L. Emmons, S. Gebreyesus, and M. Ben-Avie. (1996). "The School Development Program Evaluation Process." In *Rallying the Whole Village: The Comer Process for Reforming Education*, edited by J.P. Comer, N.M. Haynes, E.T. Joyner, and M. Ben-Avie. New York: Teachers College Press.

Heath, S.B. (1982). "What No Bedtime Story Means: Narrative Skills at Home and at School." *Language and Society* 11: 49–76.

Hord, S.M., W.L. Rutherford, L. Huling-Austin, and G. E. Hall. (1987). *Taking Charge of Change*. Alexandria, Va.: ASCD.

Huberman, M., and M. Miles. (1984). *Innovation up Close: How School Improvement Works*. New York: Plenum.

Iso-Ahola, S.E., and B. Hatfield. (1986). *The Psychology of Sports: A Social Psychological Approach*. New York: William Brown.

Johnsen, R.L., and L. Bruene-Butler. (1993). "Promoting Social Decision-Making Skills of Middle School Students: A School/Community Environmental Service Project." In *Social Decision Making and Life Skills Development: Guidelines for Middle School Educators*, edited by M.J. Elias. Gaithersburg, Md.: Aspen Publications.

Johnson, R.W. (1993). "Where Can Teacher Research Lead? One Teacher's Daydream." *Educational Leadership* 51, 2: 66–68.

Johnson, D.W., and R.T. Johnson. (1989/1990). "Social Skills for Successful Group Work." *Educational Leadership* 47, 4: 29–33.

Johnson, D.W., and R.T. Johnson. (1994). *Learning Together and Alone: Cooperative, Competitive, and*

Individualistic Learning. Needham Heights, Mass.: Allyn and Bacon.

Johnson, D.W., R.T. Johnson, B. Dudley, and R. Burnett. (1992). "Teaching Students to Be Peer Mediators." *Educational Leadership* 50, 1: 10–13.

Kavale, K.A., and S.R. Forness. (1996). "Social Skill Deficits and Learning Disabilities: A Meta-Analysis. *Journal of Learning Disabilities* 29: 226–237.

Kelly, J.G. (1987). "An Ecological Paradigm: Defining Mental Health Consultation as a Preventive Service." In *The Ecology of Prevention,* edited by J. Kelly and R. Hess. New York: Haworth.

Kessler, S. (Winter 1991). "The Teaching Presence." *Holistic Education Review* 4, 4:. 4–15.

Kessler, S., and associates. (1990). *The Mysteries Sourcebook.* Santa Monica, Calif.: Crossroads School.

Kohn, A. (1996). *Beyond Discipline: From Compliance to Community.* Alexandria, Va: ASCD.

Kolbe, L. (1985). "Why School Health Education? An Empirical Point of View." *Health Education* 16: 116–120.

Kusche, C.A., and M.T. Greenberg. (1994). *The PATHS Curriculum.* Seattle: Developmental Research and Programs.

Ladd, G.W., and J. Mize. (1983). "A Cognitive-Social Learning Model of Social-Skill Training. *Psychological Review* 90: 127–157.

Langdon, C.A. (1996). "The Third Annual Phi Delta Kappan Poll of Teachers: Attitudes Toward the Public Schools." *Phi Delta Kappan* 78, 30: 244–250.

Lantieri, L., and J. Patti. (1996). *Waging Peace in Our Schools.* New York: Beacon.

Lewin, K., R. Lippitt, and R.K. White. (1939). "Patterns of Aggressive Behavior in Experimentally Created 'Social Climates.' " *Journal of Social Psychology* 10: 271–299.

Lewis, B. (1991). "Today's Kids Care about Social Action. *Educational Leadership* 49, 1: 47–49.

Lewis, C., E. Schaps, and M. Watson. (1996). "The Caring Classroom's Academic Edge." *Educational Leadership* 54, 1: 15–21.

Lickona, T. (1991). *Educating for Character: How Our Schools Can Teach Respect and Responsibility.* New York: Bantam.

Lickona, T. (1993a). "The Return of Character Education." *Educational Leadership* 51, 3: 6–11.

Lickona, T. (1993b). "Where Sex Education Went Wrong." *Educational Leadership* 51, 3: 84–89.

Lieberman, A. (1995). Practices That Support Teacher Development." *Phi Delta Kappan* 76: 591–596.

Linney, J.A., and A. Wandersman. (1991). *Prevention Plus*

III: Assessing Alcohol and Other Drug Prevention Programs at the School and Community Level (A Four-Step Guide to Useful Program Assessment). DHHS Publication No. (ADM)91-1817. Washington, D.C.: Department of Health and Human Services.

Linney, J.A., and A. Wandersman. (1996). "The Prevention Plus III Model." In *Empowerment Evaluation: Knowledge and Tools for Self-Assessment and Accountability,* edited by D.M. Fetterman, S.J. Kaftarian, and A. Wandersman. Newbury Park, Calif.: Sage.

Lippitt, G.L., P. Langseth, and J. Mossop. (1985). *Implementing Organizational Change: A Practical Guide to Managing Change Efforts.* San Francisco: Jossey-Bass.

Lockwood, A. (1993). "A Letter to Character Educators." *Educational Leadership* 51, 3: 72–75.

Mayer, J., and P. Salovey. (1995). "Emotional Intelligence and the Construction and Regulation of Feelings." *Applied and Preventive Psychology* 4, 2: 197–208.

McElhaney, S.J. (1995). *Getting Started: The NMHA Guide to Establishing Community-Based Prevention Programs.* Alexandria, Va.: National Mental Health Association.

McGinnis, E., and A. Goldstein. (1984). *Skillstreaming the Elementary School Child.* Champaign, Ill.: Research Press.

Meadows, B.J. (1993). "Through the Eyes of Parents." *Educational Leadership* 51, 2: 31–34.

Miller, S., J. Brodine, and T. Miller. (1996). *Safe by Design: Planning for Peaceful School Communities.* Seattle: Committee for Children.

Mize, J., and G.W. Ladd. (1990). "A Cognitive-Social Learning Approach to Social Skill Training with Low-Status Preschool Children." *Developmental Psychology* 26, 3: 388–397.

Moffitt, T.E. (1993). "The Neuropsychology of Conduct Disorder." *Development and Psychopathology* 5: 135–151.

National Commission on the Role of the School and the Community in Improving Adolescent Health. (1990). *Code Blue: Uniting for Healthier Youth.* Alexandria, Va.: National Association of State Boards of Education.

Nelsen, J., L. Lott, and H.S. Glenn. (1993). *Positive Discipline in the Classroom.* Rocklin, Calif.: Prima.

Noddings, N. (1992). *The Challenge to Care in Schools: An Alternative Approach to Education.* New York: Teachers College Press.

Nummela, R., and T. Rosengren. (1986). "What's

Happening in Students' Brains May Redefine Teaching." *Educational Leadership* 43, 8: 49–53.

Parker, W.C. (1996). "Advanced Ideas about Democracy: Toward a Pluralist Conception of Citizenship Education." *Teachers College Record* 98, 1: 104–125.

Parker, J.G., and S.R. Asher. (1993). "Friendship and Friendship Quality in Middle Childhood: Links with Peer Acceptance and Feelings of Loneliness and Social Dissatisfaction." *Developmental Psychology* 29, 4: 611–621.

Pedro-Carroll, J., L. Alpert-Gillis, and E. L. Cowen. (1992). "An Evaluation of the Efficacy of a Preventive Intervention for 4th-6th Grade Urban Children of Divorce." *Journal of Primary Prevention* 13: 115–130.

Perry, B D. (1996). *Maltreated Children: Experience, Brain Development, and the Next Generation.* New York: Norton.

Postman, N. (June 1996). *The End of Education.* Presentation at the Public Education Institute, Rutgers University, New Brunswick, N.J.

Ramsey, E., and K. Beland. (1996). *Summary of a Pilot Program for a Family Guide to Second Step: Parenting Strategies for a Safer Tomorrow.* Seattle: Committee for Children.

Reimers, T., D. Wacker, and G. Koeppl. (1987). "Acceptability of Behavioral Interventions: A Review of the Literature." *School Psychology Review* 16, 2: 212–227.

Ross, D., E. Bondy, and D. Kyle. (1993). *Reflective Teaching for Student Empowerment: Elementary Curriculum and Methods.* New York: Macmillan.

Rotter, J.B. (1982). *The Development and Application of Social Learning Theory.* New York: Praeger.

Rutter, M. (1990). "Psychosocial Resilience and Protective Mechanisms." In *Risk and Protective Factors in the Development of Psychopathology,* edited by J. Rolf, A. Masten, D. Cicchetti, K.H. Neuchterlein, and S. Weintraub. New York: Cambridge University Press.

Ryan, K. (May 17, 1995). "Character and Coffee Mugs." *Education Week,* p. 37.

Shriver, T.P., and R.P. Weissberg. (May 15, 1996). "No New Wars!" *Education Week,* pp. 33, 37.

Slavin, R.E., N.A. Madden, L.J. Dolan, B.A. Wasik, S. Ross, L. Smith, and M. Diana. (April 1995). *Success for All: A Summary of Research.* Paper presented at the meeting of the American Educational Association, San Francisco, Calif.

Solomon, D., M. Watson, V. Battistich, E. Schaps, and K. Delucchi. (1992). "Creating a Caring Community: A School-Based Program to Promote Children's Prosocial Competence." In *Effective and Responsible Teaching,* edited by E. Oser, J. Patty, and A. Dick. San Francisco: Jossey-Bass.

Sternberg, R., and R. Wagner, eds. (1986). *Practical Intelligence.* New York: Cambridge University Press.

Summers, K. (Winter 1996). "Creative Training Makes a Difference." *Prevention Update,* pp. 6–7.

Sylwester, R. (1995). *A Celebration of Neurons: An Educator's Guide to the Human Brain.* Alexandria, Va.: ASCD.

Taffel, R. (1996). Teaching Values." *Parents* 71, 10: 134–136.

U.S. Department of Health and Human Services. (1996). *Trends in the Well-Being of America's Children and Youth: 1996.* Washington, D.C.: U.S. Department of Health and Human Services.

Walberg, H.J. (1984). "Families as Partners in Educational Productivity." *Phi Delta Kappan,* 84, 6: 397–400.

Weissberg, R.P., and M.J. Elias. (1993). "Enhancing Young People's Social Competence and Health Behavior: An Important Challenge for Educators, Scientists, Policymakers, and Funders." *Applied and Preventive Psychology* 2: 179–190.

Weissberg, R.P., and M.T. Greenberg. (1997). "Social and Community Competence-Enhancement and Prevention Programs." In *Handbook of Child Psychology: Vol. 4, Child Psychology in Practice,* 5th ed., series edited by W. Damon, and volume edited by I.E. Sigel and K.A. Renninger. New York: John Wiley and Sons.

Weissberg, R.P., H.A. Barton, and T.P. Shriver. (1997). "The Social-Competence Promotion Program for Young Adolescents." In *Primary Prevention Works: The Lela Rowland Awards,* edited by G.W. Albee and T.P. Gullotta. Newbury Park, Calif.: Sage.

Weissberg, R.P., M. Caplan, L. Bennetto, and A.S. Jackson. (1990). *The New Haven Social Development Program: Sixth Grade Social Problem-Solving Module.* Chicago: University of Illinois at Chicago.

Weissberg, R.P., A.S. Jackson, and T.P. Shriver. (1993). "Promoting Positive Social Development and Health Practices in Young Urban Adolescents." In *Social Decision Making and Life Skills Development: Guidelines for Middle School Educators,* edited by M.J. Elias, pp. 45–77. Gaithersburg, Md.: Aspen Publications.

Westchester County Task Force on Social Competence Promotion Instruction; R.P. Weissberg, chair. (1990). *Promoting Social Development in Elementary School Children.* New York: Westchester County

Department of Community Mental Health.

Wolchik, S., and associates. (in press). "The Children of Divorce Intervention Project: Outcome Evaluation of an Empirically Based Parenting Program. *Journal of Community Psychology.*

Wood, C. (1994). *Yardsticks: Children in the Classroom Ages 4–12.* Greenfield, Mass.: Northeast Foundation for Children.

Wynne, E., and H. Walberg. (1986). "The Complementary Goals of Character Development and Academic Excellence." *Educational Leadership,* 43, 4: 15–18.

Zins, J.E. (1992). "Implementing School-Based Consultation Services: An Analysis of Five Years of Practice." In *Organizational Consultation: A Casebook,* edited by R.K. Conyne and J. O'Neil. Newbury Park, Calif.: Sage.

Zins, J.E., and M.J. Elias, eds. (1993). *Promoting Student Success Through Group Interventions.* New York: Haworth.

Zins, J.E., C.A. Maher, J.J. Murphy, and B.P. Wess. (1988). "The Peer Support Group: A Means of Facilitating Professional Development." *School Psychology Review* 17, 1: 138–146.

Zins, J.E., L.F. Travis III, and P.A. Freppon. (1997). "Linking Research and Educational Programming to Promote Social and Emotional Learning." In *Emotional Development and Emotional Intelligence: Implications for Educators,* edited by P. Salovey and D. Sluyter. New York: Basic Books.

Appendix A: Curriculum Scope for Different Age Groups

	Preschool/Early Elementary (K–2) School	Elementary/Intermediate	Middle School	High School
Personal				
Emotion	• Can appropriately express and manage fear, helplessness, anger, affection, excitement, enthusiasm, and disappointment • Can differentiate and label negative and positive emotions in self and others • Increasing tolerance for frustration	• Expressing feelings in positive ways • Controlling own anger • Labeling observed emotions • Harmonizing of others' feelings	• Self-aware and self-critical • Harmonizing of own feelings	All areas should be approached as integrative: • Listening and oral communication • Competence in reading, writing, and computation • Learning to learn skills • Personal management: self-esteem, goal-setting/self-motivation • Personal and moral evaluations of self, actions, behaviors • Beginning to focus on the future • Exploring meaning of one's life, life in general, transcendence • Taking care of self, recognizing consequences of risky behaviors (sexual activity, drug use), protecting self from negative consequences • Harmonizing of own and others' feelings • Adaptability: creative thinking and problem solving, especially in response to barriers/obstacles • Earning and budgeting money • Planning a career and preparing for adult role • Personal career development/goals—pride in work accomplished
Cognition	• Beginning to take a reflective perspective—role taking—what is the other seeing? What is the other feeling? What is the other thinking? What is the other intending? What is the other like? • Generating alternative possibilities for interpersonal actions • Emphasis on attention-sustaining skills, recall and linkage of material, verbalization of coping and problem-solving strategies used	• Knowing about healthy foods and exercising • Times when cooperation, planning are seen; at times, shows knowledge that there is more than one way to solve a problem • Setting goals, anticipating consequences, working to overcome obstacles • Focusing on strengths of self and others • Ability to think through problem situations and anticipate occurrences	• Recognizing the importance of alcohol and other drug abuse and prevention • Establishing norms for health prevention • Setting realistic short-term goals • Seeing both sides of issues, disputes, arguments • Comparing abilities to others, self, or normative standards; abilities considered in light of others' reactions • Acknowledging the importance of self-statements and self-rewards	

	Preschool/Early Elementary (K–2) School	Elementary/Intermediate	Middle School	High School
Behavior	• Learning self-management (e.g., when waiting one's turn; when entering and leaving classrooms at the start and end of the day and other transition times; when working on something in a group or alone) • Learning social norms about appearance (e.g., washing face or hair, brushing teeth) • Recognizing dangers to health and safety (e.g., crossing street, electrical sockets, pills that look like candy) • Being physically healthy—adequate nutrition; screenings to identify visual, hearing, language problems	• Understanding safety issues such as interviewing people at the door when home alone; saying no to strangers on the phone or in person • Managing time • Showing respect for others • Can ask for, give, and receive help • Negotiating disputes, deescalating conflicts • Admitting mistakes, apologizing when appropriate	• Initiating own activities • Emerging leadership skills	
Integration	• Integrating feeling and thinking with language, replacing or complementing that which can be expressed only in action, image, or affectivity • Differentiating the emotions, needs, and feelings of different people in different contexts—if not spontaneously, then in response to adult prompting and assistance • Recognizing and resisting inappropriate touching, sexual behaviors	• Ability to calm self down when upset and to verbalize what happened and how one is feeling differently • Encouraging perspective taking and empathic identification with others • Learning strategies for coping with, communicating about, and managing strong feelings	• Being aware of sexual factors, recognizing and accepting body changes, recognizing and resisting inappropriate sexual behaviors • Developing skills for analyzing stressful social situations, identifying feelings, goals, carrying out request and refusal skills	
Key concepts	honesty, fairness, trust, hope, confidence, keeping promises, empathy	initiative, purpose, goals, justice, fairness, friendship, equity, dependability, pride, creativity	democracy, pioneering, importance of the environment (spaceship Earth, earth as habitat, ecological environment, global interdependence, ecosystems), perfection and imperfection, prejudice, freedom, citizenship, liberty, home, industriousness, continuity, competence	relationships, healthy relationships, fidelity, intimacy, love, responsibility, commitment, respect, love and loss, caring, knowledge, growth, human commonalities, work/workplace, emotional intelligence, spirituality, ideas, inventions, identity, self-awareness

	Preschool/Early Elementary (K–2) School	Elementary/Intermediate	Middle School	High School
Peers/social	• Being a member of a group: sharing, listening, taking turns, cooperating, negotiating disputes, being considerate and helpful • Initiating interactions • Can resolve conflict without fighting; compromising • Understands justifiable self-defense • Empathetic toward peers: showing emotional distress when others are suffering; developing a sense of helping rather than hurting or neglecting; respecting rather than belittling, and supporting and protecting rather than dominating others; awareness of the thoughts, feelings, and experiences of others (perspective taking)	• Listening carefully • Conducting a reciprocal conversation • Using tone of voice, eye contact, posture, and language appropriate to peers (and adults) • Skills for making friends, entering peer groups—can judge peers' feelings, thoughts, plans, actions • Learning to include and exclude others • Expanding peer groups • Friendships based on mutual trust and assistance • Shows altruistic behavior among friends • Becoming assertive, self-calming, cooperative • Learning to cope with peer pressure to conform (e.g., dress) • Learning to set boundaries, to deal with secrets • Dealing positively with rejection	• Choosing friends thoughtfully but aware of group norms, popular trends • Developing peer leadership skills • Dealing with conflict among friends • Recognizing and accepting alternatives to aggression and violence • Belonging is recognized as very important	• Effective behavior in peer groups • Peer leadership/responsible membership • Using request and refusal skills • Initiating and maintaining cross-gender friends and romantic relationships • Understanding responsible behavior at social events • Dealing with drinking and driving

	Preschool/Early Elementary (K–2) School	Elementary/Intermediate	Middle School	High School
Family	• Being a family member: being considerate and helpful, expressing caring, and developing capacity for intimacy • Making contributions at home—chores, responsibilities • Relating to siblings—sharing, taking turns, initiating interactions, negotiating disputes, helping, caring • Internalizing values modeled in family • Self-confident and trusting—what they can expect from adults; believe that they are important; that their needs and wishes matter; that they can succeed; that they can trust their care givers; that adults can be helpful • Intellectually inquisitive—like to explore their home and the world around them • Homes (and communities) free from violence • Home life includes consistent, stimulating contact with caring adults	• Understanding different family forms and structures • Cooperating around household tasks • Acknowledging compliments • Valuing own uniqueness as individual and as family contributor • Sustaining positive interactions with parents and other adult relatives, friends • Showing affection, negative feelings appropriately • Being close, establishing intimacy and boundaries • Accepting failure/difficulty and continuing effort	• Recognizing conflict between parents' and peers' values (e.g., dress, importance of achievement) • Learning about stages in adults' and parents' lives • Valuing of rituals	• Becoming independent • Talking with parents about daily activities, learning self-disclosure skills • Preparing for parenting, family responsibilities

School-related

	Preschool/Early Elementary (K–2) School	Elementary/Intermediate School	Middle School	High School
Reasonable expectations	• Paying attention to teachers • Understanding similarities and differences (e.g., skin color, physical disabilities) • Working to the best of one's ability • Using words effectively, especially for feelings • Cooperating • Responding positively to approval • Thinking out loud, asking questions • Expressing self in art, music games, dramatic play • Likes starting more than finishing • Deriving security in repetition, routines • Able to articulate likes and dislikes, has clear sense of strengths, areas of mastery, can articulate these, and has opportunities to engage in these • Exploring the environment • Self-confident and trusting—what they can expect from adults in the school; believing that they are important; that their needs and wishes matter; that they can succeed; that they can trust adults in school; that adults in school can be helpful	• Setting academic goals, planning study time, completing assignments • Learning to work on teams • Accepting similarities and differences (e.g., appearance, ability levels) • Cooperating, helping—especially younger children • Bouncing back from mistakes • Able to work hard on projects • Beginning, carrying through on, and completing tasks • Good problem solving • Forgiving after anger • Generally truthful • Showing pride in accomplishments • Can calm down after being upset, losing one's temper, or crying • Able to follow directions for school tasks, routines • Carrying out commitments to classmates, teachers • Showing appropriate helpfulness • Knowing how to ask for help • Refusing negative peer pressure	• Will best accept modified rules • Enjoys novelty over repetition • Can learn planning and management skills to complete school requirements	• Making a realistic academic plan, recognizing personal strengths, persisting to achieve goals in spite of setbacks • Planning a career/post-high school pathways • Group effectiveness: interpersonal skills, negotiation, teamwork • Organizational effectiveness and leadership—making a contribution to classroom and school

	Preschool/Early Elementary (K–2) School	Elementary/Intermediate	Middle School	High School
Appropriate Environment	• Clear classroom, school rules • Opportunities for responsibility in the classroom • Authority clear, fair, deserving of respect • Frequent teacher redirection • Classrooms and school-related locations free from violence and threat • School life includes consistent, stimulating contact with caring adults	• Opportunities to comfort peer or classmate in distress, help new persons feel accepted/included • Being in groups, group activities • Making/using effective group rules • Participating in story-based learning • Opportunities to negotiate • Time for laughter, occasional silliness	• Minimizing lecture-mode of instruction • Varying types of student products (deemphasize written reports) • Opportunities to participate in setting policy • Clear expectations about truancy, substance use, violent behavior • Opportunities for setting, reviewing personal norms/standards • Group/academic/extracurricular memberships	• Guidance/structures for goal setting, future planning, post-school transition • Opportunities for participating in school service and other nonacademic involvement • Being a role model for younger students
Community	• Curiosity about how and why things happen • Recognizing a pluralistic society (e.g., aware of holidays, customs, cultural groups) • Accepting responsibility for the environment • Participating in community events (e.g., religious observances, recycling)	• Joining groups outside the school • Learning about, accepting cultural, community differences • Helping people in need	• Understanding and accepting differences in one's community • Identifying and resisting negative group influences • Developing involvements in community projects • Apprenticing/training for leadership roles	• Contributing to community service or environmental projects • Accepting responsibility for the environment • Understanding elements of employment • Understanding issues of government
Events Triggering Preventive Services	• Coping with divorce • Dealing with death in the family • Becoming a big brother or big sister • Dealing with family moves	• Coping with divorce • Dealing with death in the family • Becoming a big brother or big sister • Dealing with family moves	• Coping with divorce • Dealing with death in the family • Dealing with a classmate's drug use or delinquent behavior	• Coping with divorce • Dealing with death in the family • Dealing with a classmate's drug use or delinquent behavior, injury or death due to violence, pregnancy, suicide, HIV/AIDS • Transition from high school to workplace, college, living away from home

Appendix B: Guidelines for Social and Emotional Education

Guideline 1. Educators at all levels need explicit plans to help students become knowledgeable, responsible, and caring. Efforts are needed to build and reinforce skills in four major domains of SEL:

1. Life skills and social competencies
2. Health-promotion and problem-prevention skills
3. Coping skills and social support for transitions and crises
4. Positive, contributory service

Guideline 2. Successful efforts to build social and emotional skills are linked to developmental milestones as well as the need to help students cope with ongoing life events and local circumstances.

Guideline 3. SEL programs emphasize the promotion of prosocial attitudes and values about self, others, and work.

Guideline 4. It is most beneficial to provide a developmentally appropriate combination of formal, curriculum-based instruction with ongoing, informal, and infused opportunities to develop social and emotional skills from preschool through high school.

Guideline 5. SEL programs engage students as active partners in creating a classroom atmosphere where caring, responsibility, trust, and commitment to learning can thrive.

Guideline 6. Academic and SEL goals are unified by a comprehensive, theory-based framework that is developmentally appropriate.

Guideline 7. SEL instruction uses a variety of teaching methods to actively promote multiple domains of intelligence.

Guideline 8. Repetition and practice are vital to the integration of cognition, emotion, and behavior.

Guideline 9. Educators can enhance the transfer of SEL from lesson-based or other formal instruction to everyday life by using prompting and cuing techniques in all aspects of school life.

Guideline 10. The integration of SEL with traditional academics greatly enhances learning in both areas.

Guideline 11. The SEL curriculum may have to be adapted for children with special needs.

Guideline 12. Coordination between the SEL curriculum and other services creates an effective and integrated system of service delivery.

Guideline 13. Staff development opportunities provide teachers with theoretical knowledge essential to teaching social and emotional skills.

Guideline 14. Staff development provides modeling and practice in experiential learning.

Guideline 15. Staff development activities are visibly and regularly supported by feedback from colleagues, administrators, and others.

Guideline 16. SEL programs are most effective when teachers and administrators adopt a long-range perspective.

Guideline 17. A caring, supportive, and challenging classroom and school climate is most conducive to effective SEL teaching and learning.

Guideline 18. Students derive more benefit from SEL programs that they help to design, plan, and implement.

Guideline 19. SEL programs and activities that are coordinated with and integrated into the regular curriculum and life of the classroom and school are most likely to have the desired effect on students, and are also most likely to endure.

Guideline 20. SEL programs that are most clearly aligned with district goals and that have the support of the district administration are most likely to succeed.

Guideline 21. When home and school collaborate closely to implement SEL programs, students gain more and the SEL program's effects are most enduring and pervasive.

Guideline 22. Adequate community involvement in and support for SEL programs enhances their effects.

Guideline 23. In selecting a specific SEL program, educators must consider identified local needs, goals, interests, and mandates; staff skills; preexisting efforts; the nature of instructional procedures; the quality of materials; the developmental appropriateness of the program; and its respect for diversity.

Guideline 24. SEL activities and programs are best introduced as pilot programs.

Guideline 25. Professional development and supervision are important at all levels.

Guideline 26. Be clear about your planning process and your view of how programs expand successfully in your setting.

Guideline 27. An SEL program or approach that addresses a wide range of life skills and problem prevention areas tends to have the most impact.

Guideline 28. Allow the necessary time and support for the program to strengthen and grow.

Guideline 29. Systematically involving students who are receiving special education helps build a cohesive program climate and increases generalization of learned skills to situations students encounter in daily living.

Guideline 30. To foster long-term commitment, it is helpful to have a designated program coordinator, social development facilitator, or a social and emotional development committee. Committees typically are responsible for seeing that the various activities needed to effectively meet program goals are carried out. They monitor SEL-related efforts inside and outside the school.

Guideline 31. Long-lasting SEL programs are highly visible and recognized. These programs "act proud" and are not "snuck in" or carried out on unofficially "borrowed" time. They do not act in opposition to school or district goals, but rather are integral to these goals.

Guideline 32. Effective SEL approaches use portfolios, exhibitions, fairs, group presentations, and print and electronic media both inside and outside of school to invite participation and encourage the involvement and commitment of the larger community. By using a variety of approaches, SEL programs extend the reach of the program beyond formal school and classroom settings, and reach out to bring others in.

Guideline 33. The longer a program is in place, the more it will have to be adapted to changing circumstances. Implementation must be monitored and the program's outcomes evaluated regularly.

Guideline 34. Persistence and commitment are essential to overcoming obstacles that may hinder start-up of the SEL program and snarl the implementation. Because problem solving involves the modeling of the skills that educators are trying to teach students, the process of resolving issues contributes greatly to the effectiveness of SEL efforts.

Guideline 35. SEL programs have clear implementation criteria and are monitored to ensure that the programs are carried out as planned.

Guideline 36. Effective SEL programs are monitored and evaluated regularly using systematic procedures and multiple indicators.

Guideline 37. SEL programs have clear outcome criteria with specific indicators of impact identified and outcome information gathered from multiple sources.

Guideline 38. To maximize the benefits of the evaluation process, SEL efforts are shared and discussed within a grade level, with adjacent grade levels, with other schools in the district, and with parents and the community to ensure that members of these groups understand and contribute to the social and emotional learning that is taking place.

Guideline 39. The results of SEL program evaluation efforts are used to refine programs and make decisions about their future course.

Appendix C: Program Descriptions, Contacts, and Site Visit Information

THERE IS NO BETTER WAY TO MAKE A DECISION ABOUT a social and emotional skills-building approach or program than by talking to those actually teaching the program or by seeing it in action. CASEL has identified a number of groups who are working in the area of social and emotional education, and it maintains a clearinghouse, resource library, and World Wide Web site to provide information and networking for those interested in information, program materials, training, or consultation.

The following section presents a sampling of programs active at the time of this writing. These were identified by CASEL and the Prevention Clearinghouse of the National Mental Health Association as having empirical support for their effectiveness, sites in varying locations, and a willingness to respond to contacts and host visits from those wishing to see programs in action, explore how they work, and learn how to get them started. In each case, there is a contact for more detailed information. Site visits were made by Linda Bruene-Butler, Lisa Blum, and Zephryn Conte between September and December 1996.

Programs That Participated in Site Visits

Child Development Project (CDP)
Developmental Studies Center,
2000 Embarcadero, Suite 305
Oakland, CA 94606-5300.
Contact persons: Eric Schaps, Marilyn Watson

Phone: (510) 533-0213, 800-666-7270
Fax: (510) 464-3670

CDP works with elementary schools to help them become "caring communities of learners" or places where children care about learning and care about one another. The program emphasizes the integrated intellectual, ethical, and social development of children, recognizing that the three areas of development are interrelated and together affect children's success in school. By deliberately incorporating these domains of development into the program design, CDP aims to deepen children's commitment to being kind, helpful, responsible, and respectful of others, as well as foster motivation for learning and development of higher-order cognitive skills. The program's multifaceted approach includes cooperative learning, a problem-solving approach to discipline and classroom management, classroom and schoolwide community building, and family involvement. The program is supported by staff development and extensive curricular and professional materials from the Developmental Studies Center in Oakland, California.

Sites: Flagship schools are located in Louisville, Kentucky; White Plains, New York; and Cupertino, California.

School visited: Hazelwood Elementary School, Jefferson County Public Schools, 1325 Bluegrass Ave., Louisville, KY 40215. Site visit contacts: Brenda

Logan, Principal; Sheila Koshewa, Project Coordinator of CDP

North Country School
P.O. Box 187
Lake Placid, NY 12946-0187
Contact person: Frank Wallace, Head
Phone: (518) 523-9329
Fax: (518) 523-4858

A residential school in Lake Placid, New York, North Country provides a family-oriented environment dedicated to the development of the whole child. In a rural setting, featuring a working farm, students learn the social, emotional, and intellectual skills needed for a full and complete life of reflection, interaction, and contribution. Some students have had difficulties adjusting to peer, community, or family life in their home settings. Thus, North Country provides an environment in which children learn to accept themselves and diverse others, as well. The school accepts elementary and middle school-aged students.

School visited: North Country School, P.O. Box 187, Lake Placid, NY 12946-0187. Site visit contact: Frank Wallace

PATHS (Promoting Alternative Thinking Strategies) Program
Prevention Research Center
Pennsylvania State University
Henderson Building South
University Park, PA 16802
Contact person: Mark Greenberg
Phone: (814) 863-0241
Fax: (814) 863-7963
Web: http://weber.u.washington.edu/~paths/
Publisher: Developmental Research and Programs
1-800-736-2630

PATHS is a curriculum-based program. Children learn to recognize, express, and manage emotions; stop and think; use verbal thought; and learn words to help mediate understanding of self and others, social problem-solving skills, and language skills for self-control. Training, staff, and logistical

support are provided by the PATHS Research Group at the University of Washington. Special materials are available for children with hearing impairments. The program focuses on all elementary grades.

Sites: Flagship sites are in the Seattle, Washington, area; rural Pennsylvania; and Nashville, Tennessee.

School visited: Hazel Valley Elementary School, Highline School District 401, 402 SW 132nd St., Burien, WA 98146. Site visit contact: Barbara Walton, Principal

Primary Mental Health Project, Inc. (PMHP)
575 Mount Hope Ave.
Rochester, New York 14620-2290
Contact Person: A. Dirk Hightower
Phone: (716) 273-5957
Fax: (716) 232-6350

PMHP, Inc., features several different programs. The oldest and most widespread is called PMHP, in which young elementary school-aged students showing early signs of risk, due to social isolation, aggression, or academic failure, are paired with Child Associates who meet with them once a week to help build a positive relationship and SEL skills. Social problem-solving programs, including ENHANCE for preschool and kindergarten, build critical thinking skills. The Children of Divorce Program is a school-based, curriculum-based short-term intervention for children undergoing this stressful life event. It has received research validation and extensive national acclaim. Focal age groups are preschool through elementary.

Sites: Flagships sites are found throughout New York State; there are more than 500 implementation sites throughout the United States and its territories.

Schools visited:
Dudley Primary School, 211 Hamilton Rd., Fairport, NY 14450. Site visit contact: Paul Earnst, Principal

Rochester City School #29, 88 Kirkland Rd., Rochester, NY 14611

Site visit contact: Ms. Vivian McCloud, Principal

Resolving Conflict Creatively Program (RCCP)
RCCP National Center
163 Third Ave., #103
New York, NY 10003
Contact person: Linda Lantieri, Director, Resolving
  Conflict Creatively Program National Center
Phone: (212) 387-0225
Fax: (212) 387-0510
E-mail: ESRRCCP@aol.com

RCCP, an initiative of Educators for Social Responsibility, provides teachers with in-depth training, curriculums, and staff development and support; establishes peer mediation programs; offers parent workshops; and conducts leadership training for school administrators. The goal is to show students they have many choices besides passivity or aggression for dealing with conflict, to give them the skills needed to make those choices in the real world, to increase their appreciation of their own and other cultures, and to show them they can play a more powerful role in creating a more peaceful world. It operates at all grade levels, with an elementary- and middle-school focus.

Sites: Flagship schools can be found throughout the New York City area and in South Orange-Maplewood, New Jersey; additional sites exist throughout the United States.

Schools visited: Maplewood Middle School, Jefferson Elementary School, Clinton Elementary School. Write to: Board of Education, 525 Academy St., Maplewood, NJ 07040. Site visit contacts: Zephryn Conte, RCCP Site Coordinator; Mary Edwards, RCCP District Liaison

The Responsive Classroom
Northeast Foundation for Children
71 Montague City Rd.
Greenfield, MA 01301
Contact person: Chip Wood
Phone: 800-360-6332; (413) 772-2066
Fax: (413) 772-2097
E-mail: nefc@crocker.com

The Responsive Classroom is an approach to integrating the teaching of academic skills and social skills as part of everyday school life. The program translates vision and beliefs into sound practices. These practices provide a classroom structure within which academic and social learning flourish. The practices grow out of teachers' daily work with children and include Morning Meeting, Classroom Organization, Rules and Logical Consequences, Choice Time, Guided Discovery, and Assessment and Reporting to Parents. Observation and research show that these practices boost self-esteem, promote prosocial behavior, and reduce problem behaviors in urban, suburban, and rural schools. Our aim is to nurture inquisitive, competent and industrious students who will use their skills to add to the positive resources of the world. The Responsive Classroom is a way of thinking about teaching and interacting with children. Although management techniques and skills are taught, it is not just a set of steps or recipes. It is an all-encompassing approach to teaching, learning, and living.

Sites: Charlemont, Massachusetts; Cincinnati, Ohio; Cortland, New York; Dover, New Hampshire; Fitchburg, Massachusetts; Springfield, Massachusetts; and Washington, D.C.

School visited: Horace Mann Elementary School, 45th & Newark Sts., N.W., Washington, D.C. 20016. Site visit contact: Sheila Ford, Principal

School Development Program (SDP)
Yale Child Study Center
55 College St., Dept. A
New Haven, CT 06510
Contact person: Edward Joyner
Phone: (203) 737-1020
Fax: (203) 737-1023

The SDP involves a systemic process that targets an entire school for change. It includes (a) a school planning and management team, which is a management policy group with representatives from the teaching staff, support staff, parent groups, and administrators; (b) a mental health team comprised of child development and mental health specialists in the school whose function includes addressing school climate concerns, as well as individual student and teacher problems and issues; and (c) a parent program that involves parents in every facet of school life, including active daily participation in school activities, policy and management issues, and general school support. The SDP introduces (a) a comprehensive school plan that establishes the social and academic goals and activities of the school; (b) staff development activities designed to address the objectives outlined in the plan; and (c) monitoring and assessment of program processes and outcomes to inform program modifications.

Sites: Flagship sites are in New Haven, Connecticut; Washington, D.C.; New York State; and Nashville, Tennessee.

School visited: Board of Education, New Haven Public Schools, 54 Meadows St., New Haven, CT 06510. Site visit contact persons: Valerie Maholmes, Ph.D., Coordinator for SDP, New Haven; Lystra Richardson, Coordinator, New Haven Public Schools

Second Step Violence Prevention Curriculum
The Committee for Children
2203 Airport Way South, Suite 500
Seattle, WA, 98134-2027
Contact persons: Barbara Guzzo, Karen Bachelder
Phone: 800-634-4449; (206) 343-1223
Fax: (206) 343-1445

Second Step is a social and emotional skills curriculum that teaches children to change the attitudes and behaviors that contribute to violence. Through multimedia lesson presentations, classroom discussion, role play, and schoolwide reinforcement, children develop emotional understanding, empathy, impulse control, problem-solving, and anger-management skills. A Family Guide to Second Step is a companion program that teaches parents of Second Step students to practice and reinforce prosocial behavior at the home. Curriculums, videos, training for professionals, implementation support, and research and evaluation are provided by Committee for Children. The program is directed to students, teachers, and parents of children from preschool to 9th grade.

Sites: Flagships sites are available throughout the United States and Canada. Implementation has taken place across North America and in seven foreign countries.

Schools visited: Kimball Elementary, 3200 23rd Ave. South, Seattle, WA 98144. Site visit contacts: Theresa Escobar, School Counselor; Barbara Guzzo, Committee for Children.

Whitworth Elementary, 5215 46th Ave. South, Seattle, WA 98118. Site visit contacts: Susan McCloskey, Principal; Barbara Guzzo, Committee for Children.

Social Decision Making and Problem Solving
Department of Psychology
Rutgers University, Livingston Campus
New Brunswick, NJ 08903
Primary Contact Person: Maurice Elias
Phone: (732) 445-2444
Fax: (732) 445-0036

For Training of Trainers, National Dissemination:
SPS Unit
240 Stelton Rd.
Piscataway, NJ 08854-3248
Contact persons: Linda Bruene-Butler, Lisa Blum
Phone: (732) 235-4939
Fax: (732) 235-5115

For Video/Media/Computer-Technology Applications:
Psychological Enterprises, Inc.
165 Washington St.
Morristown, NJ 07960
Contact Person: Steven Tobias
Phone: (973) 829-6806
Fax: (973) 829-6802

Social Decision Making and Problem Solving is a curriculum-based framework for promoting students' social competence and life skills and preventing violence, substance abuse, and related problem behaviors. Focal skills include how to understand social situations, one's feelings, and the perspectives of those involved; calm down when upset or under pressure; create personally meaningful and prosocial goals; consider alternatives and consequences to ways of reaching goals; making and enacting effective plans; and overcoming personal and interpersonal obstacles. Main curriculum foci are Readiness Skills (self-control, social awareness, and group participation), Social Decision Making Strategy Skills, and Application Skills (infusion into academics, interpersonal situations). There are curriculum materials, and parent and training manuals. Extensive applications are made to self-contained classrooms and include special education students. Video- ("Talking with TJ") and computer-based applications are a current focus. It operates from pre-K to 12th grade, with a focus on elementary and middle school.

Sites: Flagship schools include those site visited and The Children's Institute in Livingston, New Jersey; Chester, New Jersey Township; St. Charles, Illinois School District; Astor Home for Children, New York; Westchester County, New York; and sites in Arizona, Washington, Texas, New York, New Jersey, USA; Australia; India; and Israel.

Schools visited:
Watsessing School, 71 Prospect St., Bloomfield, NJ 07003. Site visit contact: Darlene Mattia, Principal Berkeley Heights, New Jersey Public Schools, 345 Plainfield Ave., Berkeley Heights, NJ 07922. Site visit contact: Mrs. Joan London, Assistant Superintendent

Bartle School, Mansfield Ave., Highland Park, NJ 08904. Site visit contact: Dr. Frank Fehn, Principal Cape May Special Services School District, Crest Haven Rd., Cape May Courthouse, NJ 08201. Site visit contact: Karalee Corson, Director

Social Development Research Group (SDRG) Raising Healthy Children Program
9732 3rd Ave., NE
Suite #401
Seattle, WA 98115

Contact persons: Kevin Haggerty and Lois Meryman
Phone: (206) 543-3188; 685-3854
Fax: (206) 543-4507
E-mail: haggerty@u.washington.edu

Raising Healthy Children, a project funded by the National Institute on Drug Abuse, seeks to reduce known risk factors for later problem behaviors while increasing protective factors among elementary school-aged students. The interventions focus on three critical socializing units—the school, family, and peer group. Intervention strategies include staff development, parenting programs and home visits for families, and social skills development for students. The strategies are designed to increase bonding between students and their school and parents; teach skills to parents and teachers to increase academic success and reduce problem behaviors; and reinforce positive norms. These strategies have been shown by earlier SDRG research to reduce children's risk for later health and behavior problems. Preliminary analysis of RHC data reveal statistically significant differences between program and comparison students in their growth in social competency over a two-year period. Evaluation efforts will continue to further our understanding of how to effectively promote children's development as healthy community members.

Schools visited:
Cedar Way Elementary School, 22222 39th Ave. West, Mountlake Terrace, WA 98043-5252. Site visit contact: Jeanne Smart, Principal

Lynnwood Intermediate. 18638 44th Ave. West, Lynnwood, WA 98037-4605. Site visit contact: Marcie Nashem, Principal

Mountlake Terrace Elementary School, 22001 52nd Ave. West, Mountlake Terrace, WA 98043-3399. Site visit contact: Pat Mourtada, Principal

Hazelwood Elementary School, 3300 204th St. SW, Lynnwood, WA 98036-6899. Site visit contact: Jane Westergaard-Nimocks, Principal

Success for Life
La Salle Academy
612 Academy Ave.
Providence, RI 02908
Contact person: Ray Hebel, Academic Dean
Phone: (401) 351-7750
Fax: (401) 444-1782
Developer: Raymond Pasi, Ph.D.
Phone: (703) 358-5400
Fax: (703) 358-5409

Success for Life is the name La Salle Academy gives to its schoolwide and curriculum-infused program in social and emotional education. Student needs in this domain are met through a wide variety of established and new school initiatives. La Salle's Goals of Community Behavior were created by the joint efforts of the principal, faculty, and student representatives, and function as the overall guideline for acceptable behavior. Other school programs range from a Big Brother/Big Sister program and Athlete Goal Sheets to a daily morning reflection. These programs are complemented by social and emotional lessons, which are explicitly taught in every academic discipline several times a year. Specific themes and related skills serve as the guidelines for what is covered in each grade. The program is unique in its blending of specific schoolwide programs with social/emotional infusion into every subject.

School visited: La Salle Academy, 612 Academy Ave., Providence, RI 02908. Site visit contact: Raymond Pasi

Acclaimed SEL Programs in Schools Not Visited

Limited time made it impossible to site visit more than a representative sampling of outstanding SEL program models. Below, we list selected programs in CASEL's database that were not visited. However, each of these models has ongoing programs that may be visited through arrangements with the contact person.

Facing History and Ourselves
National Office
16 Hurd Rd.
Brookline, MA 02146-6919
Contact person: Margo Stern Strom
Phone: (617) 232-1595
Fax: (617) 232-0281

Facing History and Ourselves is a national education and teacher training organization whose mission is to engage students of diverse backgrounds in an examination of racism, prejudice, and antisemitism in order to promote the development of a more humane and informed citizenry. By studying the historical development and lessons of the Holocaust and other examples of genocide, students explore the connection between history and current events and the choices they confront in their own lives.

Sites: In addition to the National Office in Massachusetts, Regional Centers are maintained in Chicago, Illinois; Memphis, Tennessee; New York, New York; Los Angeles, California; and San Francisco, California.

Going for the Goal (GOAL)
The Life Skills Center
West Virginia Commonwealth University
800 W. Franklin St.
Richmond, VA 32384-2018
Contact persons: Steven Danish, Alice Westerberg
Phone: (804) 828-4384
Fax: (804) 828-0239

GOAL is a 10-session, 10-hour program taught to middle school students by well-trained high school students, both in and after school. The skills taught are how to identify positive life goals, the process of goal attainment, social problem solving, identifying health-compromising and goal-diverting behaviors, identifying health- and goal-promoting behaviors, and how to seek social support. There are printed Leaders Manuals and Student Activity Guides.

Sites: Connecticut, New York, Georgia, Michigan, Virginia, Massachusetts, California, USA; Australia and New Zealand

Growing Healthy
National Center for Health Education (NCHE)
72 Spring St., Suite 208
New York, NY 10012-4019
Contact person: Urvi R. Dalal, MPH
Phone: (212) 334-9470, ext. 25
Fax: (212) 334-9845

Growing Healthy is a school-based comprehensive health education curriculum designed to meet the needs of students in kindergarten through 6th grade. Its lessons are planned and sequential with varied activities that address not only the physical, but also the social and emotional aspects of health. The curriculum is designed to help children confront today's pressing health issues such as substance use; HIV/AIDS; teen pregnancy; and violence, injury, and abuse. The program includes role play, small-group exercises, cooperative and experimental activities, as well as videos, 3-D anatomical models, games, cassettes, and optional computer software. Unlike single-topic curriculums, in 43 to 51 lessons per grade level, Growing Healthy enables students to adopt proactive attitudes and behaviors by giving them the life skills they need.

Sites: Through the NCHE office, program facilitators can be contacted for specific information in the following states: Arizona, Arkansas, California, Colorado, Florida, Georgia, Idaho, Indiana, Iowa, Kansas, Maryland, Massachusetts, Missouri, Montana, New Mexico, New York, South Dakota, Tennessee, Virginia, and Wisconsin.

"I Can Problem Solve" (ICPS)
Allegheny University
Broad and Vine Sts.
Philadelphia, PA 19102
Contact person: Myrna Shure, Ph.D.
  (Developer/Author)

Phone: (215) 762-7205
Fax: (215) 762-8625

The award-winning ICPS program teaches children (pre-K to 6th grade) thinking skills that they can use to resolve or prevent problems between themselves and other people. Extensive research has proven children as young as four can learn these thinking skills. Children are guided to think for themselves (how, not what to think), to evaluate their own ideas and to try out their own solutions. There are three basic elements to training: basic skills, problem-solving skills, and program framework. Basic skills include: problem-solving vocabulary and dialogue techniques, identification of feelings, and seeing others' points of view. Problem-solving skills focus on considering multiple solutions, consequences of these solutions, and determining best solution. The framework of the program consists of teaching lessons several times a week. Lessons are in game form and sequentially build on one another; concepts are reviewed and practiced. Children learn to apply skills to real-life situations. (Companion award-winning parent program: *Raising a Thinking Child* book and workbook.)

Sites: Throughout United States and abroad

The Mysteries Program
Institute for Social and Emotional Learning
3833 N. 57th St.
Boulder, CO 80301
Contact person: Rachael Kessler
Phone: (303) 581-0331
Fax: (303) 581-0295

Mysteries provides training and materials that give adolescent students the tools to learn to tolerate and enjoy human diversity; to develop compassion, responsibility, and empowerment; to capture the ability to play; to express joy and love; and to feel connected to community. Neglected dimensions of intelligence are emphasized: sensitivity to self and other, intuition, imagination, body wisdom, and spirituality. A Passages Program prepares educators to address social and emotional issues related to teenage transitions into, during, and after high school.

Sites: Flagship sites are in New York and California.

Positive Adolescent Choices Training (PACT)
School of Professional Psychology, Ellis Institute
Wright State University
9 N. Edwin Moses Blvd.
Dayton, OH 45407
Contact persons: Janeece Warfield, Betty R. Yung
Phone: (937) 775-4300
Fax: (937) 775-4323

PACT is a school-based skill development program designed to prevent violence among African-American and other high-risk youth. The program trains youth in three social skills (giving negative feedback, receiving negative feedback, and negotiation), anger management, and violence risk education. Videotapes and program manuals can be purchased for program implementation, and training for group leaders may be arranged. Observations may be arranged in the PACT middle school site.

Site: A comprehensive observation site is set up in a Dayton, Ohio, middle school.

Preschool Stress Relief Project (PSSRP)
Wholistic Stress Control Institute
2545 Benjamin E. Mays Dr., SW
Atlanta, GA 30311
Contact person: Gloria Elder
Phone: (404) 755-0068
Fax: (404) 755-4333

PSSRP is a substance abuse prevention and mental health program developed to provide training, consultation, and educational resources in stress management to Head Start, day care, and public school teachers. The project's goal is to enable teachers to instruct preschoolers and elementary school students living in high-risk environments to develop positive coping skills for reducing and managing stress in their lives. The project

provides workshops for parents on stress reduction techniques for families as well. Educational materials include curriculum, videos, puppets, posters, songs, stickers, coloring book, and parent workbook. Training services are also available.

Sites: Arizona, Georgia, Minnesota, New Jersey, Ohio, and Washington

Project OZ, Inc.
502 S. Morris Ave.
Bloomington, IL 61701
Contact person: Mike Dobbins
Phone: (309) 827-0377
Fax: (309) 829-8877
E-mail: OZ@dave-world.net

Project OZ has created several curriculum-based programs for special education and general education students. Special prevention modules have been created for substance abuse in grades K-12, and violence prevention for grades 4-7.

Sites: Baltimore City, Maryland; Region 5, Chicago; Decatur, Illinois; and Branson, Missouri

Reach Out To Schools: Social Competency Program
The Stone Center, Wellesley College
106 Central St.
Wellesley, MA 02181-8268
Contact person: Pamela Seigle
Phone: (617) 283-2847
Fax: (617) 283-3646

Reach Out to Schools is a comprehensive multi-year program for grades K-5. A yearlong curriculum contains 40 lessons in three competency areas: creating a cooperative classroom environment, building self-esteem and positive relationships, and solving interpersonal problems. Lessons are conducted twice each week in an "Open Circle" format. Workshops are provide to parents as well.

Sites: Flagships sites are located throughout Massachusetts: Boston, Easton, Framingham, Franklin, Holbrook, Hopkinson, Medfield, Natick, Randolph, Sherborn, Wayland, Wellesley, Westwood, and Weymouth.

The Social Competence Program for Young Adolescents (SCPP-YA)
Department of Psychology (M/C 285)
University of Illinois-Chicago
1007 W. Harrison St.
Chicago IL 60607-7137
Contact person: Roger Weissberg
Phone: (312) 413-1012
Fax: (312) 355-0559

SCPP-YA is a middle school prevention program that teaches students cognitive, behavioral, and affective skills and encourages them to apply these skills in dealing with daily challenges, problems, and decisions. It has been a core element of New Haven's systemwide, K through 12 social development curriculum instruction since 1989. The 45-session SCPP-YA has 3 modules. The first module includes 27 lessons of intensive instruction in social problem-solving (SPS) skills. These foundational lessons are followed by two 9-session programs that teach students to apply SPS skills to the prevention of substance abuse and high-risk sexual behavior. To foster the application and generalization of SPS concepts and skills to daily life, teachers are trained to model problem solving to students in situations other than formal classroom lessons, and to guide and encourage students to try out problem-solving strategies in school, at home, and in the community. Research evaluations indicate positive program effects on students' problem-solving and stress-management skills, prosocial attitudes about conflict, social behavior, and alcohol use.

Sites: The flagship site is the New Haven, Connecticut, Public Schools.

Success for All Program (SFA)
Johns Hopkins University
3503 N. Charles St.
Baltimore, MD 21218
Contact person: Barbara Coppersmith
Phone: 1-800-548-4998
Fax: (410) 516-8890

SFA is a schoolwide restructuring program for students in grades pre-K to 5. It organizes resources to focus on prevention and early intervention so that every student will succeed in reading throughout the elementary grades. Components include tutors, eight-week assessments, cooperative learning, reading and writing programs, family support and staff support teams, and a full-time site facilitator.

Sites: Elementary schools in the following states are among those that can be visited: Arizona, California, Florida, Illinois, Indiana, Kansas, Maryland, Michigan, New Jersey, New York, North Carolina, Ohio, Pennsylvania, Tennessee, Texas, Virginia, and West Virginia.

Teenage Health Teaching Modules (THTM)
Center for School Health Programs
Education Development Center, Inc.
55 Chapel St.
Newton, MA 02158
Contact Person: Christine Blaber
Phone: (617) 969-7100
Fax: (617) 244-3436
E-mail: cblaber@edc.org

To see the program in the classroom, contact:
Frances ("Kika") Brown
Health/Physical Education Teacher
30845 Ashwood Dr.
Granger, IN 46530
(219) 295-4700

THTM is a successful, nationally used, and independently evaluated comprehensive school health curriculum for grades 6 through 12. It provides adolescents with the knowledge, skills, and understanding necessary to act in ways that enhance their immediate and long-term health. The evaluation of THTM concluded that the curriculum produced positive effects on students' health knowledge, attitudes, and self-reported behaviors. As a comprehensive health curriculum, THTM addresses topics as diverse as disease prevention and control, nutrition and fitness, injury and violence prevention, mental and emotional health, and healthy relationships.

Index

Page numbers in italics refer to pages that contain figures and boxed examples.

About the Authors

Maurice J. Elias, Ph.D., is Professor of Psychology at Rutgers University and codeveloper of the Social Decision Making and Problem Solving Project. This project received the 1988 Lela Rowland Prevention Award from the National Mental Health Association, is approved by the Program Effectiveness Panel of the National Diffusion Network as a federally validated prevention program, and, most recently, has been named as a Model Program by the National Educational Goals Panel. Dr. Elias is also cofounder of the Consortium on the School-Based Promotion of Social Competence, a member of the Leadership Team of the Collaborative for the Advancement of Social and Emotional Learning (CASEL), and serves as adviser to the Rutgers-based Consortium on Emotional Intelligence in the Workplace, funded by the Fetzer Institute and cochaired by Dan Goleman. With Dr. John Clabby, he has written a practical guide for parents, educators, and mental health professionals, *Teach Your Child Decision Making* (Doubleday, 1986). Dr. Elias's other books include *Social Decision Making Skills: A Curriculum Guide for the Elementary Grades* (Author), *Problem Solving/Decision Making for Social and Academic Success: A School-Based Approach* (National Education Association Professional Library), *Building Social Problem Solving Skills: Guidelines from a School-Based Program* (Jossey-Bass), *Social Decision Making and Life Skills Development: Guidelines for Middle School Educators* (Aspen), *Promoting Student Success Through Group Intervention* (Haworth), and *Social Problem Solving Interventions in the Schools* (Guilford). Dr. Elias is married and the father of two children. He may be reached at the Department of Psychology, Rutgers University, Livingston Campus, New Brunswick, NJ 08903. Phone: (732) 445-2444; fax: (732) 445-0036; e-mail: melias@rci.rutgers.edu.

Joseph E. Zins, Ed.D., is Professor in the College of Education at the University of Cincinnati and a consulting psychologist with the Beechwood, Kentucky, Independent Schools. A licensed psychologist, he has twenty-five years of applied experience with public schools, a community mental health center, a pediatric hospital, and other organizations. Professor Zins has authored more than a hundred scholarly publications, including eight books on consultation, prevention, and the delivery of psychological services in schools. Among his books are *Helping Students Succeed in the Regular Classroom: A Guide for Developing Intervention Assistance Programs*, *Handbook of Consultation Services for Children*, *Promoting Student Success Through Group Interventions*, and *Psychoeducational Interventions in the Schools: Methods and Procedures for Enhancing Student Competence*. He also is Editor of the multidisciplinary *Journal of Educational and Psychological Consultation* and has been a member of numerous editorial boards. In addition to being a member of the Collaborative for the Advancement of Social and Emotional Learning (CASEL) and the Consortium on the School-Based Promotion of Social Competence, Dr. Zins is a Fellow of the American Psychological Association and past secretary of the National Association of School Psychologists. Professor Zins may be contacted at 339 Teachers College, University of Cincinnati, Cincinnati, OH 45221-0002. Phone: (513) 556-3341; fax: (513) 556-1581; e-mail: joseph.zins@uc.edu.

Roger P. Weissberg, Ph.D., is Professor and Director of Graduate Studies for the Psychology Department at the University of Illinois at Chicago (UIC). He is Executive Director of the Collaborative for the Advancement of Social and Emotional Learning (CASEL). He directs an NIMH-funded Predoctoral and Postdoctoral Prevention Research Training Program in Urban Children's Mental Health and AIDS Prevention at UIC, and also holds an appointment with the Mid-Atlantic Laboratory for Student Success funded by the Office of Educational Research and Improvement of the U.S. Department of Education. Professor Weissberg has published about one hundred articles and chapters focusing on preventive interventions with children and adolescents, and has coauthored nine curriculums on school-based programs to promote social competence and prevent problem behaviors including drug use, high-risk sexual behaviors, and aggression. Three recent books that he coedited are *Healthy Children 2010: Enhancing Children's Wellness, Healthy Children 2010: Establishing Preventive Services,* and *Children and Youth: Interdisciplinary Perspectives* (Sage 1997). Professor Weissberg was the Research Director for the Primary Mental Health Project from 1980 to 1982. He was a Professor in the Psychology Department at Yale University between 1982 and 1992, where he collaborated with the New Haven Public School System to establish the New Haven's Kindergarten through grade 12 Social Development Project. He has been the President of the American Psychological Association's Society for Community Research and Action. He is a recipient of the William T. Grant Foundation's

five-year Faculty Scholars Award in Children's Mental Health, the Connecticut Psychological Association's 1992 Award for Distinguished Psychological Contribution in the Public Interest, and the National Mental Health Association's 1992 Lela Rowland Prevention Award. He may be contacted at Department of Psychology (M/C 285), The University of Illinois at Chicago, 1007 W. Harrison St., Chicago, IL 60607-7137. Phone: (312) 355-0640; fax: (312) 355-0559; e-mail: rpw@uic.edu.

Karin Frey, Ph.D., is Research Associate Professor of Educational Psychology at the University of Washington and the Director of Research and Evaluation at the Committee for Committee for Children. Her research focuses on children's social and emotional development. Her basic research, looking at mastery motivation, emotional expression, and peer interaction in school settings, has been published in leading journals of child development. Her applied research documents the impact of a social-competence program on teachers and students over a period of several years. Dr. Frey has also worked in hospitals and clinics, providing social-emotional support and skill training to groups of children with special needs. She may be contacted at Committee for Children, 2203 Airport Way South, Seattle, WA 98134. Phone: (206) 343-1223; fax: (206) 343-1445; e-mail: karinf@ u.washington.edu.

Mark T. Greenberg, Ph.D., is Professor of Psychology at Pennsylvania State University. He is the coauthor of several books including *Promoting Social and Emotional Development in Deaf Children: The PATHS Project* (1993), *The PATHS Curriculum* (1995), and *Attachment in the Preschool Years: Theory, Research and Intervention* (1990). He was the Principal Investigator of the Seattle site of the Fast Track Prevention Program. He continues to direct the PATHS Curriculum Project. His primary interest is the prevention of child psychopathology through the development of prevention programs that promote healthy emotion regulation and social compe-

tence in all children. His work on the PATHS Curriculum is used in schools in Europe, Australia, Canada, as well as in the United States. He may be contacted at Prevention Research Center, Pennsylvania State University, Henderson Building South, University Park, PA 16802. Phone: (814) 863-0241; fax: (814) 863-7963;
Web: http://weber.u.washington.edu/~paths/.

Norris M. Haynes, Ph.D., is Associate Professor of Psychology, Education, and Child Development at the Yale Child Study Center and Research Director of the School Development Program (SDP). Dr. Haynes contributes significantly to the SDP's training and dissemination activities. Dr. Haynes has taught at the elementary and high school levels. He has been a professor at Howard University and adjunct professor at several other universities. He is the recipient of many honors and awards, including recognition as a Fellow of the American Psychological Association, Outstanding Young Man of America, citation in several Who's Who publications, The Crispus Attucks Award for Educational Leadership, Fulbright Scholarship, and the first Howard University Graduate School Distinguished Alumnus Award in 1994. Dr. Haynes is the author of many articles, book chapters, and a recent book titled *Critical Issues in Educating African-American Children.* He is also the author of *Promoting Motivation, Learning and Achievement Among Urban Middle and High School Students* (in press). Dr. Haynes is also coeditor of *Rallying the Whole Village: The Comer Process for Reforming Education* (1996), published by Teachers College Press, and coeditor of another book to be published by Teachers College Press titled: *Child by Child, Adult by Adult, and School by School.* He may be contacted at Yale Child Study Center, 230 S. Frontage Rd., New Haven, CT 06520-7900. Phone: (203) 785-2548; fax: (203) 785-3359; e-mail: norris.haynes@yale.edu.

Rachael Kessler is Director of the Institute for Social & Emotional Learning. She provides professional and curriculum development for schools and individual educators through consultation, inservice training, and workshops. As first chair of the Department of Human Development at Crossroads School in Santa Monica, California, Kessler pioneered one of the first curriculums to integrate emotional, social, and spiritual capacities with academic learning. Her curriculums include "rites of passage" for adolescents: students are provided a school-based structure for expressing their yearning for meaning, purpose, and connection and are offered guidance and validation to constructively navigate their deep internal and external changes. Kessler's publications include: *The Mysteries Sourcebook, A Teachers' Guide;* "Honoring Young Voices: A Vision for Education (video); "The Mysteries Program: Educating Adolescents for Today's World"; "The Teaching Presence"; and "The 'Senior Passage' Course" in Crossroads: The Quest for Contemporary Rites of Passage." She may be reached at the Institute for Social & Emotional Learning, 3833 N. 57th St., Boulder, CO 80301-3017. Phone: (303) 581-0331; fax: (303) 581-0295; e-mail: SELRachael@aol.com.

Mary E. Schwab-Stone, M.D., is a child psychiatrist with training in epidemiology. Her research has been guided by an interest in the relationship between the social environment and psychological adjustment in childhood, with a particular emphasis on children growing up in situations of social and economic disadvantage. In recent years this interest has become focused specifically on school-based programs for the prevention of psychological difficulties and the promotion of healthy development in children in urban settings. She has collaborated with the New Haven Public Schools as a program consultant, and heads the Yale-based team responsible for evaluation of their social development and prevention programming. She has served as a clinical consultant to the Special Education Program in the New Haven Schools for a number of years. After graduating from Harvard University, she earned her M.D. at Dartmouth Medical School. She did residency training in adult and child psychiatry at the Massachusetts Mental Health Center in Boston. After clinical training she was on the staff at McLean Hospital in Belmont, Massachusetts, and did part-time psychiatric practice. In 1984, she decided to pursue more actively a longstanding interest in child psychiatric research by undertaking a research training fellowship in child psychiatry and epidemiology at Columbia College of Physicians and Surgeons. She moved to New Haven in 1986 where she is currently Harris Associate Professor of Child Psychiatry at the Yale Child Study Center. She served as Acting Director of the Collaborative for the Advancement of Social and Emotional Learning (CASEL) until October 1996 and continues to serve on the CASEL Leadership Team. She may be contacted at Yale Child Study Center, 230 S. Frontage Rd., New Haven, CT 06520-7900. Phone: (203) 785-2546; fax: (203) 785-6106; e-mail: mary.schwab-stone@yale.edu.

Timothy P. Shriver, Ph.D., is President and Chief Executive Officer of Special Olympics International, and Chair of the Leadership Team of the Collaborative for the Advancement of Social and Emotional Learning (CASEL). Prior to joining Spe-

cial Olympics, Shriver was the Supervisor of the New Haven, Connecticut, Public Schools' Social Development Project, a comprehensive, K-12, primary prevention effort involving students, parents, teachers, administrators, community leaders, and scholars. The Project, which he launched in 1987, is designed to prevent substance abuse, violence, and teen pregnancy. In 1994, he helped launch CASEL, a national organization to promote effective school-based prevention programming. In that role, he continues to advocate for effective primary prevention programming in schools nationwide. Shriver has written extensively on these issues and has coauthored several publications including, "Promoting Positive Social Development and Health Practices in Young Urban Adolescents," "Involvement in Multiple Program Behaviors of Young Urban Adolescents," "No Safe Haven: A Study of Violence Exposure in an Urban Community," and "No New Wars." He may be contacted at Special Olympics International, Inc., 1325 G St., NW, Suite 500, Washington, DC 20005. Phone: (202) 628-3630, ext. 235; fax: (202) 628-0067; e-mail: timshriver@juno.com.